WARD SHOE

...TURN

A genre of superna[...] [i]mprobable products of the A[...] charts the troubled entry of the supernatural into fiction, and questions the historical reasons for its growing popularity in the late eighteenth century. Beginning with the notorious case of the Cock Lane ghost, a performing poltergeist who became a major attraction in the London of 1762, and with Garrick's spell-binding and paradigmatic performance as the ghost-seeing Hamlet, it moves on to look at the Gothic novels of Horace Walpole, Ann Radcliffe, M. G. Lewis, and others, in unexpected new lights. The central thesis concerns the intimate connection between fictions of the supernatural and the growth of consumerism: not only are ghost stories successful commodities in the rapidly commercialising book market, they are also considered here as reflections on the disruptive effects of this socio-economic transformation. Appealing to irrational emotions themselves, these texts participate in contemporary debates on the nature and direction of modern society, divided between the alternatives of a traditional model of rational leadership from above, and the acquisitive passions that drive the economy. In other words, these are not fantasies which escape into a never-never Gothic past, but works which engage with issues of the present, including the inhumane enforcement of patrilineal property laws, the obscure legal status of women, and the role of mass action in the unfolding of the French Revolution. Fantasy, it is argued, is able briefly to become a privileged mode of truth-telling, until a developing theory of the autonomy of the aesthetic abstracts literature from the realm of politics.

CAMBRIDGE STUDIES IN ROMANTICISM 12

THE RISE OF SUPERNATURAL FICTION, 1762–1800

CAMBRIDGE STUDIES IN ROMANTICISM

This series aims to foster the best new work in one of the most challenging fields within English literary studies. From the early 1780s to the early 1830s a formidable array of talented men and women took to literary composition, not just in poetry, which some of them famously transformed, but in many modes of writing. The expansion of publishing created new opportunities for writers, and the political stakes of what they wrote were raised again and again by what Wordsworth called those 'great national events' that were 'almost daily taking place': the French Revolution, the Napoleonic and American wars, urbanization, industrialization, religious revival, and expanded empire abroad and the reform movement at home. This was a literature of enormous ambition, even when it pretended otherwise. The relations between science, philosophy, religion and literature were reworked in texts such as *Frankenstein* and *Biographia Literaria*; gender relations in *A Vindication of the Rights of Woman* and *Don Juan*; journalism by Cobbett and Hazlitt; poetic form, content and style by the Lake School and the Cockney School. Outside Shakespeare studies, probably no body of writing has produced such a wealth of response or done so much to shape the responses of modern criticism. This indeed is the period that saw the emergence of those notions of 'literature' and of literary history, especially national literary history, on which modern scholarship in English has been founded.

The categories produced by Romanticism have also been challenged by recent historicist arguments. The task of the series is to engage both with a challenging corpus of Romantic writings and with the changing field of criticism they have helped to shape. As with other literary series published by Cambridge, this one will represent the work of both younger and more established scholars, on either side of the Atlantic and elsewhere.

For a list of titles published in the series, see back of book.

THE RISE OF
SUPERNATURAL FICTION,
1762–1800

E. J. CLERY

Department of English, Keele University

CAMBRIDGE
UNIVERSITY PRESS

Published by the Press Syndicate of the University of Cambridge
The Pitt Building, Trumpington Street, Cambridge CB2 1RP
40 West 20th Street, New York, NY 10011–4211, USA
10 Stamford Road, Oakleigh, Melbourne 3166, Australia

First published 1995

Printed in Great Britain at the University Press, Cambridge

A catalogue record for this book is available from the British Library

Library of Congress cataloguing in publication data
Clery, E. J.
The rise of supernatural fiction, 1762–1800 / E. J. Clery.
p.   cm. – (Cambridge studies in Romanticism: 12)
Includes bibliographical references (p.).
ISBN 0 521 45316 x (hardback)
1. Horror tales, English – History and criticism. 2. English
fiction – 18th century – History and criticism. 3. Supernatural in
literature. 4. Literature and society – Great Britain – History – 18th
century. 5. Literature publishing – Great Britain – History – 18th
century. 6. Ghost stories, English – History and criticism.
7. Gothic revival (Literature) – Great Britain. I. Title.
II. Series.
PR858.S85C58 1995
823'.087380906 – dc20   94–10649   CIP

ISBN 0 521 45316 x hardback

1000535826

CE

For my mother and father

Contents

Illustrations

Acknowledgements

My thanks to Chris Baldick, Philip Martin and Isobel Armstrong for their early encouragement; to Anita Roy, Harriet Guest, Roger Pooley, John Rogers and Charles Swan for suggestions at the revisions stage; and especially to John Barrell, who helped me navigate this project from the start, and Michael Newman, my mainstay throughout.

An earlier version of chapter 8, 'Like a heroine', appeared as 'The Politics of the Gothic Heroine in the 1790s' in *Reviewing Romanticism*, edited by Philip Martin and Robin Jarvis (Macmillan, 1992).

Introduction

A 'rise of supernatural fiction'? The idea appears paradoxical. Certainly it cannot refer to the place of the fantastic in the hierarchy of literary genres, more marginal than elevated. Its popular success has more often been described as a spread or even contagion than as a rise. This will not, then, be the chronicle of the 'rise' of a genre of ghost stories as a triumphal progress through time. What I will be discussing concerns less the career of an already recognisable category of fiction, than the conditions which made such a category possible; in other words, the subject under consideration is the emergence of the supernatural *into* fiction. For the now all-too-familiar repertoire of spectres, sorcerers, demons and vampires was not from the first unproblematically available as a resource for writers of fiction. Works like *The Castle of Otranto*, *The Mysteries of Udolpho* and *The Monk*, today identified and dealt with by literary critics as early examples of the Gothic novel, as if that label were already securely in place at their time of writing, will here be seen as breakthroughs in the difficult overcoming of barriers to the fictional use of the marvellous.

The dates 1762 to 1800 given in the title mark the extent of a problematic. The period of the study properly begins two years before the publication of *The Castle of Otranto* by Horace Walpole. The highly publicised visitations of a ghost in the East End of London, the subject of chapter 1, was an event which for us illuminates the conditions of Walpole's experiment. The varying responses provoked by the Cock Lane ghost represent both the summation of previous modes of writing and showing the supernatural, and the disclosure of new possibilities. The turn of the century marks the close of a decade which saw dramatic swings in the career of the literary supernatural, from latency to critical success to convergence with the unfolding narrative of contemporary politics; moments discussed in parts III and IV. The year 1800 announces the end of one particular struggle over the boundaries of fictional representation and the beginning of an era of acceptance. The ever-increasing proliferation of supernatural fictions through the next two centuries still shows no signs of slackening in the last years of the twentieth century.

What the significance of that acceptance and this proliferation might be for the present time is a question I will address speculatively towards the end of the Introduction. But the question will remain implicit throughout the book in my treatment of historical material. On the one hand, a primary aim is to make apparent the otherness of the past by considering what was at stake in the exclusion of apparitions from works of literature, and their eventual inclusion, for the writers and readers of the eighteenth century. The debate over representation of the supernatural belongs to a historical horizon which is not immediately accessible to us, and which consequently brings us up against the limits of our own assumptions. On the other hand, the reconstructed meaning of this debate inevitably speaks to present concerns, and is understood by the process of identifying resemblances and origins: history has an effect. Acknowledgement of the alterity of the past enables, through dialogue, reflection on the nature of the present. This enquiry attempts to think together the two horizons of understanding, past and present, in the form of 'effective history'.[1]

THE GHOST STORY-TELLING CIRCLE

Incredulus odi,[2] to disbelieve is to dislike, might be taken as the motto of enlightenment faced with the spectacle of superstition. The attitude appears epitomised in an essay by Joseph Addison from the *Spectator*, no. 12 (14 March 1711). The taciturn but observant Mr Spectator has come to London and taken a room in the home of a widow on the strict condition that he is to be left entirely to himself:

I remember last Winter there were several young Girls of the Neighbourhood sitting about the Fire with my Landlady's Daughters, and telling Stories of Spirits and Apparitions. Upon my opening the Door the young Women broke off their Discourse, but my Landlady's Daughters telling them that it was no Body but the Gentleman (for that is the Name which I go by in the Neighbourhood, as well as in the Family) they went on without minding me. I seated myself by the Candle that stood on a Table at one end of the Room; and pretending to read a Book that I took out of my Pocket, heard several dreadful Stories of Ghosts as pale as Ashes that had stood at the Feet of a Bed, or walked over a Church-yard by Moon-light; and of others that had been conjured into the *Red-Sea*, for disturbing People's rest, and drawing their Curtains at Midnight, with many other old Womens Fables of the like Nature. As one Spirit raised another, I observed that at the End of every Story the whole Company closed their Ranks and crouded about the Fire: I took Notice in particular of a little Boy, who was so attentive to every Story, that I am mistaken if he ventures to go to bed by himself this Twelvemonth. Indeed they talked so long, that the Imaginations of the whole Assembly were manifestly crazed, and I am sure will be the worse for it as long as they live. I heard one of the Girls, that had looked upon me over her Shoulder, asking the Company how long I had been in the Room, and whether I did not look paler than I used to do. This put me under some Apprehension that I should be forced to explain my self if I did not retire; for which Reason I took the Candle into my Hand, and went up into my Chamber, not without wondering at the unaccountable Weakness in reasonable Creatures, that they should love to astonish and terrify one another.[3]

This is hostility to representations of the supernatural as we would expect to find it in the 'Age of Reason'. Imagination, far from being the active faculty exalted by the Romantics, is understood as a passive medium for the imprint of external impressions, liable to be permanently disordered by the excessive input of improbabilities. The children's taste for such horrors is an 'unaccountable Weakness'. The implication is that it would be for the best if ghost stories could be withdrawn from circulation altogether.

Or is the case so predictable? For there is also the surreptitious involvement of the observer in the scene he condemns, hinted at with such subtle irony by Addison: a suggestion of identification with the attentive little boy, in the man apparently unable to tear himself away as story after story is recounted, whose pallor is remarked by another of the children, and who finally retreats rather sheepishly, unwilling – or unable? – to 'explain himself'. Above all, there is the sense of physical contrast between the huddled group by the fire, and the solitary observer seated at a table, candle by his side, book in hand. There is an air of iconic significance to this juxtaposition. The group seems to represent an order of society which achieves cohesion through its myths, a circle bound and tightened by the shared sensations of fascination and terror. With each story it draws closer together, and shrinks further from the observer marooned in his pool of light. He, with his affection of anonymity and unconvincing display of detached authority, suggests on the other hand the emptiness and isolation of rational judgement, a sentiment of loss (hardly remedied by the strange notion, which ends the essay, of a crowd of invisible 'Spectators' existing alongside the living and authorised by rational religion).

The imaging of superstition as a ghost story-telling circle is not unique to Addison, and I will be suggesting that it served for those who spoke from the position of enlightenment as an ambiguous figure of the break with the naive beliefs of the past, which in spite of their falsity formed a ground for consensus, and equally of their dissatisfaction with the relative incoherence of modern society.

In 'Winter' from *The Seasons* (1730–44), James Thomson presents the image of villagers gathered together indoors in snowy weather, exchanging tales of the supernatural.

> ... the Village rouzes up the Fire;
> While well attested, and as well believ'd,
> Heard solemn, goes the Goblin-Story round;
> Till superstitious Horror creeps o'er all.   (617–20)[4]

Thomson insists on the credulity of the listeners, and the epithet 'superstitious Horror' might seem to indicate the unfavourable light in which the occasion is to be seen. Yet soon we are being guided to view this as a scene of natural community, when the circle of superstition, generically rural, is valorised to contrast with the artificial pastimes of the disenchanted city. In the city, at the theatre, in place of the rustic spectre, 'the ghost of Hamlet stalks' (line 646) and the anonymous crowd treats traditional beliefs as a source of artificial sensation.

William Collins's 'Ode on the Popular Superstitions of the Highlands of Scotland, Considered as the Subject of Poetry' (1749–50) moves beyond ambivalence to an open avowal of admiration for the ghost-story tradition and a clear desire to emulate it. The art of the story-teller has become the prototype of imaginative creation, and superstition is transmuted into a source of poetic inspiration. But the hapless London poet, disinherited by reason, can only bring himself to make use of these forbidden riches by the ruse of offering them up as suitable material for the writings of a friend, the addressee of the poem, Scottish-born and therefore closer to the remnants of the primitive in civilised Britain.

Such airy beings awe the untutored swain:
Nor thou, though learned, his homelier thoughts neglect;
Let thy sweet muse the rural faith sustain:
These are the themes of simple, sure effect,
That add new conquests to her boundless reign,
And fill with double force her heart-commanding strain.   (30–5)[5]

Collins here tentatively proposes the integration of the supernatural into the sphere of the aesthetic, and envisages the creation of a new story-telling circle which would consist of cultivated readers enabled, by taste, to reconcile themselves to the depiction of ghosts and goblins. A modern circle of aestheticised superstition would bear witness to the 'boundless reign' of aesthetic experience, its ability to transcend the narrow dictates of reason and unite a scattered and anonymous readership with the power of its 'heart-commanding' effect. But the prescription is implicit only; the sense of enlightenment prohibition is still strong enough to prevent the poet from preaching what he obliquely practises.

How could Collins have foreseen the happy marriage of super-naturalism and modernity satirised in a print by Gillray (fig. 1)? Dated 1802, it reflects several years of the frenzied production of modern supernatural fictions, and consciously parodies the conventional image of 'rural faith' in the form of four fashionable ladies who sit enthralled around a parlour table while one of them reads aloud from M. G. Lewis's horror anthology, *Tales of Wonder!*. The renovated circle of superstition has become a reality: it is determined by the rotations of fashion and commodity consumption. Ghost stories have been restored to universality by the improbable means of a commercial system of publishing and distribution. The unreality of these tales now goes without question; 'poetic faith', the voluntary suspension of disbelief, replaces 'rural faith'. The dangers of credulity have been overtaken by the primary goal of provoking sensation.

SUPERNATURALISM AND CONSUMERISM

The rise of supernatural fictions must be understood in relation to the contemporary rise of consumerism, which has been described as the eighteenth-century 'consumer revolution'.[6] The craze for such fictions in the 1790s was made possible, of course, by the expansion of the reading public, and the devising of new methods for dis-

This attempt to describe the effects of the Sublime & Wonderful is dedicated to M.G. Lewis, Esqr. M.P.

TALES of WONDER!

1. James Gillray, *Tales of Wonder!*, 1802

tributing and marketing books. But the connection goes beyond this, to contemporary reflection on the nature and direction of modern society. The resistance to representations of the marvellous, with their illusory, irrational appeal, coincides with anxiety over the escalation of 'unreal needs'.

'Political economy', J. G. A. Pocock has written, 'is the dominant mode of Augustan political thought',[7] and within this mode the discourse of civic humanism set the terms of the critique of modernity in the eighteenth century. Civic humanism entailed support for an economy founded on the 'real' wealth of land, along with the conservative political programme this implies, and condemnation of finance capitalism, based on rumour and speculation, resulting in mushrooming profits and sudden deflations, and encouraging the spread of a luxury – excessive consumption – which would corrupt individuals and destabilise the social order. As I will try to show in chapter 6, the attacks on novels and novel-reading in this period were part of the wider opposition to consumerism. In the case of supernatural fictions, the civic humanist objection to luxury commodies in general was supplemented by the enlightenment objection to a form of writing which perpetuated irrational ideas for the sake of affect. Within these complementary frameworks, supernatural fiction figures as the ultimate luxury commodity, produced by an 'unreal need' for unreal representations.[8]

But if eighteenth-century Britain saw the growing commercialisation of spirits, it also saw a spiritualisation of commerce; a fundamental chiasmus. While ghost stories were being assimilated by a rationalised market system of publishing in the second half of the eighteenth century, the language of supernaturalism was increasingly employed to justify and universalise the characteristics of market capitalism. Earlier in the century the analogy of the supernatural had been invoked under the influence of civic humanism in a negative way. For instance, in 1720 after the collapse of the South Sea 'Bubble' – a speculative scheme on an unprecedented scale and a symbol of the rising power of the 'monied interest' – broadsheets and satirical prints drew on the imagery of superstitious belief to express the sense of mysterious, inscrutable causalities at work: the stock-jobbers are conjurors or alchemists, the investors are Gadarene swine, demoniacally possessed, and the master of ceremonies is the Devil in person.[9] Similarly, when in *The Fable of the Bees* (1714) Bernard Mandeville embraced civic humanism's negative description of acquisitiveness and luxury as 'private vices' and proposed the paradox that these were the foundation of 'public benefits,' he was promptly denounced as an Antichrist. His doctrine that a prosperous economy was the net product of the apparent chaos of selfish passions rather than of disinterested reason, the consequence of the capricious pursuit of ephemeral satisfactions rather than of reflection and self-control, presented the unacceptable picture of a modernity dominated by illusion and fantasy as surely as the superstitious past had been.[10]

However, gradually a more positive version of the spirituality of the capitalist marketplace began to be put forward. Where its critics had attributed its cultural effects to infernal agency, apologists identified commerce as an order validated by God. In *The Elements of Commerce and Theory of Taxes*, designed as a textbook for the Prince of Wales, Josiah Tucker argued that the multiplication of 'artificial needs' in modern society is entirely creditable – 'as this System of Commercial Industry is equally the Plan of Providence with the System of Morals, we may rest assured, that both are consistent with each other'. Edmund Burke opposed state intervention to alleviate the food shortages of 1795 on the grounds that 'it is not in breaking the laws of commerce, which are the laws of nature, and consequently the laws of God, that we are to place our hope of softening the Divine displeasure to remove any calamity under which we suffer, or which hangs over us'.[11]

'Economic theodicy' has been introduced as a descriptive label for this hybrid discourse, which managed to retain much of Mandeville's libertarianism while laying claim to the high moral ground previously reserved for proponents of strict moral and economic regulation. It was a formula designed to 'reinsert' economic activity in the form of emergent free market capitalism 'within the sphere of the good'.[12] The verbal trappings of providential belief are applied, by a curious twist, to the evolving social science of economics. The mechanisms of commerce are 'supernaturalised', attributed to the unsearchable will of God. Even the most outlandish characteristics of the capitalist order are to be read as signs of a guiding intelligence, as are miracles within the schema of religious revelation. While the economic passions are not positive virtues, yet they are justified by the internal checks and balances of a divinely ordained economic order, able to smooth out in moral terms even the most extreme inequalities of wealth without the need for intervention from secular authorities. The 'invisible hand' hypothesised by Adam Smith is the most famous emblem of this eighteenth-century *rapprochement*. Smith's *The Theory of the Moral Sentiments* (1759) proposes a paradox as harsh as anything in Mandeville: luxury, the 'natural selfishness and rapacity' of the rich, results in the employment and economic support 'of all the thousands who they employ in the gratification of their own vain and insatiable desires'. Again, 'private vices' are condoned for the 'public benefits' they bring, but the rough magic of the trickle-down effect is then immediately glossed as the transcendental justice of an 'invisible hand': 'When Providence divided the earth among a few lordly masters, it neither forgot nor abandoned those who seemed to have been left out in the partition.'[13]

What can we deduce from the historical coincidence of the expanding taste for commercial fictions of the supernatural and the project of a supernaturalised theory of capitalism? It may be possible to see in this chiastic relation the roots of the 'dialectic of fear' which Franco Moretti has discovered in those mass culture myths of the twentieth century, Frankenstein's Monster and Count Dracula: 'The more a work frightens, the more it edifies. The more it humiliates, the more it uplifts. The more it hides, the more it gives the illusion of revealing. It is the fear one *needs*: *the* price one pays for coming contentedly to terms with a social body based on irrationality and menace. Who says it is escapist?'[14] By the beginning of the nineteenth century literary tales of terror were being affirmed as manifestations of an autonomous realm of the aesthetic, detached from the didactic function which had guaranteed the social utility of the realist novel. What could seem more gratuitous, more free of social determinations, than this indulgence in a fantasy of fear? But given the massive scale of the operations by which the culture industry has come to supply this experience, Adorno's remark on the phenomenon of 'free time' seems pertinent: 'people first inflict upon themselves (and celebrate as a triumph of their own freedom) precisely what society inflicts upon them and what they must learn to enjoy'.[15]

But in the period that concerns us, the assimilative potential of a revived and modernised ghost-story-telling circle was still in question. At this time the literary supernatural still had the power to disturb and, by the very force of the prohibitions against it, to voice otherwise unspeakable truths. Denounced by contemporaries as the symptom of a regression to Gothic barbarism by way of consumer capitalism, the literature of terror arose in the late eighteenth century as a symptom of and reflection on the modern. To quote Adorno once more:

phantasmagoria comes into being when, under the constraints of its own limitations, modernity's latest products come close to the archaic. Every step forward is at the same time a step into the remote past. As bourgeois society advances it finds that it needs its own camouflage of illusion simply in order to subsist. For only when so disguised does it venture to look the new in the face. That formula, 'it sounded so old, and yet was so new,' is the cypher of a social conjuncture.[16]

I

Techniques of ghost-seeing

CHAPTER I

The case of the Cock Lane ghost

In the second week of January 1762, an advertisement appeared in the London daily newspaper the *Public Ledger* reporting that a young lady had been lured to London, and then imprisoned and murdered by poisoning. Sensational though this was, it was nothing to the revelation which followed a few days later: the source of the story was the victim herself, returned to the world as a ghost. She was even then holding nightly interviews at a house in Cock Lane near Holborn and, though invisible, was able to give evidence through a system of knocks, one knock signifying yes, and two knocks, no.

Fanny Lynes died in Clerkenwell, in East London, in February 1760, after an illness diagnosed as smallpox. She was bearing the child of William Kent, the husband of her deceased sister. Earlier that year they had briefly rented a room in the house of Richard Parsons in Cock Lane, before moving on after a quarrel with their landlord. Kent had enemies who had no objection to seeing him publicly disgraced: Fanny's family, on the grounds of her illicit relations with him, and especially the will by which she left most of her property to him; and Parsons himself, who had borrowed money from Kent, and had been threatened with a lawsuit when he failed to repay it punctually.[1] It was almost always in the vicinity of Parsons' daughter Elizabeth, aged 12 in 1762, that the ghostly visits began to occur; and it was Parsons who alerted a group of clergymen, henceforth the self-appointed 'managers' of the haunting, who sparked the scandal that led to the item in the *Public Ledger*.

Other newspapers picked up the story and carried regular reports on its progress, and the Cock Lane ghost quickly became the talk of London. Familiarly known as 'Scratching Fanny' for her habit of making loud scratching noises in response to impertinent questions, she began to attract crowds to the haunted house day and night. Queues of carriages coming from the West End blocked the Strand.

The taverns and alehouses in the neighbourhood overflowed with thirsty sightseers. The interest of the murder case diminished as interest in the spectacular mode of the accusation grew. With a ghost so open to public scrutiny, there was bound to be more at stake than the criminal indictment of one man. Here at last, it seemed, after decades of inconclusive debate, was a chance for believers and sceptics to settle once and for all the question of the existence of spirits.

In early February 1762 Dr Samuel Johnson agreed to serve as a member of an 'investigating committee' into the ghost affair set up by the Methodist sympathiser Lord Dartmouth. The committee included both believers and sceptics, and they resolved to put the ghost to the test. Johnson wrote a report of their deliberations that was duly published in the *Public Ledger*.

The supposed spirit had before publicly promised, by an affirmative knock, that it would attend one of the gentlemen into the vault, under the church of St. John, Clerkenwell, where the body is deposited, and give a token of her presence there by a knock upon her coffin: It was therefore determined to make this trial of the existence or veracity of the supposed spirit.[2]

In Charles Churchill's caricatured version of the event, 'Pomposo' (Johnson) is joined by two others: 'SILENT ALL THREE WENT IN, ABOUT / ALL THREE TURN'D SILENT, AND CAME OUT'.[3] The knock never came, and though some were resolved to try further tests, Johnson resigned himself once more to doubt.

In the meantime writers and booksellers did their best to broadcast the debate, and cash in as they could. Among the catchpenny pamphlets in support of belief was a *History of Ghosts, Spirits and Spectres* by an anonymous clergyman, and a complete history of 'Scratching Fanny' herself. Two new editions appeared of Drelincourt's *A Christian Man's Consolation against the Fears of Death*, prefaced by Daniel Defoe's famous and authenticated report of 'The Apparition of Mrs Veal'. On the side of scepticism there was *Anti-Canidia: or, Superstition Detected and Exposed, & C.*, and *The Mystery Reveal'd*, attributed to Oliver Goldsmith. William Hogarth hastily revised the print *Enthusiasm Delineated* to include the latest scandal, and put Cock Lane (emblematised as a hammer-bearing ghost at the top of a thermometer of enthusiasm) in the context of a series of supernatural frauds under the new title *Credulity, Superstition, and Fanaticism. A Medley* (fig. 2).[4]

2. William Hogarth, *Credulity, Superstition, and Fanaticism*, 1762

Elsewhere, commercial exploitation neglected to assume even the appearance of serious engagement. There were broadside ballads, among them 'Cock-Lane Humbug' ('The town it long has been in pain / About the phantom in Cock-Lane'), poems and prints which

treated the ghost as pure farce. The Drury Lane and Covent Garden
theatres responded to the affair by staging rival productions of
Addison's comedy *The Drummer: or, The Haunted House*. Although the
play had failed on its first showing in 1715 and had not been revived
since, in the present atmosphere of ghost-mania success was guaranteed, or so the new prologue to the Covent Garden production
implied with humorous cynicism:

> If in this credulous, believing age,
> We bring a harmless Ghost upon the Stage,
> Some will perhaps conclude – in hopes of gain,
> We've lur'd the Knocking Spirit from Cock-lane.[5]

In its new context the play gained a dimension of knowingness. The
high point of each performance came when one of the characters
stated, out of the assumptions of another era, ''Tis the solitude of the
Country that creates these Whimsies; there was never such a thing as
a Ghost heard of at *London*.'[6] For now a ghost had become one of the
most fashionable metropolitan diversions.

   As well as presenting *The Drummer*, Covent Garden added a
'Ghost scene' to the pantomime *Apollo and Daphne* performed before
the king and queen in February. The following month Garrick at
Drury Lane struck back with a hugely successful new Interlude, *The
Farmer's Return*, in which the level-headed Farmer teases his astonished family with an account of his meeting with the 'ghoast' in the
capital,

> FARMER: *I* ask'd her *one* thing –
> WIFE: What thing?
> FARMER: If yo', dame, was true?
> WIFE: And the poor soul knock'd *one*.
> FARMER: By the zounds, it was *two*.[7]

Hogarth produced an engraving of Garrick as the Farmer which
was used as the frontispiece to the printed edition of the play, while
Zoffany's painting of the actor in the same role made his reputation
when it was shown at an exhibition at the Society of Arts in April.

   The great success of Garrick's play was due to the comic disruption of expectations, its inversion of the standard mapping of superstition, credulity in the countryside and scepticism in the town.
Here, instead, a sceptical rustic mocks the credulity of the city-folk;
a straightforward enough device. But if we extend the frame of the
theatrical spectacle to include the spectators, the city-folk them-

selves, their laughter, self-directed, could be taken to relate to a more complex perception, something exceeding the simple defeat of expectations; a new object, a new joke, beyond the country/city opposition. It is not that the city has regressed into superstition; there is nothing to distinguish the crowds who rush to Cock Lane to witness the haunting from the crowds who congregate at Drury Lane to mock it. It is as though the urban relocation of the supernatural has effected a change in the very nature of superstition. The audience's laughter seems to mark a transition, a displacement of the old opposition of belief and scepticism, truth and error. It celebrates the wresting of the invisible world from the sphere of religious doctrine, and its incongruous, hilarious embrace by the fashion system of the city. Freed from the service of doctrinal proof, the ghost was to be caught up in the machine of the economy; it was available to be processed, reproduced, packaged, marketed and distributed by the engines of cultural production. All spirits, whether spuriously real or genuinely fictional, will from this time be levelled to the status of spectacle: this was Garrick's underlying message. The town has added the supernatural to its list of commodities. The epistemological status of the supernatural, the truth or falsity of ghosts, is marginalised, a merely academic issue. The supernatural, deregulated, was going *laissez-faire*.

It is difficult for us, the inheritors of this 'spectacular' supernatural, to appreciate the impact and far-reaching implications of Garrick's joke. In order to do so we must go back to the end of the previous century and retrace the paths leading to Cock Lane, recovering the range of meanings attached to the supernatural and its representation in order to understand how the events of 1762 came to figure as a reversal of traditional expectations, and an illumination of new possibilities. The well-documented opinions of two members of the crowd who visited the ghost, Samuel Johnson and Horace Walpole, offer points of departure for the investigation of two techniques for ghost-seeing that posit two distinct objects: a 'real' supernatural and a 'spectacular' supernatural. Yet the opposition of the two terms will prove to be only apparent. For the spectacle of the supernatural, the production of ghosts as entertainment, emerges out of the ideological division between believers and sceptics which characterises the problematic of the 'real' supernatural. Johnson represents the impasse in the debate over the reality of spirits; Walpole, its supersession through the hedonistic acceptance of ghosts as a fiction, the move on which the founding of a popular genre of supernatural fiction will depend.

THE 'REAL' SUPERNATURAL

James Boswell was intrigued by the reputation for credulity that clung to Johnson in the aftermath of the Cock Lane affair. What had led him to expose himself to public ridicule? Boswell tackled him with typical intrepidity on this sore point more than once, and in his *Life of Samuel Johnson* attempted to make clear the nature of Johnson's commitment to the supernatural. Its source was doubt: an extreme horror of death which made proof of the immortality of souls an urgent necessity. This proof a spirit perceptible to the senses would provide. True, there was plenty of evidence for the reality of apparitions, and therefore of life after death, in the testimony, past and present, of those who claimed to have witnessed them. But could it be credited? Reason demanded something more concrete. Faith and tradition were together subordinated to a problem in epistemology: Can an immaterial being become materially perceptible, and if not, how can it be known to exist? The question of ghosts, Johnson said, was 'a question, which, after five thousand years, is yet undecided; a question, whether in theology or philosophy, one of the most important that can come before the human understanding'.[8] Johnson came to the ghost debate as a 'candid enquirer after truth'.

The truth that Johnson was after was essentially the truth of seeing, the truth of empirical philosophy. Sight was privileged above the other physical faculties in Locke's theory of mind to an extent that it became a metaphor for knowledge. Where did a truth that correlated seeing and knowing, and that elevated immediate experience above the authority of tradition, leave the invisible, supernatural agencies alleged by religious orthodoxy? Locke, following Bacon, had tried to moderate the secularising tendency of empiricism by positing separate and coexisting realms of knowledge, human and divine. But this was a shelving of the problem rather than a resolution. In the absence of material proof, the issue tended to revolve around the value of testimony. The need to demonstrate the existence of the invisible necessitated a resort to the tools of language and narrative. The desire for vision gave rise to a practice of writing.

As a means of guaranteeing truth, the exchange of experience through language represents a considerable fall from direct sense-perception. The ideal ghost scenario would therefore approximate the procedures of experimental science: a hypothesis would be formulated with otherworldly aid, a trial would be carried out to test it and the results compared to the prediction; the authenticity of both the hypothesis and its supernatural source could then be either confirmed or disproved. An aspiration towards scientific rigour lies behind Johnson's report to the newspaper on the testing of the Cock Lane ghost by the 'investigating committee', cited at the beginning of the chapter: the descent into the crypt of St John's was a controlled experiment, with premises ratified by the hypothesised ghost itself. If the 'supposed spirit' gave signs of its presence at an agreed time and an agreed place its reality would be established. In the event the promised induction was unforthcoming, the 'existence or veracity' of the ghost was unsustainable, and the value of the narrative itself, void.[9]

By attempting to construct a narrative that would serve as material proof of the supernatural, Johnson was maintaining a project which had begun a century before.[10] In the 1660s, attested apparition narratives had been offered as an antidote for the spread of atheism, for 'if there be once any visible ghosts or spirits acknowledged as things permanent, it will not be easy for any to give a reason why there might not be one supreme ghost also, presiding over them all and the whole world'.[11] The influence of Hobbes's attacks on superstition and his arguments for the corporality of the soul inspired Joseph Glanvill, a member of the Royal Society, to demonstrate the existence of spirits, and of witches as the agents of spirits, on rational grounds.[12] In the preface to *A Blow at Modern Sadducism* (1668) he called for an extension of scientific knowledge to include the supernatural: 'as things are for the present, the LAND of SPIRITS is a kinde of AMERICA, and not well discover'd *Region*'. Included in the work, as 'Palpable Evidence of Spirits and Witchcraft,' was an account of the case of a poltergeist at Tedworth in Wiltshire, a haunting which Glanvill personally investigated at the time it took place. In contrast to the rousing rhetoric employed elsewhere in the work, this story was written in a plain and circumstantial style, with no attempt to heighten the drama. A key element is the description of an incident where Glanvill himself sees mysterious movement inside a 'Linnen Bag' hanging in one of the rooms of the house, 'I stept and caught it by the upper end with one Hand, with which I held it, and drew it through the other, but found nothing at all in it' – thus demonstrating the presence of a spirit. Later referred to by the author's friend and editor as 'Mr Glanvil's *Experiment*', the episode typifies the way scepticism, rather than faith, set the terms of this project: phenomena are open to doubt until they have been put to the test.[13]

The preface to Richard Baxter's *The Certainty of the World of Spirits. Fully Evinced by Unquestionable Histories of Apparitions and Witchcrafts, &c.* (1691) explains how the author's own doubts concerning supernatural revelation led him to place faith on a 'firm foundation and rooting' by collecting all '*sure Evidence* of *Verity, Surely Apprehended*,' and how he then realised that 'all confirming helps' of 'Apparitions, and other sensible Manifestations of the certain existence of Spirits of themselves Invisible, was a means that might do much with such as are prone to judge by sense'.[14] As Michael McKeon has remarked, the documentary narratives of the supernatural 'speak to skepticism and atheism in the only language they will understand'.[15] The style of these stories was determined by the dialogue with a projected sceptical interlocutor.

And ultimately it is rhetoric, rather than logic, that carries the burden of persuasion. The apparition narratives were intended to quell disbelief by the patient, methodical and exhaustive display of facts: proper names of objects and people, exact measurement of distances of time and space, precise recollection of speech and actions. Here, monotony became a virtue. In order to refute those Devil's advocates who claimed, in Glanvill's words, 'that the stories of *Witches, Apparitions*, and indeed every thing that brings tidings of another world, are but *melancholick Dreams*, and *pious Romances*',[16] every circumstantial detail, every possible guarantee of the trustworthiness of the witnesses was to be painstakingly documented.

But in the latter condition, the need to establish the authority of witnesses, lay the problem; however internally persuasive the incidents of the narrative, they were still mediated by the intolerable veil of testimony. The dream of an intrinsically credible, rational ghost story was an impossible one. As Hume wrote in his essay 'Of Miracles', 'The same principle of experience, which gives us a certain degree of assurance in the testimony of witnesses, gives us also, in this case, another degree of assurance against the fact, which they endeavour to establish; from which contradiction there necessarily arises a counterpoise, and mutual destruction of belief and authority.'[17] The improbability of the tale casts doubt on the authority of the tale-teller; the dubious reputation of the tale-teller will henceforth undermine belief in his tale.

By the retelling of 'objective' ghost stories, Glanvill, More, Baxter, and later Johnson attempted to restore on a rational foundation the lost coherence offered by superstition; the former three aiming to win back the sceptics in the cause of a unified social body, and Johnson to persuade the sceptic in himself. As if in an effort to deny the impossibility of fulfilling the aim, the compilation of narratives tended to become an end in itself. The image of the ghost-story-telling circle, discussed above in the Introduction,[18] is curiously recalled, for instance, in *Saducismus Triumphatus, Or, Full and Plain Evidence Concerning Witches and Apparitions &c.* (1681; edited and published by Henry More from manuscript papers Glanvill left at his death), which is perhaps most interesting as the record of a large network of correspondents energetically involved in the exchange of apparition narratives. Named individuals scattered throughout the country were evidently united by the activity of writing up and communicating newly discovered incidents for the benefit of an appreciative audience; readers were invited to join by sending the editor new material.[19] Moreover, by the simple device of shifting the evidence of probability from internal to external grounds, from logic and circumstance to the more traditional guarantee of the quality and quantity of the witnesses,[20] the evidence of the shared belief in the supernatural in other times and other places, among the highest as well as the low, could be used to create the vision of a companionable, world-wide, trans-historical community of ghost-seers.

This notion of a reassurance of faith through force of numbers is introduced by Johnson into his oriental tale *Rasselas* (1759), when the poet Imlac takes refuge from the scepticism of Rasselas in a consensus that spans time and space, a global chorus of witness:

That the dead are seen no more ... I will not undertake to maintain against the concurrent and unvaried testimony of all ages, all nations. There is no people, rude or learned, among whom apparitions of the dead are not related and believed. This opinion, which, perhaps, prevails as far as human nature is diffused, could become universal only by its truth: those, that never heard of one another, would not have agreed in a tale which nothing but experience can make credible. That it is doubted by single cavillers can very little weaken the general evidence.[21]

The same willing surrender of intellectual individualism, or singular cavil, before the united voice of 'all ages, all nations' is found in Addison's essays on ghosts and witches from the *Spectator*. In no. 110 (6 July 1711) he carefully dissociates himself from the superstitious rumour-mongering of servants and villagers by referring to Locke's description of night terrors as a product of the association of ideas, inculcated by nursery tales.[22]

At the same time I think a person who is thus terrified with the imagination of ghosts and spectres much more reasonable than one who, contrary to the reports of all historians, sacred and profane, ancient and modern, and to the traditions of all nations, thinks the appearance of spirits fabulous and groundless. Could I not give myself up to this general testimony of mankind, [he cautiously adds] I should to the relations of particular persons who are now living, and whom I cannot distrust in other matters of fact.

Yet only a week later, in no. 117 (14 July 1711), the Spectator is speaking of his 'hovering faith' with regard to witches. Once again the 'Relations that are made from all Parts of the World' are there, but, inconsistently, they are no longer found conclusive. The doubting, questioning self of empiricism has been resurrected to challenge the pacified self of religious doctrine and external probability: 'my Mind is divided ... I believe in general that there is ... but at the same time can give no Credit to any Particular Instance'.[23]

But beyond the problems of demonstration and testimony, with their resulting tensions, the most serious threat to the project of the 'real' supernatural was perhaps the impossibility of determining the way in which the stories were read. Worse than the sceptics' charge that they encouraged superstition in the ignorant was the suspicion that they might merely be supplying a popular taste for the marvellous. The Cock Lane ghost's double career as both the subject of serious religious debate and as a kind of vaudeville attraction illustrates a tendency to slippage which was from the start a feature in the dissemination of apparition narratives. The authors and editors of the narratives were well aware of the risk that their publications might be misread or misappropriated, that idle curiosity or pleasure might subvert the didactic message. Glanvill voiced this unease: 'I have no humour nor delight in telling Stories, and do not publish these for the gratification of those that have; but I record them as *Arguments* for the confirmation of a Truth.'[24] Similarly, in the preface to *The Certainty of the World of Spirits*, Richard Baxter tried to pre-empt, by an exhaustive examination of his own motives for writing the book, the suspicion that it might have been produced to 'please Men with the strangeness and Novelty of useless Stories'. But there was no way of ensuring, however truthfully and plainly the accounts were set down, that the audience would not be illicitly gratified by them.

However much anthologists might fear the abuse of their stories, and insist defensively from time to time that they were merely sops to 'those of the lower sort' unable to rise to the level of abstract reflection, the fact was that stories, not argument, were the basis of the success of their works. In Glanvill's case this meant a grudging increase in the narrative part of his retort to Sadducism. Eventually his bookseller refused to reprint the work 'so often printed already' unless 'he had some new Matter of that kind to add, which might make this new Edition the more certainly saleable'.[25] Others more actively exploited demand. George Sinclair's *Satans Invisible World Discovered* (1685) contained a ratio of narrative to doctrine of 8:1, compared to 8:13 of *Saducismus Triumphatus*, and this factor is likely to have been decisive in its enduring success.[26] Sinclair has been cited as a key example of the progress of the apparition narrative from the didactic to the literary, for not only did he offer the reader a greater number of stories, he also told them more artfully – a strategy which would ensure their survival in the literary anthologies of a later generation.[27]

Daniel Defoe's *A True Relation of the Apparition of One Mrs Veal*, the most celebrated apparition narrative of all, is another example of this trend towards literariness and commercial acumen. Soberly factual as it appears, a comparison with other contemporary accounts of the ghost reveals Defoe's superior editing and enhancement of the raw material, blending vivid and credible circumstance with moral message and even adding a touch of suspense at the point when the spectre evades the welcoming kiss of her friend.[28] In the course of the story a religious tract entitled *The Christian's Defence Against the Fears of Death*, by Charles Drelincourt, is enthusiastically recommended by the apparition; 'Since this happened', muses the narrator, Drelincourt's work has been 'bought up strangely'. No wonder then that Defoe's tale was appended to *The Christian's Defence* in its many editions printed after 1707. Should the reader harbour doubts about these endorsements from the beyond, assurance is given in the Preface that the eye-witness, Mrs Bargrave, 'never took the value of a Farthing'.[29]

It seems that the category of the 'real' supernatural, as elaborated in the factual form of the apparition narrative, was always, irresistibly, on the way to becoming a 'spectacular' supernatural, a species of fiction. Hume, recognising no distinction between an irrational and a 'rational' ghost story, observed the potential of the pleasurable emotions aroused by the supernatural to overturn the criterion of truth: 'The passion of *surprize* or *wonder*, arising from miracles, being an agreeable emotion, gives a sensible tendency towards the belief of those events, from which it is derived. And this goes so far, that even those who cannot enjoy this pleasure immediately, *nor can believe these miraculous events*, of which they are informed, yet love to partake of the satisfaction at second-hand and by rebound ...' (emphasis added).[30] Hume's backward glance at a regressive feature of human nature and human society emphasises that narratives of the supernatural, least of any narrative type, can escape their exchange-value, their rhetorical dimension; their effect is such that 'even those who cannot enjoy this pleasure immediately', the pleasure of shared religious enthusiasm, even they can 'partake of the satisfaction at second-hand and by rebound', delighting in the performance alone, and in the irresistible power of discourse to rouse emotion. In making this observation Hume unknowingly predicts the rise to authority of hedonistic and aestheticised versions of the supernatural which will render the problem of belief indifferent, and restore the ghost story to universal currency – only this time in the form of a commodity, a fiction to be bought and sold. The social body will then be able to draw its coherence, not from traditional belief, but from the unconditional pleasures on offer in the marketplace. If collective truth is no longer attainable, let there be collective fantasy, a phantom collectivity.

THE 'SPECTACULAR' SUPERNATURAL

Horace Walpole recorded his visit to Cock Lane in a letter to his friend George Montagu:

I could send you volumes on the ghost; I went to hear it – for it is not an *apparition*, but an *audition*. – We set out from the Opera, changed our clothes at Northumberland House, the Duke of York, Lady Northumberland, Lady Mary Coke, Lord Hertford, and I, all in one hackney coach, and drove to the spot; it rained torrents; yet the lane was full of mob, and the house so full we could not get in – at last they discovered it was the Duke of

York, and the company squeezed themselves into one another's pockets to make room for us. The house, which is borrowed, is wretchedly small and miserable; when we opened the chamber, in which were fifty people, with no light but one tallow candle at the end, we tumbled over the bed of the child to whom the ghost comes, and whom they are murdering there by inches in such insufferable heat and stench. At the top of the room are ropes to dry clothes – I asked, if we were to have rope dancing between the acts? – we had nothing; they told us, as they would at a puppet-show, that it would not come that night till seven in the morning – that is, when there are only prentices and old women. We stayed, however, till half an hour after one.[31]

Johnson's melancholy failure to ground the spirit world in truth is here replayed as farce. It goes without saying that Walpole is a sceptic; there is no hint of the interests that drew Johnson to become involved in the case, not even a shade of hesitation regarding the truth status of the phenomenon. But it is surely not scepticism that has brought Walpole and his party out in the pouring rain, braving discomfort and disease to stand in a stifling, overcrowded room, and made them wait until half past one in the morning for something they have been told will not happen. Since there is nothing to see, or even to hear – for as Walpole points out this was to be an 'audition' not an 'apparition' – what is the purpose of their visit? They are there because this is the place to be. After putting in an appearance at the opera, Cock Lane, with its scandalous reputation, serves as a diverting 'afterpiece', an amusingly original recreation, its 'piquancy' counteracting the stink. In spite of the lack of event the structure of spectacle is in place.

In the instance of the 'real' supernatural, we observed how the pressures imposed by a commercial mode of publishing motivated a drift towards entertainment values in the *writing* of apparition narratives. An investigation of the 'spectacular' supernatural will disclose another drift from the criterion of truth to that of entertainment, but here it is scepticism determining a *mode of reception* for the purported appearance of marvels which initially ridicules and rejects, but ultimately prepared the way for affirmation. Out of the tensions inherent in a problematic defined by the seriousness of scepticism and faith emerge complementary forms of production and consumption positing a new object: the spectre as spectacle.

Just as the stringently factual stories of Glanvill could not contain their affective dimension, so the ridicule of scepticism could not repress the compulsive element of fascination which threatened to

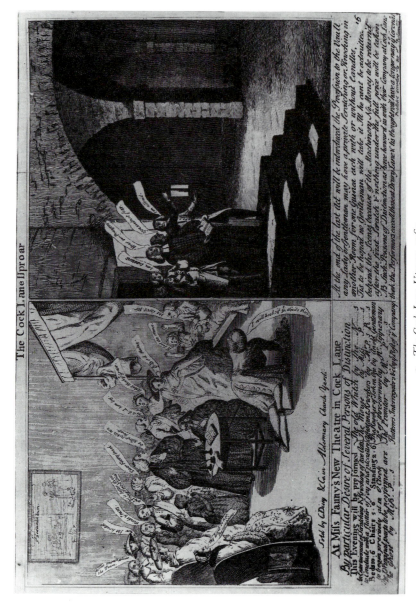

3. *The Cock Lane Uproar*, 1762

reify in a new and indestructible form the object of mockery. A spectacular conception of the supernatural does not stand over and against the problematic which disputes the question of reality, it is the product of its unresolved contradictions. Walpole's text is a document of transition: suspended between the negation of scepticism and the revalorisation of aesthetics.

Logically, scepticism requires the exclusion of the unbelievable from representation. *Incredulus odi*: that which cannot be believed must inspire disgust. Satire already involves a violation of this central tenet, for in castigating its object, it reproduces it. And the *way* it was typically reproduced was via the metaphor of theatre. Like a stage play, a haunting is based on illusion, and is subject to demystification. But the reproduction of a haunting as theatre equally provides the basis for a new attitude: it implies that whether genuine or false, a ghost attracts audiences like a stage play. A literal identification becomes possible whereby the marvellous is hedonistically accepted as a spectacle like any other, and the question of belief is marginalised. Thus Walpole remarks at the conclusion of his account, 'The most diverting part is to hear people wondering *when it will be found out* – as if there was anything to find out; as if the actors would make noises where they can be discovered.' There is no truth detached from the representation; only the internal truth of the illusion itself.

The visit of Walpole, the Duke of York and company to Cock Lane was duly commemorated in a print which uses the analogy of theatre as a satirical device (fig. 3). *The Cock Lane Uproar* advertises 'Miss Fanny's New Theatre ... An Entertainment of Scratching and Knocking in two acts' presented at the request of 'Several Persons of Distinction'. The finale will be the investigating committee's 'Procession to the Vault' – an occasion, as we know, involving Samuel Johnson – which the audience is invited to join, but "Tis to be hoped no Gentleman will take it Ill he cant be admitted behind the Scenes because of the Machinery'. Here the intent is all demystification, a fact reinforced by the framed pictorial reference within the wider frame of the proscenium arch. This represents the case of Mary Tofts, whose claim to have given birth to a litter of rabbits in November 1726 was, after a medical examination, upheld by Nathanael St Andre, anatomist to George I's household. 'The deception convinced several other doctors and a great part of the general public, following St Andre's lead, and the

4. *English Credulity, or the Invisible Ghost*, 1762

controversy that followed was fought with batteries of squibs and pamphlets.'[32] Theatricality is here firmly tied to the example of an earlier, well-known fraud, preventing the acceptance of Cock Lane as sheer entertainment.

In another print dedicated to the affair, *English Credulity, or the Invisible Ghost in Cock Lane* (fig. 4), there is also theatrical reference: the celebrated comedian Samuel Foote stands among the watching crowd cursing his luck at missing the opportunity of including 'Scratching Fanny' in his latest farce.[33] But once again the principal aim is to establish the event as a counterfeit by 'quoting' other notorious instances, yet again incorporated into the scene of Elizabeth Parsons' bedroom as pictures on the wall, this time with the captions 'Bottle Conjuror' and 'Eliz. Canning & the Angel'.

The 'Bottle Conjuror' referred to a fantastical event that was actually announced as a theatre performance but in the end achieved proverbial status on the sole basis of an advertisement in the *General Advertiser*, 16 January 1749, which went as follows:

At the New Theatre in the Haymarket, this present day, to be seen a person who performs the several most surprising things following; viz. First he takes a common walking cane from any of the spectators, and thereon he plays the music of every instrument now in use, and likewise sings to surprising perfection. Secondly, he presents you with a common wine-bottle, which any of the spectators may first examine; this bottle is placed on a table in the middle of the stage, and he (without any equivocation) goes into it, in the sight of all the spectators, and sings in it: during his stay in the bottle, any person may handle it, and see plainly that it does not exceed a common tavern bottle.

Those on the stage or in the boxes may come in masked habits (if agreeable to them), and the performer (if desired) will inform them who they are.[34]

The *beau monde*, among them the Duke of Cumberland, the king's brother, crowded into the theatre that evening along with the mob. They were the first to leave when rioting followed the non-appearance of the 'Bottle Conjuror.'

Elizabeth Canning, a domestic servant, disappeared for nearly a month in January 1753 and on her return claimed to have been abducted and locked up alone without food for the whole of this period before managing to escape. The two women she accused, a brothel-keeper and a gypsy, were tried and sentenced, but after further enquiries Canning herself was charged with perjury. London split into rival camps, there was daily rioting outside the Old Bailey during the trial and the Lord Mayor, the man responsible for bringing the case against Canning, was violently attacked by her supporters. Horace Walpole referred to the fabulous claim – that she had been sustained during her imprisonment by heavenly spirits – in a letter to a friend: 'For my own part, I am not at all brought to believe her story, nor shall, till I hear that living seven-and-twenty days without eating is among one of those secrets for doing impossibilities, which I suppose will be at last found out, and about the time that I am dead, even some art of living for ever.'[35] Popular protest against the trial of Canning came near to causing the collapse of the Lord Mayor's control over the City, and the memory of it led the Lord Mayor at the time of Cock Lane to act cautiously over that affair.[36]

In both these earlier cases, as in that of Mary Tofts, something that had been presented as real was eventually exposed as pure fabrication. None of them involved a return of the dead, but they shared with the Cock Lane ghost an element of the fantastic which might tempt credulity. The satirical prints, by triggering remembrance of the earlier incidents, sent the message that supernatural fraud was a recurrent fever of the age. There is another common feature in each of these episodes: the significant involvement of members of the elite in an affair otherwise represented as the result of popular superstition. The royal household, for instance, featured in the fiascos of Mary Tofts, the Bottle Conjuror and Cock Lane (the Duke of York who accompanied Walpole was George III's son), officials of the City of London in that of Elizabeth Canning. But this shared feature draws attention to a difference: Mary Tofts provoked furious controversy and the public humiliation of the medics and clergymen involved; after the hoax of the Bottle Conjuror rioting ensued; the trial of Canning, too, led to physical violence. Each time, social tensions were precipitated around a binary inherent in the paradigm of the 'real supernatural': high/reason vs low/superstition. It was an opposition symbolically disrupted by any apparent credit given to the marvellous by the elite. Their subsequent, temporary, loss of caste became the subject of gleeful derision in newspapers and prints.[37] The symbolic hierarchy could, on the other hand, be enforced from below, *vide* Elizabeth Canning, to the point where political hierarchy was threatened. There are faint traces of the carnivalesque in these inversions. In the advertisement for the

Bottle Conjuror the elite section of the audience is invited to attend in masks, but only in order to be unmasked by naming in the subsequent broadsheets.

Although Cock Lane was frequently represented as one of a whole succession of fake miracles, its significance was not exhausted by this frame of reference. Here there would be little controversy and no rioting. Social tension persists in the representation of impostures and in the events themselves as long as they remain essentially within the problematic of the 'real' supernatural; as long as the analogy of 'theatre' remains largely an instrument for the unmasking of falsity. But once the literal sense of theatricality begins to take precedence over the metaphorical, once the oppositions of truth and error, credulity and scepticism, are dismantled, tension is dissolved, for divisions of rank within the audience are relatively insignificant within the context of spectacle. There is democracy at the level of epistemology: the elite are not expected to 'know better'. In a theatre the spectators produce the spectacle by the unified focus of their gaze, and are reciprocally united by it as an audience. The collective gaze fixed on the scene of the haunting at Cock Lane constitutes it as a performance, while simultaneously enabling the self-recognition of the audience as consumers drawn together by a common appetite for novelty.

It was a recognition of the novelty value of Cock Lane that led Charles Churchill in his satirical poem *The Ghost* to describe it as 'Fanny's Lecture Theatre', rivalling the attractions of the Punch and Judy show and Thomas Sheridan's popular series of talks on oratory, then in progress.[38] In the same spirit, at Drury Lane, Kitty Clive sang (to the tune of 'For He's a Jolly Good Fellow') a 'peroration' dedicated to the ghost-as-spectacle:

> With wonder each year we the old year out do,
> We scorn to consider how far a tale's true;
> 'Tis enough that 'tis talked of, and that the thing's new.
> Which nobody can deny . . .[39]

When the new prologue to Addison's *The Drummer* stated, 'Some will perhaps conclude – in hopes of gain, / We've lur'd the Knocking Spirit from Cock-Lane' it evokes a phantom *preconceived* as a theatrical entertainer, passing from one engagement to another; a movable fiction.

The ghostly visitations in Cock Lane were exposed as a fraud on 21 February 1762, when a wooden block used to produce knocking and scratching was found in young Elizabeth Parson's bed. The conspirators were sentenced the following January: Richard Parsons to two years' imprisonment and to stand three times in the pillory; his wife to one year in prison, and Mary Frazer, the ghost's usual interrogator, to six months. When Parsons appeared in the stocks the crowd treated him kindly and made a money collection on his behalf. It seems right that the instigator of the affair should have had some recompense for a supernatural fiction that seems to stand as portent to the dozens of supernatural fictions which would be circulating successfully by the end of the century.

Against the expectations of rationalists, the invisible world was not to be demystified, deactivated and nullified by contact with a modern world of commerce and enlightenment. On the contrary: the smooth absorption of the ghost story into the rationalised apparatus of commercial production would depend on the material's continuing powers of fascination. As we will see in the following chapter, the mixed feelings of terror and pleasure that had threatened to subvert the didactic intentions of the writers of apparition narratives were already in the process of being theorised and deliberately exploited on a systematic basis, in the different contexts of dramatic criticism and theatrical practice. Abandonment of the question of belief appeared to make little or no difference to the intensity of response. On the contrary, the mental state of suspension in doubt was itself in the course of becoming a fetish; certainty would abolish this source of abject pleasure. Doubt concerning the existence of spirits would increasingly operate as a mechanism of fictions to which individuals might voluntarily subscribe.

CHAPTER 2

Producing enthusiastic terror

The affair of the Cock Lane ghost became a spectacle, but the fiction it represented was not of the kind to generate aesthetic experience. The girls in their boarding schools who, the newspapers reported, were too frightened to go upstairs to bed during the height of the scandal were a rarity among a public more inclined to laugh than shudder. For the development of the emotion of fear as the mode of reception proper to fictions of the supernatural we need to look to critical writings on drama and changes in theatrical practice. The naturalistic technique of acting which evolved around the middle of the eighteenth century showed the manner in which ghost-seeing was to be enjoyed: a lesson in subjective sensation. Where the spectre in Cock Lane had begun as a 'real' ghost and evolved into fiction, here we will be discussing fictional ghosts which are rendered 'real' in the minds of the audience.

In this matter, as over the question of the truth of ghosts, Joseph Addison again appears as an arbiter, showing that different ways of seeing the supernatural were as much the product of specific discursive fields as of personal opinion. We have seen how in the format of the periodical essay, an arena for the display of conscience and civic responsibility, Addison scrupulously wrestled with the epistemological problems raised by a sober supernatural, the object proper to this context. A few years after, in the entirely different context of comic drama, the same writer was able to present in a spirit of laughing cynicism a fraudulent supernatural, with the moral that 'ghosts' and sharp practice are generally found together. There is no inconsistency; the conventions of each form of writing determine the nature of the object. The horizon of *The Drummer; or The Haunted House* is secular not only without apology, but with assiduous guarantees. In

33

the Prologue the ladies are promised 'you shan't be frightened'; the ghost is a sham, 'Made up of Flesh and Blood – as much as you'.[1] Addison's introduction of the supernatural is not rhetorical, aimed at stirring the passions and gratifying a love of the marvellous, but farcical, a mere masquerade that the audience is party to from the outset, and in terms of dramatic value interchangeable with any other instrument of deception.[2]

Beside these alternatives, of an authentic supernatural dealt with in terms of faith and reason and a patently false supernatural treated as a theatrical contrivance, there is a third perspective found in another set of ruminations from the *Spectator*, no. 44 (20 April 1711). Here what is being legislated is the realm of the aesthetic; the essay concerns the various means for provoking terror and pity that have been successfully employed by playwrights, and their as yet doubtful legitimacy: 'there is nothing which delights and terrifies our *English* theatre so much as a ghost, especially when he appears in a bloody shirt. A spectre has very often saved a play, though he has done nothing but stalked across the stage, or rose through a cleft of it, and sunk again without speaking one word.'[3]

There is more than a touch of satire in the wording of this remark, a detached amusement at observing that extremes of emotion are reducible to the formula of a bloody shirt and a trap-door. Yet satire, and the cautious qualification that 'there may be a proper season' for the terrible effects of phantoms, thunder-claps and alarms, is evidently a strategy to disarm anticipated opposition; for Addison goes on to affirm that objects of terror, 'when they only come in as aids and assistances to the poet ... are not only to be excused, but to be applauded'.

Addison was not the first to make a claim for the revaluation of the supernatural as a resource of theatrical effect. Dryden and the critic John Dennis had tried to justify the introduction of ghosts on stage with bold assertions of the freedom of the artist (backed by classical precedent) which seem to anticipate nineteenth-century aestheticism: 'an Heroick Poet is not ty'd to a bare representation of what is true, or exceeding probable'.[4] But this doctrine bore fruit only in the tentative experiments of Dryden's *The Conquest of Granada* (1670) and Otway's *Venice Preserv'd* (1682). The attempt was weakened by the need to defend a *contemporary* writing practice in relation to the debate on the 'real' supernatural,[5] and Dryden's powerful declaration of liberty is followed by some curious vacillations over the truth-status of spirits. Addison's case, in contrast, has the strength of limitation. Ignoring the problem of creating new representations of spirits, he concentrates instead on the effect of such representations in existing works, their poetic capacity, celebrated by Dennis, for 'producing ... enthusiastic Terror'.[6] And while for Dennis 'enthusiasm', etymologically 'a god-inspired zeal', would have linked the terror inspired by poetic writing to a religious function, Addison's secular treatment warrants a sense of 'enthusiasm' closer to the modern subjectivism of 'intense interest' or 'passionate zeal'.[7]

The affirmation of the tragic ghost takes to the limit the suspension of disbelief on which all dramatic effect depends. It is not simply an object of terror, as a real ghost might be. Nor is it a source of the detached amusement to be derived from a mock ghost. The effect it produces is pleasurable in so far as the object is known to be fictitious and enjoyed as part of the dramatic artifice, but terrible in that, simultaneously, disbelief is suspended far enough for the passions to operate *as if* the object were a reality. Given that there is no room for the supernatural in a rationalistic world, the making 'real' of ghosts in the response to dramatic fiction necessarily involves enhanced sense of the possibilities of the aesthetic, and of its separateness. Only in art could ghosts have an affective afterlife. Valorisation of the supernatural as a source of aesthetic pleasure, the awakening of a sensibility detached, not only from truth, but also from probability is the sign of an autonomous sphere of art in the process of formation.

At the same time as it points to the future, Addison's view naturally relies on the authority of the classical past. His privileging of the emotions of pity and terror evokes Aristotle's discussion of tragedy in *Poetics*; so too, his discussion of dreadful murders and tortures, among the various mechanisms that provoke these emotions, owes something to the Aristotelian definition of *pathos*, translated as 'passion' in a contemporary edition and defined as 'an Action which destroys some Person, or causes some violent Pains, as an evident and certain Death, Torments, Wounds, and all such things'.[8] While the category did not overtly include preternatural beings, the example of Seneca, pervasive in the revenge tragedies of the Renaissance, was enough to secure the place of ghosts in the evolving dramatic theory of the eighteenth century – though not as yet in its writing practices; anything other than the comic representation of the mock-supernatural would open Addison and his fellow dramatists to the charge of promoting superstition.

The *Spectator* essay unequivocally sanctions the use of the supernatural to achieve *pathos*, pleasure through a fiction of suffering. Yet there is a small anomaly in the argument that suggests the effect may not in the end be fully achievable in theatrical practice, or possibly even desirable in that context. The mildly derisory picture of the effects of current stage practice already quoted is followed by the question 'Who can *read* the speech with which young Hamlet accosts [the ghost] without trembling?' Although *Hamlet* was one of the most frequently presented plays of the era, Addison implies that the complete experience of its terrible scenes required a private reading. He does not himself comment on the slippage; I would suggest that it registers the influence of another authorising source, Longinus' treatise *On the Sublime*. This work, like its successors in eighteenth-century aesthetic theory, focuses on the psychological interaction of the individual with an object in nature or a text. The eighteenth-century sublime has been construed as a primary conceptual instrument for the projection of an atomised modern subject.[9] The sublime seems to entail a turning of cultural and aesthetic theory away from problems of public, dramatic representation and the collective response of the audience towards the sphere of private aesthetic consumption and the psychosomatic economy of a single representative individual. This turn may scarcely be visible at the time Addison was writing,[10] but already a new hierarchy had been introduced. The emotions of pity and terror described by Aristotle were involuntary and universal; the sublime initiates a rarification of emotion as a mode of aesthetic response; sensibility, or imaginative empathy, becomes a faculty to be cultivated according to the external criteria of taste. Addison's private thrilling to the ghost scene from *Hamlet* bears witness to an *educated* sensibility – at the very least it required the ability to read (and to purchase books), at most the talent to visualise mentally, like the poet, the physically unrepresentable; altogether a different matter from the Pavlovian reaction of the theatre crowd to the sight of a blood-stained shirt. It may also be plausible to detect in this elitism a desire to contain unknown and incalculable potentials. 'To what Excess ... wou'd it not *move*, were *Hamlet's Character* as strongly *represented*, as *written!*' exclaims Aaron Hill of Shakespeare's tragedy in the *Prompter*, innocently and enthusiastically enough.[11] But while the power of art to move the passions remained in important respects new and uncharted territory, it might be for the best if theatre failed to reproduce the sublime experience of reading tragedy.

GARRICK AND THE RHETORIC OF FRIGHT

In the meantime, pantomime remained the dominant mode of representing the supernatural on stage. The prototypical spirits of the age were not the elder Hamlet and the other solemn revenants of revenge tragedy, but the devils of Marlowe's *Doctor Faustus*, with their fireworks and grisly practical jokes. A popular favourite was the witches' interlude from William Davenant's version of *Macbeth*, introduced in 1674 and in repertoire for seventy years, where an infernal song-and-dance routine is completed by flying machines.[12] Above all, there were the harlequinades, spectacular entertainments in which Harlequin magically transmutes from ballad-seller to ostrich, from washerwoman to rider in an equestrian statue, all in a succession of slapstick chases, which in the case of *Harlequin a Sorcerer* end with Harlequin carried off to hell, accompanied by lightning flashes and four devils mounted through trapdoors, by the illogical device of raising the entire stage, scenery and all, into the flies.[13] It was this form of the marvellous that Pope denounced for its hectic and unmeaning variety in *The Dunciad*:

> All sudden, Gorgons hiss, and Dragons glare,
> And ten-horn'd fiends and Giants rush to war.
> Hell rises, Heav'n descends, and dance on Earth:
> Gods, imps, and monsters, music, rage, and mirth,
> A fire, a jigg, a battle, and a ball,
> 'Till one wide conflagration swallows all   (III.235–40)

adding, in the *Dunciad Variorum*, a censorious note to these lines observing that farces of this kind were attended 'by persons of the first quality in *England* to the twentieth and thirtieth time'.[14] Like the performance of the Bottle Conjuror, another (would-be) staging of the supernatural with the emphasis on spectacle mentioned in the previous chapter, the harlequinade attracted a cross-class audience, but it had not shaken off the association with 'low' credulity and superstition sufficiently to make the shared pleasure in the marvellous the basis of unification, rather than of social tension.

Pantomime was readily classified in opposition to legitimate drama: the marvellous versus nature; the irrational versus reason; spectacle versus meaning; sound (music, effects) versus language. In an anonymous sketch *A Dialogue in the Shades, between the Celebrated Mrs. Cibber, and the no-less Celebrated Mrs Woffington* the two actresses find *Hamlet* and *Othello* no match for the harlequinade when it comes to drawing a full house: 'The multitude are incapable of distinguishing; and if their ears are but tickled, and their sight gratified, they re-echo applause, and go away contented.'[15] Garrick declared war on the sensuous and the low when he became manager of Drury Lane in 1747, with a public agenda in verse:

> 'Tis yours this night to bid the reign commence
> Of resumed nature, and reviving sense;
> To chase the charms of *sound* the pomp of *show*,
> For useful mirth and salutary woe.[16]

But the new regime did not signal a decline of supernaturalism. On the contrary, the banishment of pure spectacle was to be accompanied by a new method of ghost-seeing, whereby the naturalness of response would recuperate the improbability of the object.

Garrick entered the theatre scene in 1741 like the answer to a prophecy; capable of embodying the most powerful passions suggested in Shakespeare with a verisimilitude that critics had imagined impossible. A few years before, Aaron Hill, in the essay on *Hamlet* mentioned above, had written of the eponymous hero:

The *Poet* has adorn'd him with a succession of the most opposite Beauties, which are *varied*, like *Colours* on the *Chameleon*, according to the different *Lights* in which we behold him: – But the PLAYER, unequal to his *Precedent*, is for-ever, his *unvaried* SELF. We *hear* him, indeed, *call'd* Hamlet: but we *see* him, Mr *Such a One*, the ACTOR – the Man who would act *any* Stage Character, to perfection, must borrow the *Serpent's* Dexterity, to *flip out of his Skin*, and leave his *old Form* behind him.[17]

Now the Man had arrived, the man who Diderot would later observe was capable of displaying, in the space of five or six seconds, every successive nuance in the spectrum of emotions from wild delight to horror and black despair.[18] Here was the actor capable of playing the ghost scenes from *Hamlet* with sublimity, as the German writer and traveller Lichtenberg testifies in a passage I will quote at length:

Hamlet appears in a black dress, the only one in the whole court, alas! still worn for his poor father, who has been dead scarce a couple of months. Horatio and Marcellus, in uniforms, are with him, and they are awaiting the ghost; Hamlet has folded his arms under his cloak and pulled his hat down over his eyes; it is a cold night and just twelve o'clock; the theatre is darkened, and the whole audience of some thousands are as quiet, and their faces as motionless, as though they were painted on the walls of the theatre; even from the farthest end of the playhouse one could hear a pin drop. Suddenly, as Hamlet moves towards the back of the stage slightly to the left and turns his back on the audience, Horatio starts, and saying: 'Look, my Lord, it comes', points to the right, where the ghost has already appeared and stands motionless, before anyone is aware of him. At these words, Garrick turns sharply and at the same moment staggers back two or three paces with his knees giving way under him; his hat falls to the ground and both his arms, especially the left, are stretched out nearly to their full length, with the hands as high as his head, the right arm more bent and the hand lower, and the fingers apart; his mouth is open: thus he stands rooted to the spot, with legs apart, but no loss of dignity, supported by his friends, who are better acquainted with the apparition and fear lest he should collapse. His whole demeanor is so expressive of terror that it made my flesh creep even before he began to speak. The almost terror-struck silence of the audience, which preceded this appearance and filled one with a sense of insecurity, probably did much to enhance this effect. At last he speaks, not at the beginning, but at the end of a breath, with a trembling voice: 'Angels and ministers of grace defend us!' words which supply anything this scene may lack and make it one of the greatest and most terrible which will ever be played on any stage. The ghost beckons to him. With eyes fixed on the ghost, though he is speaking to his companions, freeing himself from their restraining hands, as they warn him not to follow and hold him back. But at length, when they have tried his patience too far, he turns his face towards them, tears himself with great violence from their grasp, and draws his sword on them with a swiftness that makes one shudder, saying: 'By Heaven! I'll make a ghost of he that lets me!' that is enough for them. Then he stands with his sword upon the guard against the spectre, saying: 'Go on, I'll follow thee', and the ghost goes off the stage. Hamlet still remains motionless, his sword held out so as to make him keep his distance, and at length, when the spectator can no longer see the ghost, he begins to follow him, now standing still and then going on, with sword still upon guard, eyes fixed on the ghost, hair disordered, and out of breath, until he too is lost to sight. You can well imagine what applause accompanies this exit. It begins as soon as the ghost goes off the stage and lasts until Hamlet also disappears. What an amazing triumph it is ...

The ghost was played by Mr. Bransby. He looked, in truth, very fine, clad from head to foot in armour, for which a suit of steel-blue satin did duty; even his face is hidden, except for his pallid nose, and a little to each side of it.[19]

Like an apparition narrative, this record abounds in circumstantial detail; but with a decisive alteration of purpose, for what it seeks to make palpable to the reader is not the apparition, but Hamlet/ Garrick's response to it. The behaviour of Hamlet is recounted in the present tense, for dramatic immediacy, and in exact sequence, to approximate 'real time'. Precise description of details, the fall of the hat or the placement of the fingers, is periodically interrupted by tributes to their effect: exclamation ('alas!') and sudden out-bursts of panegyric ('the greatest and most terrible'); involuntary breaks in the thread of the narration that bear witness to the explo-sive power of the performance even in recollection. Put beside this the bland and perfunctory evaluation of the ghost in his satin suit ('very fine'), with the slightly absurd preponderance of the 'pallid nose', and a new dispensation of interests becomes clear. What has gripped the spectators with terror is the vision of terror itself. Gar-rick's body acts as a lightning-rod for the transfer of passion. An anonymous essayist of roughly the same date remarks of Garrick in the same scene, 'he preserved Shakespear's fire undiminished, faith-ful as the electric, and sent the animated shock of nature's flame home to the heart'.[20] In art, the empiricist injunction against the transfer of experiences of the miraculous could be overcome. The perfect simulation of fear was a flare which transfigured by refrac-tion its supposed source, the otherwise stolidly earthbound spectral visitant, and could persuade the viewer that this was indeed an object worthy of the passion.

   This curious reversal of cause and effect is the principle theme of the earliest and best-known tribute to Garrick's playing of the ghost scenes. In *Tom Jones* (1749) the hero takes his chronically supersti-tious companion Partridge to see Shakespeare's tragedy at Drury Lane. The play begins, the ghost makes its first appearance, but in spite of Jones's assurances Partridge refuses to believe 'the man that was in the strange dress'[21] was intended for a ghost: 'Though I can't say I ever actually saw a ghost in my life, yet I am certain that I should know one, if I saw him, better than that comes to.' Then comes 'the scene between the ghost and Hamlet, when Partridge gave that credit to Mr Garrick, which he had denied to Jones, and fell into so violent a trembling, that his knees knocked against each other'.[22] In the light of Fielding's scepticism, the superstitious reac-tion of Partridge is lamentably vulgar, and Jones and the sophisti-cated town-bred members of the audience sitting near by have a good laugh at his literal interpretation of the action on stage. But Lichtenberg's account suggests that by the 1770s the literal interpretation has become the norm and the very notion of superstition, let alone the stigma, has vanished as a factor in the audience's reception. A specific technical innovation at Drury Lane may have a bearing on the contrast between Fielding's and Lichtenberg's versions of the performance. In the 1760s footlights on stage and black-outs in the auditorium replaced the diffused light of chandeliers, intensifying the relation of audience to the dramatic action on stage, while it reduced, or at least blurred and generalised, awareness of the behaviour of other members of the audience. Not only did this promote the power of dramatic illusion, but it also made possible the replacement of a socially complex experience of theatre-going, involving a continuous awareness of rank and clique, conversation, argument, flirtation and the risk of rioting, with a situation in which individuals are isolated and interpellated as passive subjects while being united by the shared experience of a vision.

A key feature of the literal response is the transference of the physical symptoms of fear from actor to spectator. In *Tom Jones* this is conceived of as farce. Garrick's recoil 'with his knees giving way under him' in Lichtenberg's account translates into Partridge's knocking knees. Once again, at a distance of over twenty-five years, Lichtenberg freely admits that the actor's expression of terror 'made my flesh creep'; and the tremulous audience, sharply contrasting with their detached counterparts in *Tom Jones*, are praised for possession of 'the greatest sensibility'.

Fielding's logic operates within a different paradigm, one in which the pantomime ghost and its technological delights prevails. It has not evolved beyond the instance in *Joseph Andrews* when, searching for an adequate simile for the expression of surprise imprinted on Lady Booby's face, the narrator invites the reader to recollect 'the Faces, in the Eighteen-penny Gallery, when through the Trap-Door, to soft or no Musick, Mr. *Bridgewater*, Mr. *William Mills*, or some other of ghostly Appearance, hath ascended with a Face all pale with Powder, and a Shirt all bloody with Ribbons'.[23] We find ourselves back within the problematic of the 'real' supernatural, which entailed practices of representation that were crudely mechanical and transparently artificial, and interpreted any emotional response in the spectator as evidence of the grossest credulity.

The reverse side of the same coin was Johnson's verdict on the acting triumph of his former pupil: writes Boswell, 'He was of a directly contrary opinion to that of Fielding ... who makes Partridge say, of Garrick, "why, I could act as well as he myself" ... For when I asked him, "Would you not, sir, start as Mr Garrick does, if you saw a ghost?" He answered, "I hope not. If I did, I should frighten the ghost." '[24] Johnson's attitude is, at root, indistinguishable from that of Fielding, overdetermined both by rationalist distaste for the exhibition of emotion and empiricist disregard for the affective dimension of the supernatural. They are immune to Garrick's naturalistic enchantment because they stand outside the conceptual boundaries within which it can take effect.

It may at first seem paradoxical that the new method of naturalistic acting by all accounts achieved its greatest triumph in a simulated encounter with the supernatural. But what the spectator in fact witnesses in the performance is the supersession of the ghost as an autonomous object, and its internalisation by the expressive sensorium of the perceiving actor. It cannot be 'seen' directly by the audience; vision is mediated by a new form of cognitive mapping. The body of the actor playing Hamlet becomes the locus of a system of exchanges, refractions and identifications joining the members of the audience, the ghost, and the ghost-seer on stage himself. First there is the simple triangular relation of perception: the Ghost is perceived and registered as an object in the mind of Hamlet (as played by Garrick); the association of ideas and consequent emotions that the Ghost produces in Hamlet are externalised in bodily form and impressed as an object of vision in the mind of the audience, who are then able to interpret the nature of the Ghost within the fictional framework of the drama. But the audience's intense emotional engagement with the action on stage is produced by another, supplementary series of interactions. Superimposed on the relation of seeing subject to seen object is an intersubjective relation. In order to infer the nature of the Ghost by means of Hamlet's actions and physiognomy, the audience must double back, put itself imaginatively in the place of Hamlet and reduplicate, through empathy or identification, the process of cognition that Hamlet makes manifest by his involuntary gestures.

On the basis of this mechanism, Garrick's mimicry of internal states spreads by sympathetic contagion to the individual members of the audience. They were moved and astonished by a physical eloquence transcending language. The *London Chronicle* for 2 Jan.

1772, published a poem allegedly by a young man deaf and dumb from birth, written after being taken to see Garrick in the part of Hamlet:

> When Britain's Roscius on the Stage appears,
> Who charms all eyes, and (I am told) all ears;
> With ease the various passions I can trace
> Clearly reflected from *his* wondrous face;
> Whilst true conceptions with just action join'd,
> Strongly impress each image on my mind;
> – What need of *sounds?* when plainly I descry
> Th'expressive FEATURES, and the *speaking* EYE;
> That Eye, whose bright and penetrating ray,
> Does *Shakespear*'s meaning to my soul convey. –
> Best Commentator on Great SHAKESPEAR's text!
> When Garrick acts, no passage seems perplext.[25]

During a performance by Garrick and Mrs Pritchard of the 'dagger scene' from *Macbeth*, comparable for terror to the *Hamlet* ghost scenes, 'a foreigner, who knew no English, was so upset . . . that he fainted away'.[26] 'To what excess', Aaron Hill had speculated, would the audience not be moved if an actor could equal the potency of Shakespeare's words. Now it appeared they were not only equalled for effect, but surpassed. No wonder Hamlet's meeting with a ghost emerged as one of Garrick's most celebrated set-pieces – the affinity lay with a technique of acting that bordered on the miraculous.

Yet this aspect of the marvellous with its sensational impact on audiences seems to have led to none of the anxiety we might have expected on the basis of our reading of Addison. Garrick's gift was wonderful, but it was not, to the trained eye, incalculable, inexplicable or even unpredictable. For behind the miracle of acting lay a body of knowledge, a knowledge of the body – a taxonomy of the passions. So that while Garrick might appear to communicate in a language so natural that it became transcendent, rendering superfluous even that most generic of human tools, verbal expression, those in privileged possession of this knowledge of the body could read Garrick himself as if he were a book, an encyclopedia of emotions made visible, or perhaps better, a dictionary. Like a linguistic sign, the units of paralinguistic communication employed by Garrick had two parts, a material substance and a conceptual referent as closely joined as the two sides of a sheet of paper. The mental states of 'pity', 'awe', or 'grief' were embodied by habitual and classifiable configurations of face and body, 'true conceptions with just actions join'd'. In the phrase of Aaron Hill, an idea of passion was 'muscularly stamped' on the face and body.[27] So closely linked are these emotions with their outward physical signifiers that the connection was readily and frequently described as 'natural'. Yet the observation that the signs of passion could be displayed at will and out of context, apparently unattached to genuine feeling, argued that the connection was arbitrary. Diderot called this delusory commingling of nature and art 'the paradox of the actor', but went on to unravel the paradox in favour of technique. The actor does not – cannot humanly – feel everything he shows night after night. The 'natural' priority of the mental over the physical is reversed; the signs of feeling are reified and infinitely reproducible.[28]

The years of Garrick's greatest success coincide with a period of intense interest in the art of public speaking.[29] We have already noted how the Cock Lane ghost's 'auditions' were compared to Thomas Sheridan's contemporary series of 'Lectures on Elocution'. With respect to the project of codifying the union of expressive action with speech, Garrick was, of course, exemplary. His genius was precisely for sudden transitions between clearly discrete emotional states, rather than the, to us, more familiar method of gradually building a psychologically coherent character.[30] William Cockin, dedicated his *Art of Delivering Language* (1775) to the actor, claiming that 'the doctrine laid down in the following essay agrees exactly with your own sentiments'. In the Introduction to *Elements of Elocution* (1781), John Walker explained that his system of notation was intended to convey the practices of a good speaker, 'and this, had that great actor and excellent citizen Mr Garrick lived, I should have exemplified in some of his favourite pieces'.[31] *The Art of Speaking* (1763) by James Burgh is one of the most comprehensive of these works of codification. The actions and demeanour proper to each passion are itemised in turn; a second section gives sample texts under the heading of one primary emotion, while other more transient sensations corresponding to the spoken lines are listed in the margin as a guide to gesture. The description under 'Fear' can be set beside Lichtenberg's account of the 'ghost scene' from *Hamlet* or Hogarth's portrait of Garrick as Richard III, horror-struck by the vision of his murdered victims (fig. 5).

5. William Hogarth, *Garrick as Richard III*, c. 1740

Fear violent, and sudden, *opens* very wide the *eyes* and *mouth*; shortens the nose; draws *down* the *eye-brows*; gives the *countenance* an air of *wildness*; covers it with deadly *paleness*; draws *back* the *elbows* parallel with the sides; *lifts* up the open *hands*, the fingers together, to the height of the breast, so that the palms face the dreaded object, as shields opposed to it. One *foot* is drawn *back* behind the other, so that the *body* seems *shrinking* from the danger, and putting itself in a posture for *flight*. The *heart beats* violently; the *breath* is fetched *quick* and *short*; the whole *body* is thrown into a general *tremor*. The *voice* is *weak* and *trembling*; the *sentences* are *short*, and the *meaning confused* and *incoherent*.[32]

Later in the book the famous scene from *Hamlet* is taken to exhibit 'Terror. Discovery of secret Wickedness', with such marginal instructions as 'Alarm.', 'Start', 'Tremb.'. The 'dagger scene' from *Macbeth* is chosen to exemplify 'Plotting. Cruelty. Horror'.

Rather than attempting, like Diderot, to undo the 'paradox of the actor', Burgh simply tightens the knot. There is no discrimination of art and nature in his picture of fear; the minute arrangement of limbs could only be the product of conscious control, the violently beating heart would be difficult if not impossible to imitate voluntarily, or to show. The confusion was the equivalent in theory of the *necessary* obscurity surrounding Garrick's practices and their effect.[33] Through the audience's act of identification the physical rhetoric of passion is naturalised, technique is masked, and emotion can pass unhindered from actor to viewer. Yet the actor's ability to engage identification is itself evidence of superlative technique. Naturalisation *reveals* skill even as it conceals it. If the individual spectator does not share the complete lack of aesthetic sense of Partridge in *Tom Jones*, and can retain a partially detached position of judgement, she or he will be able to join the general acclaim for a great demonstration of stagecraft. Now you see it, now you don't; sensibility and understanding flicker. But time would tell. What had appeared lifelike spontaneity at the beginning of Garrick's career became by the end of it analysable, through repetition, as a series of 'turns' and 'strokes'.

Where does all this leave the supernatural? In the context of theatre, a locus which combines unresolved the irrational play of imagination and desire with demonstration of the verities of protopsychology, the supernatural emerges redefined as a tributary of art. Within the regime of the aesthetic the ghost-seer could abandon her or himself to the involuntary flux of sensation, untroubled by the need to judge the perceived object by the standard of truth. Truth lies elsewhere, in the objectification of emotional states, classified and graded.[34] The significance of a spectre is to be determined by the quality and intensity of the feeling it arouses. In any scene of haunting, fear is the true object of the aesthetic, the apparition a mere catalyst. This will hold true for the fiction of the supernatural, which could perhaps more properly be called 'the fiction of fear of the supernatural'. Valorisation of a species of emotional response, authentically displayed and effectively contagious, carries over to legitimise its cause.

But before such a fictional practice can be established, a further prohibition must be overcome. Like Addison, Garrick successfully effected a recuperation of spirits as aesthetic images by a respect for limits. His practice is confined to works of the past, and of course the works of Shakespeare above all. Never is there a suggestion that the writers of the present enlightened age should apply themselves to increasing the stock of images that could provoke delightful terror. I will be discussing in the following chapter the model of historical progress that determines this rule. At this point I want simply to indicate the contradictory impact of the rule, as registered in the work of a contemporary poet.

Fear has become something that can be seen, known, valued and desired aesthetically. It is personified and wooed in William Collins's 'Ode to Fear':

> Thou, to whom the world unknown
> With all its shadowy shapes are shown;
> Who see'st appalled the unreal scene,
> While Fancy lifts the veil between:
> > Ah Fear! Ah frantic Fear!
> > I see, I see thee near.
> I know thy hurried step, thy haggard eye!
> Like thee I start, like thee disordered fly
> For lo, what monsters in thy train appear! (1–9)[35]

But although the poem represents one stage in the overcoming of the enlightenment refusal of spectral representation, it at the same time reveals, consciously dramatises, a tension which arises from the new dispensation. With the valorisation of spirits as a source of the sublime, the predicament of the modern poet stranded by secularism begins to be felt. The opening invocation to Fear is therefore no routine matter: Fear is 'seen' not only in order to flaunt the poet's skilful use of *prosopopoeia*, but because she *must* be seen, as a pre-condition for sublime utterance.

The urgency becomes apparent when the poem is read as a narrative beginning with the second and third stanzas before returning to the first. Shakespeare and the tragedians of ancient Greece, we learn, were the privileged intimates of Fear and they were able to communicate through their poetry the 'divine emotions' she inspired, above all by utilising the legend and folklore of the supernatural. In modern times this source of inspired feeling has been cut off; the invisible world that Shakespeare knew so familiarly has been 'un-known', falsified and disallowed by reason. Now only 'cottage-maids believe', though the supplicant of the 'Ode', half facetiously, half in desperation, promises to 'Hold each strange tale devoutly true' in return for the ability to read the works of the past with the feelings of an earlier, more credulous, audience. But there is no possibility of a genuine return. The emotion of fear is the one remaining point of access to an otherwise lost realm of poetic inspiration, a guardian of the threshold dividing the natural and the supernatural. Any access will be purely imaginary – a vicarious

experience like that of the audience at the performance of *Hamlet* –
but will enable a rehabilitation, by means of affect, of that exploded
object, superstition. It is fear personified that the poet hopes will
'teach' him by example to equal Shakespeare's powers of expression:
'And I, O Fear, will dwell with thee!'

Looking back at the first stanza, we can recognise it as the
fulfilment in anticipation of this final wish. The poet has been
granted his merger with Fear: by the power of apostrophe – that
emblem of poetic vocation[36] – and by personifying description, he is
able to visualise her, and, by catching her example, wins access to
the 'world unknown'. In evidence of this, the strophe itself exhibits
the symptoms of a body possessed by fear. The opening quatrain
hurries breathlessly towards the identification of 'Thou'. On first
reading, the effect of the revelation in line 5 that 'Thou' is 'Fear'
could be compared to coming face to face at the end of a corridor
with the pursuing fiend you had hoped was behind you. But the
initial, seemingly perverse, flight *towards* Fear is of a piece with the
logic of the complete poem: Fear, far from being evaded, needs to be
actively sought out. The following couplet testifies by its metre and
syntax that she has been found. The strong, irregular rhythm
mimics the violent heartbeats of James Burgh's recipe for the
passion. The repetitions figure 'the *breath* . . . fetched *quick* and *short*';
the sentences, too, are appropriately short 'and the *meaning confused*
and *incoherent*.' This is not to point out any extraordinary correspondence between Burgh and Collins – the symptoms are standard
enough – but to suggest that what is taking place in both cases is a
textbook lesson in fear. The poet 'knows' the 'hurried step' and
'haggard eye' of Fear, and from recognising these indicators, inter-
nalises them: 'Like thee I start, like thee disordered fly.' The success
of this manoeuvre is demonstrated by the consequence: 'For lo, what
monsters in thy train appear!' Fancy has lifted the veil and the poet,
now identified with Fear in mind and body, can, like her, gain entry
to the 'world unknown'.

But the 'flashback' ordering of the poem, happy ending coming
before crisis, must of course be taken into account, for its effect is
one of irony: the brief moment of affirmation is passed before we are
told what it is affirming, and from the start of the second stanza
the creative voice of the poet gradually dwindles into regretful
retrospect and pleadings. The poet we meet in the final stanza can
only dream, hopelessly, of writing the first. The visionary power

displayed at the start is retrospectively exposed as the illusory wish-fulfilment of the plaintive last lines. The structure of the 'Ode to Fear', a broken circle, insists that a difficulty has yet to be resolved. As in Collins's 'Ode on the Popular Superstitions of the Highlands of Scotland', referred to in the Introduction, the poet is divided between the desire to exploit the supernatural for aesthetic effect, and a guilty consciousness of the enlightenment prohibition against any such usage, exposing a general problematic which would also have a determining effect on Walpole's novel, *The Castle of Otranto*.

Like the addressee in Collins's 'Ode', Garrick in the ghost scenes from *Hamlet* acted for his contemporaries as a personification of fear and a figure for imitation. He was a legislator of taste, like Addison, but also a populariser and audience-builder: 'Garrick ... corrected the audience's taste: he taught them, by the greatness of his acting, to know those nice touches of nature, which they were till then strangers to. When he acted, the audience saw what was right.'[37] The taste for supernatural terror he left in his wake, while it did not overcome all obstacles, went some way towards establishing the conditions in which fantastic fiction would be produced by popular demand.

II

The business of Romance

CHAPTER 3

The advantages of history

EXEMPLARY HISTORICISM

In February 1765 the *Monthly Review* recommended *The Castle of Otranto* to its readers, promising 'considerable entertainment' to those 'who can digest the absurdities of Gothic fiction, and bear with the machinery of ghosts and goblins ... for it is written with no common pen; the language is accurate and elegant, the characters are highly finished; and the disquisitions into human manners, passions and pursuits, indicate the keenest penetration, the most perfect knowledge of mankind'.[1]

But in a later issue the *Monthly Review* was forced to revise its verdict:

While we considered [*The Castle of Otranto* a translation] we could readily excuse its preposterous phenomena, and consider them as sacrifices to a gross and unenlightened age. – But when, as in this edition, [it] is declared to be a modern performance, that indulgence we offered to the foibles of a supposed antiquity, we can by no means extend to the singularity of a false tale in a cultivated period of learning. It is, indeed, more than strange that an Author, of a refined and polished genius, should be an advocate for re-establishing the barbarous superstitions of Gothic devilism! *Incredulus odi*, is, or ought to be a charm against all such infatuation.[2]

Three months divided the two judgements. The cause of this turnaround was the appearance in the interim of a second edition of the book including a new preface, signed with the initials 'H. W.'. *The Castle of Otranto* was revealed to be a modern scandal rather than an ancient curiosity, a sinister hoax rather than a naive genuine article. The reviewer was, in effect, faced with two entirely different works. One was a relic of the middle ages, attributed to 'Onuphrio Muralto, Canon of the Church of St. Nicholas at Otranto' and translated from old Italian by a certain 'William Marshall, Gent.'.

53

This work was a 'gothic' fiction in the accepted, historical sense. The other, resembling the first almost word for word, was shown by a new preface to be a 'modern performance', and the added initials 'H. W.' hinted that the writer was no obscure eccentric but a man of rank and influence. This was something unprecedented and untenable – a *'gothic* story', as the newly introduced subtitle insisted, with a *modern* author. Chronology was confounded.

The reviewer's double response makes clear the limits of a 'horizon of expectation', the system of critical norms that determines whether or not a new work is to be considered acceptable.[3] A work of the distant past that includes the supernatural or the wonderful falls within that horizon; a modern work that does the same will be beyond the pale. The supernatural is admitted to representation on condition that it exists *only* in representation, as fiction, myth or superstition, without claims to external reality. Here the issue is not, as it was in the case of the Cock Lane ghost or the performances of *Hamlet*, ways of *seeing* the supernatural, whether as an object of truth, an entertainment or a source of aesthetic pleasure. The fictionality of superstitious phenomena is taken for granted by the critic. Attention is turned instead to legitimate and illegitimate ways of *showing* and *reading* the supernatural as an exclusively literary phenomenon. The marvellous machinery of the first edition of *Otranto* is 'digestible'; its supposed antiquity warrants the use of a discourse of taste. The motto *incredulus odi*, to disbelieve is to dislike, is temporarily suspended. But the rule returns in force once the hoax is uncovered, freezing the operations of taste and proscribing pleasure.

A model of historical progress is manifest in the critic's double-take, and, equally, in the nature of the trick that caused it. Historicity, the criterion of historical authenticity, underwrites them both. Rationally speaking, ghosts and goblins are not *true*, but when they appear in the literary artifacts of past ages, they are *true to history*, accurate representations of an obsolete system of belief: a stance we might call *exemplary* historicism. For the enlightened reader, ancient romances are at once fictions *and* historical documents. The same standard that allows for the depiction of irrational impossibilities in works from the distant past must therefore disallow it in modern fictions. 'The publication of any work, *at this time*, in England, composed of such rotten materials, is a phenomenon we cannot account for', wrote another reviewer of *Otranto*, who guessed at the imposture from the start.[4] For modern fictions are also historical documents, and self-authenticating modernity has a stake in their sustained realism. Description gives rise to prescription: a nation guided by reason, in an age of reason, will not produce modern literary works which could be mistaken for the products of the age of superstition; if such a work does appear, it must not be countenanced.

On the one hand, then, by the 1760s critical discourse was actively working to produce the taste and demand for literary antiquities among the reading public, and helping to overcome enlightenment objections to the representation of the marvellous. On the other hand, it imposed the rule that such representations could only be enjoyed in a work of the past, when it could be accompanied by awareness of their out-moded absurdity. For a number of authors the logical response to this message was forgery. The lesson of the unfavourable critical reception given to Gray's and Collins's experiments in the 'Gothic' style was perfectly clear. If the public's appetite for Gothicism was to be tapped by living authors, it had to be done under cover of fake antiquity. *The Castle of Otranto* was one result, Thomas Chatterton's 'Rowley' poems (1769) were another. But the most successful fakes of all were James Macpherson's prose poems *Fingal* and *Temora*, which many continued to believe were the work of 'Ossian' well into the nineteenth century. There is no need to speculate on Macpherson's personal motives for the hoax. It is enough in this context to remark that the poems were an obliging answer to an urgent invitation. On the basis of his *Fragments of Ancient Poetry* (1760), Macpherson was commissioned by a group of Scottish patriots full of classical learning, among them Hugh Blair, Adam Ferguson, David Hume and James Boswell, to go to the Highlands and come back with an epic poem in Gaelic to rival Homer. This he promptly did; and the late eighteenth-century reading public had what it desired, a work in the image of its own enthusiasms and prejudices, the past as it was meant to be. 'Ossian' was quickly translated into nine European languages and converted into an icon of Romanticism by Goethe's *Sorrows of Young Werther*, becoming the favourite author of Napoleon.

As a representation of the supernatural, the text of Ossian's poems bears witness to its own ambiguous status. A post-Romantic reader would imagine that the enthusiasm the poems inspired depended on an unmediated sympathy with the alien world of the ancient Celts, where the dead and the living exist in a single dimension. But in the official editions of the poems the framework of antiquarian scholarship becomes part of the representation, quite objectively, in the format of each page. The first two books of *Fingal*, for instance, testify to Macpherson's astute management of the problem of reproducing superstition for the eyes of an enlightened audience. There are two passing instances of the supernatural in Book 1: the reappearance in his native country of the ghost of the slain hero Trenar, and the shrieking 'ghosts of the lately dead' prophesying destruction. Both of these are counterbalanced by extensive annotation at the bottom of the page, filling the modern reader's presumed vacuum of belief with historical truths concerning ancient Scottish folklore. The following book begins with a more sustained and structurally integrated passage of supernaturalism: Connal is visited by the apparition of his friend Crugal and warned of his army's coming débâcle on the battlefield. Here a different paratextual strategy is employed: comparative quotation of passages from Homer and Virgil, both in the original languages and in translations by Pope and Dryden, occupy two half pages. This method, which is regularly, not to say compulsively, practised throughout the poem, highlights the ambivalence of the whole project. The aim is both to legitimate a literary novelty by association with the classical canon, and at the same time to suggest that anything the classical authors had done a native bard could do as well if not better. Only the fact that this was precisely what the work's audience wanted to hear can explain why the ceaseless pointing out of parallels did not at once expose *Fingal* for what it was, gothic adapted to the model of the classical canon.

The critical apparatus of the text sent the progressivist message expected of the antiquary, framing a document of superstition with historical knowledge. But the critical dissertations which were appended to the epics implicitly criticise the progress of commerce and enlightenment. 'The genius of the highlanders has suffered a great change within these few years', Macpherson states, before going on to describe how improved communications with the rest of Britain, the introduction of trade and manufactures with the consequent reduction in leisure, the breakdown of the clan system, migration and the changed tastes of those who return, have all led to the erosion of the native poetical tradition.[5] Blair in his commentary suggests that, contrary to the assumptions of enlightenment, the writings of Ossian represent a meridian of the human spirit which the present age cannot aspire to: 'The two dispiriting vices, to which Longinus imputes the decline of poetry, covetousness and effeminacy, were as yet unknown.'[6] He refers to a section of Longinus' treatise *On the Sublime* entitled 'The Decay of Eloquence', which proposes that 'the love of money, that insatiable craving from which we all now suffer, and the love of pleasure make us their slaves, or rather, one might say, sink our lives (body and soul) into the depths'.[7] The civilising of the Scottish Highlands, the furthest outpost of the kingdom, was a drama enacted before the eyes of eighteenth-century intellectuals. A major literary work, said to derive from a culture which was only now in the course of vanishing, was a natural focus for ambivalent attitudes towards the direction of modernity, encouraging the articulation of a position in which primitivism, the aesthetic discourse of the sublime, and anti-capitalist political discourse were all linked.

Public debate over the authenticity of the 'Ossian' and 'Rowley' poems dragged on for years; MacPherson refused to speak and Chatterton died before the publication of his works. Prominent among the zealots for truth was Samuel Johnson, this time ranged on the side of the sceptics, apparently undeterred by the outcome of the Lauder 'plagiarism' affair in which he had unluckily involved himself.[8] Quixotically Johnson, with a bemused Boswell in tow, scoured the extremities of the British Isles for evidence of deception, an *ad hoc* literary police force. On his tour of the Highlands in 1773 he had the opportunity of interrogating the natives on the existence of Gaelic in written form, the results confirming his conviction that no old manuscripts of the 'Ossian' poems could be produced to prove their authenticity. Three years later Johnson and Boswell were journeying to Bristol, where an interview with a local pewterer 'who was as zealous for Rowley, as Dr. Blair was for *Ossian*', an examination of some 'original manuscripts' and a view of the ancient chest in which they were purported to have been found, alike failed to impress.[9] Johnson stood for a historicism uncontaminated by primitivism. In his view the works of 'Ossian' were not only worthless as historical documents; by their very success in simulating gothic 'wildness' they were rendered aesthetically and morally worthless, quite apart from the question of authenticity. He said of *Fingal*, 'a man might write such stuff for ever, if he would *abandon* his mind to it'; it had 'no end or object, design or moral'. His reply to the question 'whether he thought any man of a modern age could have written such poems?' is indicative: 'Yes, Sir, many men, many women, and many children.'[10]

Johnson's response to 'Ossian' is worth dwelling on, because it is closely tied to what was probably the most important and influential statement of exemplary historicism with regard to fiction, his essay on the nature and function of the modern novel in *The Rambler*. Here, observation of present taste, understood in contrast to the taste of the immediate past, is converted into a principle of legislation:

The works of fiction, with which the present generation seems more particularly delighted, are such as exhibit life in its true state, diversified only by accidents that daily happen in the world, and influenced by passions and qualities which are really to be found in conversing with mankind ... Its province is to bring about natural events by easy means, and to keep up curiosity without the help of wonders: it is therefore precluded from the machines and expedients of the heroic romance, and can neither employ giants to snatch away a lady from the nuptial rites, nor knights to bring her back from captivity; it can neither bewilder its personages in desarts, nor lodge them in imaginary castles.[11]

Johnson gives a number of reasons why the novel should adhere to probability and reject marvels. For a start, the audience of today is more demanding, more worldly and knowledgeable. Any deviation from reality would be rejected. Conversely, and more importantly, books of this kind are most often read by the young, the ignorant, and the idle, to whom they serve as guides to conduct, and introductions into life. The ideal type of the novel-reader is the Lockeian *tabula rasa*, a blank tablet, an unformed mind. Correspondingly the critic takes the role of tutor or wise father. Authors are advised to show extreme caution, and avoid imposing on the inexperienced 'unjust prejudices, perverse opinions, and incongruous combinations of images' which may ruin the reader for everyday life. The rest of the essay, more than half of it, is concerned with qualifying the demand for realism, to preclude the depiction of 'mixed characters', heroes combining good and bad qualities. The question of representation is displaced by the problem of rhetoric. In a work that successfully depicts its characters in terms of real human behaviour, as opposed to the outlandish stereotypes of romance, the reader, and particularly the young reader, will be drawn into a process of identification. They will 'hope by observing [an adventurer's] behaviour and success to regulate their own practices, when they shall be engaged in a like part'. Probability is not enough; in order to fulfil the function of teaching by example, the author must select from nature according to propriety, in pursuit of a universal conception of what reality *should* be. In the final analysis, it is because narratives need not practise 'historical veracity', in the sense of passive imitation, that they are valuable for the purposes of moral education. The ideal of mimesis or imitation has undergone a series of turns: imitation of life is agreeable to the modern reader and is consequently a quality which defines modern fiction, but through the impressionable medium of the reader, the novel has the power to cause life to imitate fiction; therefore fictional imitation of life must be subordinated to the interests of morality, and remain a vehicle rather than becoming an end in itself.

The concept of fictional example, a variation of the doctrine *utile dulci*, the useful with the agreeable, was the dominant definition of what the modern novel was and what it was meant to do for the remainder of the eighteenth century, until rival accounts – aesthetic, psychological and political – strengthened in the 1790s. As the touchstone of a language of critical evaluation for fiction it was far more pervasive than the discourse of the sublime, for instance. It is a measure of its monopoly that it was applied to the first edition of *The Castle of Otranto* in the passage from the *Monthly Review* quoted at the beginning of this chapter. The novel is, properly speaking, disqualified from an exemplary role in Johnson's sense by the stigma of its antiquity, its gothic 'absurdities', but it is nevertheless praised for its possession of peculiarly eighteenth-century virtues of imitation. Its language is 'accurate and elegant', its characterisation 'highly finished', it shows a 'perfect knowledge' of mankind. There was, it would seem, no other vocabulary with which to express the pleasure derived from *Otranto*, a pleasure not usually connected with antique texts. Like 'Ossian', improbabilities notwithstanding, it suited the taste of the times remarkably well, and the unsuspecting critic would soon know why. Once the hoax is uncovered the catalogue of virtues becomes a list of grievances. The didactic principle of example accorded fiction extraordinary powers to corrupt or improve, with no allowance for the reader's reflective distance. In this respect, *Otranto*, an unprecedented amalgam of exemplary polish and gothic roughness, posed a peculiarly dangerous threat. The combination in a modern work of improbability *and* convincing realism was a possibility unforeseen by Johnson. As the critic remarked, it was 'more than strange that an Author, of a refined and polished genius, should be an advocate for . . . Gothic devilism!'

If we were to look for something like a scientific 'control' to test the claims of the argument up to this point, we might note the appearance, two years before publication of *The Castle of Otranto*, of Thomas Leland's *Longsword*. This was openly a modern fiction in the romance mode, catering to the same demand for images of the gothic past as Macpherson, Walpole and Chatterton, yet its critical reception was universally favourable and unproblematic. This success can be attributed to the decision to exclude any hint of the supernatural or marvellous. *Longsword* was presented unequivocally as a work of the present which depicted the medieval age in the manner approved by the present; as one reviewer described it, 'a new and agreeable species of writing, in which the beauties of poetry and the advantages of history are happily united'.[12] It offered 'the advantages of history' – an informative picture of the past which illustrated progress while stimulating through its strangeness – but without corrupting the faculty of judgement with fantastic improbabilities.

THE CASTLE OF OTRANTO I: PREFACES

The abrasive effect of *The Castle of Otranto* was unique. While other writers attempted to manage the divergent tendencies of the historicist critical code to their own benefit either by forgery (Macpherson, Chatterton) or compromise (Leland), Walpole exposed its incoherence by inviting orthodox assumptions which were then shown to have no foundation. It is true that Walpole's own explanation of the hoax was rather different; he claimed it was the defensive action of a nervous innovator, and this seems plausible enough in view of the hostile critical reaction the work provoked once his authorship became known. Yet if his strategy had had the deliberate aim of breaking down and reforming the outlook of the reading public on supernatural fiction, it could not have been more effective. The readers who eagerly bought up the first edition and established its reputation took their pleasure from the tale within the terms of a legitimating set of presuppositions; they quickly found that they had invested in a variety of fiction that was condemned by some authorities as wholly illegitimate. But while magazine critics railed, the public continued to buy and read and, in private, literary friends and acquaintances felt free to express their approval. On the basis of the difference between the first two editions of *Otranto*, a shock metamorphosis, a new stage in the career of the supernatural was publicly initiated.[13]

The discourse of the critic in the *Monthly Review* was summoned into voice by the familiar signals of the first preface, only to be undermined by the second. The first preface counterfeits the idioms of historicism and fictional example, and actively canvasses in response the conventional assumptions of the review. The second preface reveals the first to be a parody-in-advance of the terms in which the critic will condemn and reject *Otranto*.

The second preface also alters the meaning of the first by suggesting that the spurious antiquarian account of the work's origins in the late gothic era is a disguised account of its true origins in the present.

Letters were then in their most flourishing state in Italy, and contributed to dispel the empire of superstition, at that time so forcibly attacked by the reformers. It is not unlikely that an artful priest might endeavour to turn their own arms on the innovators; and might avail himself of his abilities as an author to confirm the populace in their ancient errors and superstitions.[14]

The trope of the spread of learning driving out superstition is a cliché in the language of enlightenment. With a technological determinism worthy of Marshall McLuhan, it places the printing press at the centre of world historical progress. The present, witnessing an unprecedented diffusion of print and rapid expansion of the reading public, represented the glorious culmination of this progress. The trope was often applied in the comparison of ancient and modern times, but it was also relevant to the more topical contrast between the liberties of British civil society, where freedom of information reigned, and foreign despotic and papist institutions raised on ignorance, secrecy and superstition. A third context was the debate over the organisation and responsibilities of the modern publishing industry itself, which I will discuss further. Walpole, with what will appear in retrospect transparent irony, takes a symbolic struggle between the powers of light and darkness with strong contemporary associations and projects it into a murky Italian past.

The potential irony of the first preface intensifies with the reference to the 'artful priest', the author of the tale named as 'Onuphrio

Muralto' on the title page, who will later be revealed as Walpole himself – an identification reinforced by the approximate translation of 'Walpole' to 'Muralto'. Ironic, because it is precisely *as* a designing demagogue, a propagator of the 'barbarous superstitions of gothic devilry' that Walpole will be denounced. Like the priest, he is guilty of hijacking the primary instrument of reform, the press, and reintroducing fabulous lies by means of the widely circulated form of popular fiction.

Here the language of historical progress intersects with debate on the power of fiction and the proper methods of directing it to useful and moral ends. The critics, straight-faced and earnest, will reverse against Walpole his own teasing assertion in the first preface that 'Miracles, visions, necromancy, dreams, and other preternatural events, are exploded now even from romances.' As the *Monthly Review* put it, the 'singularity of a false tale' is incompatible with 'a cultivated period of learning'. At the intersection of the discourse of enlightenment and the fiction controversy, 'superstition', the other-to-be-subjugated, is subsumed by a much nearer anxiety, the threat of an unregulated, hedonistic, irrational consumption of print.

Like superstition, hedonistic consumption is a manifestation of the passions without the guidance of reason. The ruling theory of material progress held that the economic passions, which include self-interest and the love of luxury, are the basis of national prosperity, but that they must be reined in and coordinated for the public good under the rational direction of wise governors. This view was scandalously challenged by Bernard Mandeville, who argued in *The Fable of the Bees* that the private vices of greed and luxury would translate into the public benefits of a healthy national economy and strength abroad without the need for moral or political intervention, a position not far from the *laissez-faire* of classical liberal economics. I want to suggest that Walpole's prefaces represent a similar scandal, disguised in the first instance and later confirmed by the second edition. The scandal would be magnified by the fact that the author was himself a Member of Parliament, in principle one of the 'wise governors', as it was thirty years later in the case of 'Monk' Lewis.

Mimicking the shocked tones of a champion of progress, Walpole observes in the first preface, 'Such a work as the following would enslave a hundred vulgar minds beyond half the books of controversy that have been written from the days of Luther to the present hour.'[15] 'To the present hour' precisely, for the statement lexically hooks into the critical discourse that speaks of the reading public's 'enslavement' by authors of fiction who calculatingly manipulate the passions, and Walpole obliquely confesses himself guilty of just this. Not are his remarks concerning the latter-day value of *Otranto* as mere entertainment or a faithful picture of 'the *manners* of the times' as innocent or banal as they must at first have seemed. A work of the barbaric past may be presented as entertainment but it can have no useful moral for the enlightened present, no exemplary power beyond the illustration of progress itself. But this is far from being the case with a modern work of fiction, which must justify and redeem its fall from truth to illusion with a clear moral function. Walpole will go on to refuse a moral function outright in the second preface, and already in the first he obligingly draws attention to this heterodoxy, pointing out, in the role of translator, the 'author's defect' in not finding a more useful moral than that '*the sins of the fathers are visited on their children to the third or fourth generations*'.[16] In the same fashion, the detached stance of the antiquarian who simply offers the public, without censorship, a faithful record of 'things as they were' disguises the amoral modern author, happy to cater to the regressive public taste for the marvellous because he accepts, without judgement, 'things as they are'.

In the second preface, the position of economic amoralism just outlined is rearticulated in aesthetic terms. In a well-known passage, the author speaks of a 'new route' in fiction, and of a 'blend of the two kinds of romance, the ancient and the modern'. The idea for a blend is based on the perceived deficiencies of these two existing types. Modern fictions are overly mimetic, cramped by their imitation of nature.[17] Ancient fictions are too wildly improbable, their delineation of character, especially, is too unnatural, Walpole appears to suggest, to allow a modern reader a viable point of identification. Both the proposal to salvage the extravagances of the past, and the criticism of an aesthetic of nature that really amounted to an ethic, are controversial. But how do they engage with the social and economic issues just mentioned?

First, by context: the preface quickly launches into a digression addressed to Voltaire, establishing that Shakespeare is Walpole's model and defending the presence of comedy in the tragedies from the criticisms of the Frenchman. At the same time Walpole is challenging orthodox opinion at home, and inviting the charge from

the *Monthly Review* that he defended 'all the *trash* of Shakespear . . .
what that great genius evidently threw out as a necessary sacrifice to
that idol the *caecum vulgus* [blind masses], he would adopt in the
worship of the true God of Poetry'.[18] The excision of comic elements
from the tragedies in the interests of increased probability and
decorum had long been a part of English theatre practice. The Fool
was removed from *King Lear* after Nahum Tate's 1681 revision and
Garrick, as part of his drive for the moral reformation of Drury
Lane, left the Porter out of *Macbeth*, and would experimentally cut
the Gravediggers from *Hamlet* in productions between 1773 and
1776. Generic impurity opposed the canons of neoclassicism and
detracted from the function of moral illustration. Voltaire helped to
alter the terms of the argument with his regular attacks on Shakespeare from 1733 to 1776, inadvertently shifting the issue from the
universal rules of drama to the question of nationhood and its
expression in literature.[19] He provoked a whole series of patriotic
defences of various disputed aspects of the plays; Walpole's rehabilitation of genre hybridism in Shakespeare is matched, for instance,
by Elizabeth Montagu's attempt a few years later to rehabilitate the
preternatural in Shakespeare on the grounds of national tradition.[20]
In both these instances, the exemplary function of literature is
discounted. Walpole and Montagu alike ignore the objection that
drama which included gross improbabilities like ghosts and fairies,
or promiscuously mixed comedy and tragedy, threatened to lapse
from the role of instruction and elevation to mere unredeemed
entertainment, from didacticism to aimless affectivity. Accordingly,
when Walpole and Montagu's revaluations are resisted and condemned, it is rationalised as resistance to a groundling's-eye-view of
the drama; the passive, uncritical, sensuous pleasure of the spectacle. It is therefore not incidental that Walpole's argument is
framed in terms of rank, as the right of the fictionalised domestic
servant to laugh '[h]owever grave, important, or even melancholy,
the sensations of princes or heroes may be'.[21]

   Walpole's lengthy aside on drama illuminates the libertarian
language of the opening proposal for a new mode of fiction. The
powers of fancy have been dammed up and cramped, in his view, by
the same prescriptions, the same critical strictures, as are aimed at
Shakespeare. The subordination of fiction to moral instrumentality
is refused. In place of this function, 'boundless realms of invention'
are evoked, the rhetoric of artistic individualism or 'Original

Genius' favoured by theorists of the sublime, also prompting related, optimistic ideas of the infinite vistas of commercial opportunity. The absolute value of freedom is novelty, 'creating more interesting situations'; suggesting the joint centrality of artistic invention and the fashion system in that most commercially up-and-coming literary form, the novel.[22] In effect, Walpole had spotted a gap in the market. He decided to try and reconcile the 'powers of fancy' with 'the rules of probability'. The success of the first edition has vindicated his venture, and encouraged him to reveal his authorship and point the way for 'men of brighter talents' to build on his entrepreneurial foundations.

But this vision of liberty is not without its tensions. The remark that 'the great resources of fancy have been dammed up, by a strict adherence to common life' removes the notion of moral instrumentality at the same time as it metaphorically introduces an idea of economic instrumentality by representing fancy as a property, a natural resource. Meanwhile, the author's deferential address to 'the public' masks a more complex relation involving both antagonism and dependency. On the one hand, there is the memory of the claim that '[s]uch a work as the following would enslave a hundred vulgar minds' relocated in present fears concerning the addictive, pathological nature of the pleasures of fiction, and the powers wielded by the novelist over the sensibilities of her or his readers. On the other hand, there is the reverse possibility, raised in the simple, submissive boast 'the public have applauded the attempt', that an author, having asserted the independence of fiction from moral ends, its social uselessness, may become in turn a slave to the whims of the audience, what Oliver Goldsmith termed a *'child* of the public',[23] a weather-vane for changing fashions. In this vision the law of supply and demand reigns supreme, and fiction is reinstrumentalised by the operations of the market and reconstituted as a leisure commodity.

This possibility is raised more provocatively in the final sentence of the second preface: 'Such as [*Otranto*] is, the public have honoured it sufficiently, whatever rank their suffrages allot to it.' The polite language of the republic of letters is misapplied to convey the message, 'this is a bestseller, so to hell with the critics'. A hierarchical, judgemental conception of taste is supplanted by 'kitchen taste' relating to a 'culinary' or entertainment art, based on a gustatory model, subjectivist and non-evaluative; *de gustibus non est disputandum* or 'each to his own taste'.[24] The word 'rank' does double service here: not only indicating the indifference of the author to critical hierarchy, but also playfully mauling the cherished correlation of social rank and the proper exercise of taste. The rather forced use of 'suffrages' may, too, be an attempt to crank up the level of critical reaction one degree closer to hysteria, its radical political connotations overlaying the radical (unthinkable) prospect of a 'republic of consumption'.

The two prefaces of *The Castle of Otranto* raise the spectre of a thoroughgoing transformation in the relation between literary fiction and society, not in order to analyse or resolve the questions or difficulties involved in such a change, certainly; more, if I can change the metaphor, to wave it like a red rag in the face of the opposition. Yet we find there not only a proposal for a new kind of reading-matter, but the outlines of a new mode of fiction reading, one which still largely determines our expectations today. By justifying supernatural fiction, in defiance of paternalist critical dogma, with an appeal to a hedonistic, self-gratifying version of aesthetic pleasure, Walpole also established the historical connection between economic and fictional 'invisible hands'. In *The Theory of the Moral Sentiments* (1759) Adam Smith first posited the 'invisible hand' as a metaphor for the workings of an economic unconscious; the system achieves its providential end of the general good of the whole through the unknowing agency of individuals driven only by greed and self-interest.[25] In *Otranto* the invisible hand represents a *laissez-faire* of fictionality; in thematic terms an inscrutable force again manipulating and ultimately subordinating human agency in the interests of a 'moral' goal (to be discussed in the following chapter); in performative terms a willing subjection of the passions, unconstrained by didactic, rationalist imperatives, to the unsearchable and unknowable in imagination.

The founding work of the Gothic genre did not appear out of the blue, the harbinger of a Romantic revolt against the repressive rationalism of the Enlightenment. The aim of this chapter has been to show how thoroughly the event of *The Castle of Otranto*, its critical reception, its address to the public in the prefaces, its very newness, was determined by a complex of values and assumptions already in place. Walpole's innovation becomes visible through the reproduction of a system of norms, a horizon of expectation, which is then thrown into crisis. In the next chapter we will see how far the disturbing implications of the mere *idea* of a modern supernatural fiction are carried through to the themes and techniques of the novel's narrative.

> opening realistic mimesis
of Romance (incl preface)
→ big helmet.

CHAPTER 4

Back to the future

GOTHIC ALLEGORY

For much of the eighteenth century the term 'gothic' was used
loosely to describe any time from the fall of the Roman Empire to
the reign of James I.[1] But from the 1760s the Scottish 'historical
school', including James Steuart and Adam Smith, began defining
feudalism in a more analytical way, as a distinctive stage in historical evolution with a prevailing mode of subsistence giving rise to
characteristic social, intellectual and political structures. At around
the same time, Richard Hurd was effecting a similar change in
literary history. In *Letters on Chivalry and Romance* (1762), he drew on
French scholarship in order to explain the cultural logic of the
gothic era: 'Chivalry was no absurd and freakish institution, but the
natural and even sober effect of the feudal policy; whose turbulent
genius breathed nothing but war, and was fierce and military even
in its amusements.'[2] By the same token, ancient romances could not
be judged by anachronistic modern standards.[3] Tales of enchantment, with all their apparent irrationality, 'shadowed out' the
realities of their times: giants 'were oppressive feudal Lords, and
every Lord was to be met with, like the Giant, in his strong hold, or
castle', their wretched and equally violent dependants 'were the
Savages of Romance'.[4] The fantasies of the past were by this means
rendered comprehensible and thereby tolerable for the modern-day
reader; but what would be the result if the same explanatory method
were applied to a supernatural fiction of the present?

The continuing popularity throughout the eighteenth century of
chap-books recounting fabulous legends of giants and witches
encouraged the working-class radical Thomas Spence, in 1782, to
propose a materialist interpretation of these stories in the manner of
Hurd. The chap-book giants, he suggests, represent the social con-

flict of landlord and tenant: 'I can compare them and their Castles to nothing but the Giants, and their Castles in Romances, who were said to be a Terror and Destruction to all the People around.' Spence was an occasional writer of chap-books himself, and, unlike Hurd, he regarded social allegory as a communicative act, rather than a spontaneous product of the 'genius' of the age. The legends 'must certainly have been invented for a Satire against Landlords'. And in the same spirit of political polemic Spence titled his last periodical journal *The Giant-Killer*.[5]

In the previous chapter we saw how Walpole's two prefaces together invited an allegorical reading of the fiction of *Otranto*'s medieval origins as a satire on the prejudices and anxieties of modern literary criticism. But when we come to the narrative of *Otranto* itself, the question of materialist interpretation becomes more complex. No contemporary reader, so it seems, took up the challenge to decode Walpole's ghostly giant, as Spence did the chap-book giants. An explanation for this can be found in the dictates of exemplary historicism already discussed. As long as superstition is taken to be the cultural index of a primitive society, and its absence defines modernity, modern supernatural fiction is unthinkable, let alone unreadable. When the unthinkable occurs in the form of *The Castle of Otranto* there is no language of interpretation available to deal with it. Or rather, the only available method for interpreting supernatural fictions – rational demystification with reference to the shortcomings of a society that could require such fictions – would produce a reading subversive of the progressivist schema itself. If tales of the marvellous can be read as allegories of an imperfect, irrational social structure, then a revival signified regression. It would be many years before *Otranto*'s negative capability, if we can call it that, could be safely defused and assimilated by critical techniques grounded in aesthetic rather than historicist principles. The following reading of *Otranto* as a social allegory will be an attempt to fill the place of a missing interpretation. It will focus on the perpetuation of 'gothic' violence, injustice and irrationalism in an enlightened age, a phenomenon which Walpole invokes as the natural basis for a contemporary nightmare. This is the interpretation which the practice of historicist criticism at the time licensed but could not, for the sake of its own validity, carry out.[6]

But at the same time, a referential, enlightenment interpretation of *Otranto*, reducing its myth to nature, will clearly not exhaust the significance of the work for its contemporary readers. Allegory in this context presumes a logically inferred connection between literary sign and socio-historical referent, whereas the supernatural takes effect through an appeal to the emotions. The meaning of the text is inseparable from its affect, its impact on the reader, the feelings of fear, suspense, curiosity and sympathy which it attempts to arouse. The question of reference – what does it mean? – must be joined to another question which remains latent in eighteenth-century criticism – How does it work? It is latent rather than absent, because it is visible for us even in the conventional terminology of the time, the 'machinery of the supernatural'. The term refers to those sensationalist devices common to classical drama and Drury Lane pantomime which have the 'ghost in the machine' lowered from a crane in the flies or raised through a trap-door. The audience gasps and meaning is sublimated in sensation.

The specific mechanism of affect in *Otranto* is plainly set forth in the second preface. Unnatural events in the plot are to be mediated for the enlightened reader through the naturalistic, credible responses of the characters to them. The metaphysical devices of medieval romance and the psychological realism of the modern domestic novel are combined to produce a hybrid in which the characters 'think, speak and act, as it might be supposed mere men and women would do in extraordinary positions'.[7] We discover again in this model the triadic relation of supernatural affect evinced in Garrick's simulacrum of ghost-seeing and in the psycho-somatic language of Collins's 'Ode to Fear'. The modern consumer of ghost stories must be taught the physiology of superstitious fear by example, via sympathetic identification with a fictional witness. The meaning of the supernatural in *Otranto* for its eighteenth-century audience is inseparable from the formal method which produces affect. The fact that the conventions of characterisation employed in the narrative were found to be stale, clumsy and unconvincing even by the following generation of readers only serves to demonstrate that its techniques of persuasion were specific to the moment of its production. I will later be discussing evidence for the contemporary reception outside the periodical press which suggests that Walpole's declared aims were successful.

THE CASTLE OF OTRANTO II: INTERPRETATION

One of the most striking features of the narrative for the latterday reader is the lavish supply of clues. We need to recall that as a self-conscious exercise in a new species of writing, *Otranto* needed also to serve as an education in a new mode of reading, to provide a sort of hermeneutic cushioning for the British public's first faltering steps into the territory of the Gothic. The reader will never be permitted to suffer the torments of unsatisfied curiosity for more than a few paragraphs.[8]

Accordingly, the whole logic of the supernatural appearances in the story springs open like a secret drawer with a faulty catch on the very first page, with the declaration of the prophecy that hangs over Manfred, Prince of Otranto: '*That the castle and lordship of Otranto should pass from the present family, whenever the real owner should be grown too large to inhabit it*'.[9] A series of apparitions follow in confirmation, building to a climax over the five-part structure of the book, in which the action is limited, as in a neoclassical play, to approximately 24 hours. In the first chapter a monstrous helmet lands in the courtyard of the castle, killing the false Prince Manfred's son and heir, and a giant armour-clad leg and foot is glimpsed through a door in the castle by two servants. In chapter three a mysterious knight arrives with a hundred gentlemen bearing an enormous sword which spontaneously falls to the ground beside the helmet. In chapter five the maidservant Bianca reports seeing on the banister of the great staircase 'a hand in armour as big, as big – I thought I should have swooned'. Finally the gigantic fragments are reconstituted in the form of Alfonso, the murdered Prince, 'dilated to an immense magnitude'. As the walls of the castle fall down around him in ruins, the vision pronounces the name of his heir before solemnly ascending, 'accompanied by a clap of thunder', towards heaven. There are three other uncanny episodes, involving a portrait that descends from its frame, a bleeding statue, and an animated skeleton, more monitory than directly portentous.

The supernatural, it is made clear from the outset, arrives to announce and correct a lapse in the rightful possession of property. A 'real' or natural condition of ownership is assumed by the words of the prophecy. When this is lost, the disruption summons the intervention of surreal forces, which take a monstrous shape that appropriately reflects the monstrousness of the original crimes of murder and usurpation. But there is a hesitation in the dynamic of revenge and restoration. With a turn of phrase typical of Walpole's whimsical, throwaway style, it is stated that the present, irregular, state of affairs will end, not 'when', but 'whenever' certain conditions are fulfilled. The supernatural is in no hurry. The wrath of heaven descends not on the usurper, but on his luckless grandson and great-grandchildren. Already there is a hint of the arbitrary ways of the powers of right that will throw the reader's sympathies and antipathies into question, undermine the 'moral' of the story, and have a decisive, ironising effect on an allegorical reading. The ambiguity at the opening is reflected in the gratuitously violent and sensational resolution of the story. There is to be no simple restoration; the unusually physical phantom leaves the castle in ruins.

We can establish for a start, at any rate, that the declared function of supernatural agency in the tale is to support 'reality' of possession, an authenticity dependent on inheritance, the transmission of property and title through a family's male line.[10] 'Real' ownership is constituted by the correspondence of 'house' in two senses: dwelling-place and ancestral lineage. The obvious parallels with *Macbeth* immediately suggest one possible line for a historical interpretation of the novel. In Shakespeare's play, the crimes of regicide and usurpation, outrages against providential order, give rise to a sympathetic revulsion in nature. Unnatural portents and visions are reinforced by the repetitive imagery of outlandish disproportion: the 'giant's robe / Upon a dwarfish thief' (v. ii.21–2). *Macbeth* conservatively restates the divine right of kings. But in spite of Walpole's notorious fascination with things royal and genealogical, it would be difficult, given the moral ambivalence of the prophecy that carries over into the narrative itself, to discover any straightforward legitimist message in *Otranto*. On the contrary, external evidence might justify speculation that it represents an ironic, 'Whig' rewriting of *Macbeth*. Walpole's joint personal and political inheritance as the son of Robert Walpole, who was described by his admirers as the great parliamentary defender of constitutional monarchy against the threat of royal prerogative, led him to regard Shakespeare's tragedy with a rather brash familiarity. In the years before the Revolution in France, he liked to characterise himself as a 'quiet republican', content to see the 'shadow of monarchy, like Banquo's ghost, fill the empty chair of state' as an obstacle to worse evils of ambition and tyranny.[11] At Strawberry Hill he kept a copy of the Magna Carta on one side of his bed and the warrant for the execution of Charles I on the other, as if to boast that no royal spectre was going to murder *his* sleep. The firmly established associations of the name 'Walpole' with the bloodless civil war which persisted in this century between king and parliament would inevitably, for better or for worse, form part of the subtext of the novel for the readers of the time. Here, however, I intend to focus on a slightly different aspect of the Walpole inheritance, in which the issue of sovereignty is subsumed by the more general issue of property and ownership.

Montague Summers was one of the first, though not the last, to remark that it is the haunted castle, rather than any of the assorted heroes or villains, that takes the role of protagonist in the majority of Gothic fictions, embodying the influence of the past over the present, the dead over the living. From *The Castle of Otranto* onwards this priority is reflected in their titles. 'The buildings seem to acquire a personality ... of their own.'[12] Formally speaking, inanimate property takes on independent life; the existence of its inhabitants is subordinate to the unfolding of its fate. But *Otranto* was not simply a backward-looking evocation of a feudal order in which the relationship to a landed estate determined personal identity; it represented, in fantastical but recognisable form, aristocratic ideology as it persisted in modern times. By the second half of the eighteenth century, debate over the divinely appointed succession of kings was effectively dead, whereas patrilineal inheritance of land and title continued to be a live issue. Indeed, it could be said that the moment when the providential doctrine of kingship was revoked, in 1688, was the point at which aristocratic ownership of land became sacralised in its place, and the following century was to be the scene of a ceaseless struggle to maintain the legitimacy of the aristocracy's continuing political and economic domination of a rapidly changing society on the basis of a mystique of land. Civic humanism perpetuated in a modified, civil, form the feudal equation of possession of estate and service in arms, deriving from this formula the landowner's political 'personality', and the justification of his social and economic power. The quasi-feudal prophecy that hangs over the Castle of Otranto resonates with very topical assumptions concerning the correspondence of estate and natural hierarchy, far from new but driven into aggressive articulacy by the growth in economic importance of the bourgeois, commercial sections of society.

A narrative that opposed 'real' ownership and lordship to a disordered state of things in which monstrous phantoms ran amok was by no means necessarily a flight of Gothic fancy. I have already referred in the Introduction to the phantasmagorical imagery of the conservative discourse which sought literally to demonise the new manifestations of market capitalism in the 1720s, as it reasserted the providential necessity of a primarily agrarian economic order. For opponents of a market economy, the difference between real and unreal modes of ownership was clear-cut. Mobile property, bound up in the unstable, 'imaginary', mechanisms of speculation and credit, was the threatening alternative to the system of heritable wealth derived from land rents, which laid claim to the values of stability and, by avoiding the abstraction of capital investment and profit, natural law.

But apparent support in *The Castle of Otranto* for an authentic or real claim to property and social status on the basis of genealogy soon becomes insecure. The supernatural is summoned into action by a violent infringement of natural right, but the violent means it uses to repair the damage compromises the claim to right. While the gigantesque manifestations signify the loss of natural order, they also, through the goal of reinstating order, act as a metaphysical extension of it. The concept of a harmonious identity of owner and property, self and object, takes on a demoniacal objective fatality which disrupts and dominates the lives of all the characters. The most important organising structure in the narrative is the opposition between subject and object, between the characters with their desires, intentions and affections and the principle of property objectivised as the supernatural phenomena which obstruct their wishes at every turn. The anticipated course of actions motivated by natural emotion – family affection, lust or romantic love – is persistently interrupted when it crosses the designs of divine providence, and is redirected with generally disastrous consequences. Even the true heir, Theodore, does not escape this rule: his beloved Matilda is accidentally murdered in a supernaturally instigated case of mistaken identity, and the final lines of the story refer to his compromise marriage to Isabella, 'persuaded [that] he could know no happiness but in the society of one with whom he could forever indulge the melancholy that had taken possession of his soul'.[13] Furthermore, it becomes apparent that the same principle of patrilineal descent that threatens Manfred also motivates his own illegitimate attempts to perpetuate his family line. The family portrait that opens the novel shows how the laws of inheritance can undermine the ties of kinship and marriage: Prince Manfred favours his sickly and unpromising son Conrad, neglects Matilda, his beautiful and virtuous daughter, and reproaches his wife Hippolita for her inability to give him more sons. The personality of Manfred himself, prototype for the Byronic hero, is represented as a casualty of the same laws: 'The circumstances of his fortune had given an asperity to his temper, which was naturally humane.'[14] And, as in innumerable sentimental novels, the two young heroines, Matilda and Isabella, face the conflict between a prudential marriage dictated by the claims of property and title, and love.

Walpole was ideally placed to provide a vision of aristocratic mores combining the effects of delight and terror. His own family background guaranteed ambivalence, for although his father came from a substantial gentry family, the policies he pursued as prime minister led him to be portrayed by Tory propagandists as an arch-enemy of the landed interest.[15] Robert Walpole was regularly accused by his enemies of corruption and embezzlement, and his provision of sinecures for his sons added fuel to these suspicions. When Horace Walpole's older brother inherited the family estate after their father's death in 1745, annuities from government places became his only source of income. With this dependent, client status, ignominious in terms of the aristocratic ideology that equated citizenship with independent landed wealth, he was a sitting target for slander. In 1782 years of humiliating criticism led him to publish a self-justifying pamphlet, 'Account of My Conduct Relative to the Places I Hold under Government and Towards Ministers', which to an extent anticipates Edmund Burke's counter-attack on the 'Noble Lord' who questioned his acceptance of a government pension. In the latter work Burke offers a thoroughly demystifying account of the 'vast landed Pensions' enjoyed by the present nobility on the basis of long histories of servile obedience and confiscation.[16] Walpole does not go so far, but he ventures to suggest that estates were often unfairly gained and that a 'country gentleman has very little grace in complaining that any other unprofitable class is indulged by the laws in the enjoyment of more than an equal share of property, with the meanest labourer or lowest mechanic'.[17] In this context Walpole's love of feudal knickknacks and the minutiae of genealogy, notorious among contemporary observers,[18] begins to look like an ingenious form of revenge. His first publication was *A Catalogue of the Royal and Noble Authors of England* (1757), in which he took the opportunity to annoy the defenders of rank and custom with his sweeping and belittling literary judgements. The house at Strawberry Hill was acquired from the proprietor of a London toyshop, and the happy coincidence was not lost on the new owner as he systematically transformed the building into what we would call today a 'theme park' treatment of aristocratic ascendency.[19] As the feudal origins of the aristocratic order were turned into the plaything of a whimsical hobbyist, its present legitimacy was symbolically diminished.

In reality, the legal provisions for the maintenance of landed inheritance were actually strengthened in the eighteenth century, notably by introduction of the device of 'strict settlement'. Michael McKeon has usefully summarised the sharp difference of scholarly opinion on the social tendency of this law, some claiming that 'it reinforced primogeniture and patrilineal principles by stabilizing the landed estate, limiting the life tenant's powers of alienation and thereby ensuring the descent of the entail in the male heir'; while others hold that 'the guaranteed provisions for daughters and younger sons which the settlement facilitated were its most important aim and the intergenerational transfer of land its desired effect', thereby signalling the waning of patrilineal principles. McKeon concludes that the device made apparent the conflict of interests inherent in the system of inheritance itself.

By attending thus closely and explicitly to the mediation of distinct family interests, the strict settlement only emphasized their divergence, separating out elements which, by the less scrupulous and self-conscious consensus of aristocratic ideology, were less problematically comprehended within the general category of 'family'. The strict settlement helped make the perennial and implicit tension between male owner and male heir, and between patrilineal interests and kindred interests, an active one; and so it both reinforced patrilineal principles and undermined them.[20]

But the contradictions of the system become most clearly visible at the point where the system is challenged, rather than merely modified. Criticism of strict settlement presupposes a post-aristocratic view, the perspective of bourgeois capitalism with a different category of 'family' and a different concept of the relation between self and property, founded on contract rather than genealogy. From such a perspective the laws regulating ownership of land are exposed as dehumanising superstition. A departure from natural law, the critic might say, is bound to occur when the hoarding instinct native to man, and rational within bounds, is permitted to become a ruling passion and institutionalised by government. In these terms Henry Home condemned the English legislature for instituting 'a most irrational power, that of making an entail' enabling 'every land-proprietor to fetter his estate for ever; to tyrannize over his heirs; and to reduce their property to a shadow, by prohibiting alienation; and by prohibiting the contracting debt, were it even to redeem the proprietor from death or slavery'. Home's rhetorical antithesis, by which the integrity of an insentient object is raised to a highest principle, becoming 'in effect a mortmain', a dead hand potentially endangering human life and freedom, anticipates Marx's comment that 'The civilized victory of moveable capital had precisely been to reveal and create human labour as the source of wealth in place of a dead thing [i.e. land].'[21] The values that originally underlay the system have been estranged, defamiliarised, and the system is understood only as an intolerable, irrational, universal threat to human self-determination and the bonds of familial affection. The supernatural in *The Castle of Otranto* figures an equivalent contradiction between the traditional claims of landed property and the new claims of the private family; a conflict between two versions of economic 'personality'.[22]

The first few pages of *Otranto* represent the manner in which contradiction is employed in the whole. The sketch of a family group is not very different, apart from its antique setting, to the opening lines of many sentimental novels. Psychological relations are established, a marriage ceremony is about to be performed, when news arrives that the bridegroom has been killed by a giant helmet. The helmet marks a new development in narrative technique precisely on the basis of its gross improbability. A helmet, a mere thing, has usurped the plot, has become the subject, the moving force of the narrative, to the bewilderment of the characters. The helmet 'knows' the plot in a way they, and the readers, do not. The crushing of Conrad by the helmet represents a subordination of character to plot – and this subordination is significant, for however notional the idea of a 'Conrad' may have been, it was introduced under the rubric of probability, within a logic of psychological relationships and with a past history and future prospects. Instead of fulfilling the functions of 'actant' in the narrative, he is himself reduced to a thing, 'dashed to pieces' like a china teacup.

The transgressive nature of this transformation, this 'thingifi-cation', is witnessed in the language which represents the event through the eyes of Manfred:

Shocked with these lamentable sounds, and dreading he knew not what, he advanced hastily – But what a sight for a father's eyes! – He beheld his child dashed to pieces, and almost buried under an enormous helmet, an hundred times more large than any casque ever made for human being, and shaded with a proportionable quantity of black feathers.[23]

The immediacy of Conrad's death, the pathos of the event, is likewise buried – under an accumulation of information about the helmet, which takes on the compelling quality of a fetish. Conrad's diminishment is reflected in the organisation of the sentence. Half way through, the helmet displaces Conrad as the affective centre of the statement of the event, so that it should come as no surprise to us when we are told in the following paragraph of the astonishment of observers at Manfred's insensibility to the death of his adored son and contrasting fascination with the 'tremendous phaenomenon': 'He touched, he examined the fatal casque; nor could even the mangled remains of the young prince divert the eyes of Manfred from the portent before him.'

It becomes clear that the affective use of the appellations 'father' and 'child' ('what a sight for a father's eyes!') was a mockery and amounts to a scandal when set against sentimental or affectional standards of kinship, standards repeatedly invoked in *Otranto* only to be violated. A rhetoric of family relationships is used to enhance the shock value of the distance between human affectivity and reifi-cation. As Manfred is seduced away from his fatherly role by the fantastic spectacle of the helmet, so the language of kinship, of personhood, grates even absurdly here against the language of appraising, impersonal description: 'an hundred times more large', 'shaded with a proportionable quantity of black feathers'. The stately rhythm of the latter clause represents a bottleneck in the affective flow, the circulation of sensible words, around the repre-sentation of the central fact of the incident.

Half a century after the first appearance of *Otranto*, it was pre-cisely on the basis of such writing that William Hazlitt would dismiss the novel in his *Lectures on the English Comic Writers* as 'dry, meagre and without effect'. 'The great hand and arm, which are thrust into the court-yard, and remain there all day long', he states with some exaggeration, 'are the pasteboard machinery of a pantomime ... They are a matter-of-fact impossibility; a fixture, and no longer a phantom.'[24] Once the literary supernatural has been vindicated by an appeal to the absolute value of imagination, *Otranto*'s supernaturalism will inevitably appear meagre. It was addressed to a specific crisis in the experience of its eighteenth-century audience, a fantasy of the dissociation and homicidal confrontation of self and social forms, a spectacle which for a passing moment inspired delicious terror; whereas in later years the same dissociation would be romanticised and affirmed.

Walpole liked to imagine his work would have the purgative effect of catharsis.[25] Tears, as much as terror, feature in the few clues to the book's intended and actual reception outside the pages of the periodical press. In the dedicatory sonnet to the novel, the author appealed to Lady Mary Coke for tears to mark the hard fate of Matilda. His correspondence with friends after the publication of *Otranto* contains similar hints. Thomas Gray reported to him that after reading the book he and some of his companions at Cambridge University had difficulty going to sleep at night and 'cried a little'. When Walpole sent a copy to another friend, a M. De Beaumont, he modestly remarked in the covering letter, 'If I make you laugh, for I cannot flatter myself that I shall make you cry, I shall be content.' George Hardinge did not hesitate to flatter the author: 'I could have cried (*once in my life*) at the first conversation between Manfred's daughter and the imprisoned peasant ... I could have loved such tears, and felt a sensual kind of enjoyment in shedding them.'[26]

In 1761 Rousseau's novel of sentiment *La Nouvelle Héloïse* had appeared, 'a key event in the history of tears'.[27] Its astonishing effect made weeping the measure of a literary work's success with the public. It also confirmed beyond all doubt the novel's triumph over romance. Credibility was of the essence: if a character could not be believed in there could be no intersubjective exchange, no identification, no sympathy, no reason for reading further. It was said that the rise of the novel represented the supersession of the appeal to wonder by the principle of compassion.[28] Walpole's innovation was to bring together wonder and compassion, broadening the parameters of sympathy to include experience of the miraculous and the terrible, and artfully extending the limits of what could be felt by the reader as 'real'.

CHAPTER 5

The value of the supernatural in a commercial society

THE SUPERNATURAL SUBLIME

It is not altogether surprising, given the complexities of the experiment, that 'men of brighter talents' did not at once follow Walpole down the new route he had struck out. In 1772 an anonymous tale of Norman times entitled *The Hermitage* was published, which included visions, portents, a scene of supernaturally instrumented devastation on a par with *Otranto* and, possibly for the first time, introduced a wicked double-dealing monk. It sunk almost without trace, in spite of the editor's care to point out its exemplary usefulness: 'The work, in general, inculcates resignation to the will of Heaven, filial reverence, and universal love.'[1] Fantastic fiction, it seemed, could not compete with the realist novel on its own didactic territory.

The obvious solution was an independent theoretical justification for use of the supernatural. This is what Anna and John Aikin aimed to provide with their essay 'On the Pleasure Derived From Objects of Terror', which appeared in a collection of miscellaneous critical writings in 1773. Here the arguments popularised by Burke's *Enquiry into the Origin of our Ideas of the Sublime and Beautiful* (1757) were applied specifically to tales of the marvellous and supernatural. The essay begins by considering the pleasure taken in scenes of human affliction: here the cause is easily discovered, for nature systematically connects satisfaction with any emotion which, like sympathy, is 'productive of the general welfare'. The delight in terror, on the other hand, seems to present a real paradox. The evidence for it is universal yet difficult to explain. Ghost stories and tales of natural disasters are alike greedily 'devoured by every ear'. Tragedy has ever been the most popular literary genre, and a chronological checklist of the terrible follows, including Greek and Roman tragedy, Shakespeare and Otway, Milton's 'Il Pensoroso' and

Collins' 'Ode to Fear'. It also includes 'Old Gothic Romance and the Eastern tale' which 'however a refined critic may censure them as absurd and extravagant, will ever retain a most powerful influence on the mind'. Two explanations for the phenomenon are offered. The first involves the suggestion that the irresistible desire for stories of this kind is not a consequence of positive pleasure, but rather the alleviation of the 'pain of suspense': 'We rather chuse to suffer the smart pang of a violent emotion than the uneasy craving of an unsatisfied desire.' Hence the experience of children 'chained by the ears' to 'frightful stories of apparitions'. This explanation, although non-evaluative, conforms to the historicist paradigm that sees the passion of wonder as a regressive element in human nature.

But a second and quite different etiology is then produced to explain delight caused by productions of a 'sublime and vigorous imagination'. This stems from the primitivist strand in exemplary historicism but, as in Burke, it breaks loose of its origin to form a psychological account of the sublime. The taste for horrors arises from the resistance of the mind to the torpor induced by humdrum reality:

A strange and unexpected event awakens the mind, and keeps it on the stretch; and where the agency of invisible beings is introduced, of 'forms unseen, and mightier far than we', our imagination, darting forth, explores with rapture the new world which is laid open to its view, and rejoices in the expansion of its powers.[2]

Elsewhere the authors speak of the 'ventilation' of the mind by 'sudden gusts of passion', of prevention of 'the stagnation of thought' by 'a fresh infusion of dissimilar ideas'.[3] This quasi-medical account of the necessity of representations of the supernatural in literature can be readily traced to parallel passages in Burke, where he proposes that the mind, unhindered, naturally falls into a state of indifference caused by 'stale unaffecting familiarity', and prescribes artificial terror as a remedy.[4] An organic model of historical development, from childhood to maturity to the threat of old age (regression), is skeletally present in Burke's theory, underlying the empiricist language; most notably in the opening section on novelty, where the active principle of curiosity found in children is said to give way to langour and vacuity of mind through force of habit. He takes from primitivism the valorisation of figurative language and the powers of imagination, but instead of merely opposing them to the debilitating effects of luxury in an affluent commercial society, he recommends them as antidotes. The delicate organs controlling the faculty of imagination, the mind's powers of image-making, intimately connected to the senses and the passions, must be 'shaken and worked', just like the other bodily parts, if they are not to become unusable. The means is terror. The effect on the subject is a combination of pain caused by exertion and delight caused by clearing the parts of 'a dangerous and troublesome encumbrance'.[5] And the final, providential cause of the sublime as exercise for the mind is self-preservation, the proper and harmonious functioning of selfhood, in mind as in body.

The Aikins move from a theory of the cause of pleasure to a theory of the effects of pleasure, and consequently to prescription of the type of fiction likely to have the most beneficial effect on the mind. Walpole, as 'editor' of the first edition of *Otranto*, had discussed the tale using a psychosomatic discourse close to that of Burke's sublime: 'Terror, the author's principal engine, prevents the story from ever languishing; and it is so often contrasted by pity, that the mind is kept up in a constant vicissitude of interesting passions.'[6] In the second preface he had presented his novel as a remedy to the common run of realist fictions. Along similar lines the Aikins follow their exposition with praise of the *Arabian Nights*, *The Castle of Otranto* ('a very spirited modern attempt upon the same plan of mixed terror, adapted to the model of Gothic romance') and above all the tomb scene in *Ferdinand Count Fathom* ('the most strongly worked-up scene of mere natural horror that I recollect'). They adjoin their own sample, 'Sir Bertrand. A Fragment', designed to bear out the thesis that wildly fanciful adventure will produce more pleasure than one which attempts to stick closer to nature. These examples form the ammunition for an attack on the dullness of modern fiction, which begins in the essay on terror and gathers strength in the following essay, which reconsiders the question of pity as a function of reading. In contrast to the health-giving tale of terror, the average sentimental novel is represented as the essence of morbidity and perversion. The author, 'like an inquisitor', sadistically computes the amount of suffering that can be extracted from their virtuous heroes while the reader's limited stock of sensibility is 'wasted' on illusions 'without advantage'. Whereas Gothic romances 'elevated the mind' modern novels 'tend to depress and enfeeble it'.[7]

The unavoidable inference of this diagnostic imagery is that the book-buying public is a body in perpetual danger of relapse. The notion was common in early descriptions of the mechanisms of consumerism. In *The Case for Authors* (1758), for example, James Ralph relates, in an extended metaphor comparing the fashions of the book market to the fluctuations of a diseased body, how book-sellers maintain control through their ability to 'feel the Pulse of the Times' and prescribe accordingly: 'Hence the Cessation of all Political Carminatives, and the Introduction of Cauterides, in the shape of Tales, Novels, Romances &c.' and the change from 'a Course of Composers and Amusers' to 'State-Stimulatives of the most daring and dangerous kind'.[8] The business of the writing trade is the supply of 'artificial necessaries': 'Infatuation! Phrenzy! – Be it so! – By the Statute of modern Uniformity, Luxury is the idol all worship – There is a Luxury of the Mind as well as of the Senses – Of Those who administer to the latter, Authors stand the foremost', enlarging 'the Bounds of our Happiness'.[9] Ralph's economic pragmatism comes remarkably close to the remedial theory of the sublime. Was the literature of terror an answer to the ills of commercial society, or merely another manifestation of it, a new revolution in the cycle of fashion? Perhaps, as an antidote, it was both poison and cure.

CLARA REEVE AND *THE OLD ENGLISH BARON*

It was not until 1777, thirteen years after the publication of *The Castle of Otranto*, that a viable successor appeared. In that year Clara Reeve had *The Champion of Virtue* printed privately in Colchester. The following year a revised version was brought out by the London publishers Dilly, to whom the author had sold the copyright for £10, with a new title, *The Old English Baron*. The event raises a number of questions. Why was there such a long wait before another author tried to consolidate Walpole's success? Why did the consumer-conscious booksellers apparently fail to recognise the marketability of this type of fiction, and encourage its production? What resistance remained to the publication of supernatural fictions, and then, on what basis did Reeve attempt to overcome it?

In market terms, the reasonably enthusiastic consumption of Walpole's 'modern romance' had not been converted into 'productive consumption'. It did not create 'the need for *new* production'.[10] Indeed, after a flurry of editions, legitimate and pirated, *Otranto* itself would not be republished until 1782. The concept of a modern mode of 'Gothic Story' was seemingly immobilised by the reputation of *Otranto* as a one-off novelty or caprice. This may help to explain why, when finally a work arrived which openly imitated the design of *Otranto*, it also took the form of a corrective. Reeve's criticisms and revisions of Walpole stem from Johnson's theory of the exemplary function of the novel. When in her preface she urges the need to keep within 'the utmost *verge* of probability', verisimilitude is not seen as an end in itself. The 'business of Romance' is first 'to excite the attention' and secondly 'to direct it to some useful, or at least innocent, end'.[11] For Reeve, as for Johnson, Richardson is the writer who most perfectly unites these two imperatives. *The Old English Baron* was dedicated to Richardson's daughter, Mrs Bridgen, who gave advice for the changes to the second edition.

By these standards *The Castle of Otranto* is judged by Reeve and found wanting. Successfully to unite ancient romance and modern novel, 'there is required a sufficient degree of the marvellous, to excite the attention; enough of the manners of real life, to give an air of probability to the work; and enough of the pathetic, to engage the heart in its behalf'. Although it fulfils two of the categories it fails in the first by an excess of wonders: 'the machinery is so violent, that it destroys the effect it is intended to excite'. A ghost is acceptable: 'we can conceive, and allow of, the appearance of a ghost'. An enchanted sword and helmet are credible within limits, but not a 'sword so large as to require an hundred men to lift it; a helmet that by its own weight forces a passage through a court-yard into an arched vault, big enough for a man to go through'. The walking portrait and skeleton monk are equally ruled out.

When your expectation is wound up to the highest pitch, these circumstances take it down with a witness, destroy the work of the imagination, and, instead of attention, excite laughter. I was both surprised and vexed to find the enchantment dissolved, which I wished might continue to the end of the book; and several of its readers have confessed the same disappointment to me: The beauties are so numerous, that we cannot bear the defects, but want it to be perfect in all respects.[12]

In the course of her chatty, anecdotal critique Reeve quietly shifts the boundaries of fictional example. Set beside a murderous flying helmet a simple ghost begins to look almost commonplace.[13] Suddenly, without fanfare, the supernatural has slipped back into the realm of truth, though now it can only be the looking-glass truth of fiction. A ghost may be truthful enough to appear in a story that exemplifies and instils the laws of moral conduct.

Reeve takes Walpole's plot, of peasant providentially revealed as heir, and carefully purges it of ambiguities. Now the usurper directly suffers the consequences of his actions, and his offspring, who providentially die in childhood, are mentioned only in passing and in retrospect, his wife not at all. In addition, the confrontation of malefactor Lord Lovel and true successor, his nephew, Edmund Lovel alias Twyford, is now mediated by the introduction of a third party, the former's brother-in-law, Baron Fitz-Owen. The Baron buys the castle with its haunted east apartments from Lovel and presides there as virtuous paterfamilias and kind patron of Edmund before his true identity is discovered. With the loss of *Otranto*'s monstrous, unmediated disproportion of right and wrong, there are many, many niceties of right conduct to be negotiated here between the Baron and his sons, between the family of Fitz-Owen and Edmund, who has a filial affection for the Baron but is set to oust him from his property, and between all of these and Edmund's champion, Sir Philip Harclay, a friend of his murdered father, who is nonetheless able to recognise the noble nature of the Baron. Etiquette rivals providence as the ruling agency of this story. By the midpoint of the book all supernatural occurrences are finished. They have consisted of Edmund's vision of the ghosts of his real parents, which may have been a dream, and the sound of footsteps, groans, and the flashes of light which lead him to the place where his father's body was hidden. The narrative mystery is dispersed and the reader is initiated into the technical mysteries of the redistribution of land. Sir Philip challenges Lord Lovel to a trial by combat and wins. 'Lord Lovel fell, crying out that he was slain. I hope not, said Sir Philip, for I have a great deal of business for you to do before you die.'[14] From this point the knights and barons remove their armour and, figuratively speaking, roll up their shirt sleeves. Marriage, the conventional romance vehicle for the resolution of differences, waits on the sidelines while Baron Fitz-Owen's cash payment for the castle and estate is weighed against the twenty-one years of rent owing to Edmund. The following day Sir Philip is still agitating for surrender of furniture and farm stock in place of arrears until 'Lord Fitz-Owen slightly mentioned the young man's education and expences'[15] and hard bargaining is suspended in favour of sentiments of obligation and respect.

Reeve redefines the harsh conditions of real ownership depicted by Walpole by liberalising them. Her model includes the possibility of alienation (sale of land) at the owner's will, and the voluntary disposal of property (unconstrained by entail) in accordance with the dictates of feeling. In this version of gothic times, law and feeling are not antithetical; property does not face the sensible individual as an alien, autonomous necessity, programmed by providence to crush and reify. It is a vision so thoroughly, optimistically and complacently bourgeois that any conflict of this kind is unimaginable, even as a phenomenon of the past. The assorted fifteenth-century noblemen have the appetites and (idealised) instincts of eighteenth-century men of commerce. There is a homespun emphasis on the circumstantial at the expense of the dramatic, which connects it with the apparition narrative. As J. M. S. Tompkins observes, 'it is this homely and practical streak that differentiates *The Old English Baron* from any other Gothic story whatever; nowhere else do we find knights regaling on eggs and bacon and suffering from the toothache'.[16] Providence is secularised and domesticated and inhabits every courteous word, every exchange of tears. The work of the supernatural is merely to dress and decorate this moral order, whetting the appetite of the reader for the edifying restoration of right.

Reeve's reconception of the 'business of Romance', her rewriting of *Otranto* as *Pamela* in fancy-dress with the spice of the paranormal, an illustrative conduct-book for the proper correlation of wealth and virtue, redirected the modern romance from novelty status to the professional mainstream. It began to make romance-publishing and romance-writing look like a viable business. Reeve never married, and after her father's death in 1755 she was financially independent. It is not known whether writing was her only means of support, but remarks in her later work *The Progress of Romance* (1785) show she was a narrow observer of the book market. There she discusses among other practical matters the copyright laws, the prejudicial techniques of reviewers and their habit of reprinting excessively long extracts without payment to the author and the threat of pirating anthologies. The project of *The Old English Baron* needs to be understood in prudential terms. When Reeve guarantees that she will trim her imagination in accordance with critical standards of acceptability, it is a sign of business sense as much as the mouthing of proprieties expected of novelists. Walpole had no need of compromise: he could privately publish a drama (*The Mysterious Mother*) that for moral reasons could never be performed; or write surreal fantasies (*Hieroglyphic Tales*) too wild to be published in his lifetime. He was one of the 'Voluntiers' (*sic*) or 'Holiday-Writers' that James Ralph denounced for undercutting writers' fees in *The Case for Authors*.[17] Reeve's point was that he undercut the working moral basis for fiction, and in doing so cut off a promising new mode from its potential audience.

The periodical press was the most visible institution enabling critical opinion to intervene in the sale and circulation of books.[18] *The Old English Baron* obtained good reviews in the *Critical Review* and the *Monthly Review*, although the latter still carped on the introduction of ghosts. But another less direct, less secure but potentially more decisive means of influencing distribution was through the institution of the circulating library. Sales of novels were divided between the retail trade on the one hand and the book clubs and circulating libraries on the other. The circulating libraries had by this time proved a valuable outlet for the disposal of fiction. Although originally booksellers had perceived them as a threat, it soon became clear that they in fact increased demand. Books were expensive in this period relative to the cost of living and the libraries offered an opportunity to sample them before an investment was made; 'thousands of books are purchased each year, by such as have borrowed them from the libraries and after reading, approving of them, and becoming purchasers'.[19] But readers did not necessarily want to buy books which had no literary status and lost their entertainment value after one reading. The rise of the novel was based on a commercial system of borrowing. As the libraries grew in number they accounted for an increasing proportion of sales; the writer Elizabeth Griffith remarked that out of an edition of 1,000 copies 'the Circulating Libraries take off 400'.[20]

Supernatural fictions along the lines of *Otranto* should have been the ideal commodity for the libraries. They offered a novel alternative to the standard merchandise of sentimentalism, and dealt in unrepeatable effects of suspense and shock perfectly suited to the library system, which by keeping the narratives in perpetual circulation kept them perpetually new as they changed hands. Instead, in the period up to the 1790s, pure commercial interest was counterbalanced and constrained by the representation of the library as a civic institution with moral responsibilities. This tension had a history as long as that of the circulating library itself. The initial *exclusion* of novels may have been an enabling condition. Of the four candidates for the title of first circulating library listed by Alison Adburgham, two at least were unlikely to have kept novels.[21] Allan Ramsay's Edinburgh library and the dissenting minister Samuel Fancourt's Universal Library in Fleet Street ('The Gentlemen and Ladies' Growing and Circulating Library') opened for business in 1726 and 1740 respectively, in a period when 'novel' described a bawdy or lowlife tale unfit to be openly read by the polite. By 1743, when the library at the Blue Bible in the Strand was opened by William Bathoe, Richardson and then Fielding had achieved the break-through which made narrative fictions acceptable fare for the most modest young lady.

A book's inclusion in the library catalogue depended, at least in theory, on its moral credentials. That this was not always the case in practice was a fact which, already by the 1750s, was provoking expressions of alarm in periodicals and treatises on conduct and education. What was worrying about the library was its potential, probably not yet actual, indiscrimination: the promiscuous assort-ment of reading-matter it made available, and its casual, not to say anarchic, willingness to lend any book to any reader able to pay the subscription fee. Anxiety focused on novels and the multitude of works that exploited Richardson's winning formula without his care for moral propriety. Although many novelists dutifully rehearsed Johnson's creed from the *Rambler* in their prefaces, novels were fast becoming emblematic of unregulated social and economic forces, and the erosion of established hierarchies of value and authority. Their commercial success undermined standards of taste; their direct appeal, to young women in particular, subverted the rulings of pedagogy; their easy availability at cheap rates through the libraries contravened parental control. Under pressure of these fears, the libraries were increasingly associated by critics with novels alone, and were pictured as conduits for the ever-multiplying quan-tities of degraded and degrading fiction. Writing in the early 1780s, Reeve characterises this period as one in which 'the press groaned under the weight of Novels, which sprung up like Mushrooms every year ... They did but now begin to increase upon us, but ten years more multiplied them tenfold. Every work of merit produced a swarm of imitators, till they became a public evil, and the institution of circulating libraries, conveyed them in the cheapest manner to every bodies hand.'[22]

Reeve's solution to the problem of representing the supernatural was shaped in response to these united critical and commercial factors. It ensured success in the case of *The Old English Baron*, but at the same time it brought new problems. On the one hand it signally failed to fulfil the criterion of sublimity, a validation of the supernatural which was growing in authority. On the other hand, it initiated an ambiguity that *Otranto* with its wildness had avoided. What are the side-effects of making ghosts more plausible? The *Gentleman's Magazine* suggested in a review of Reeve's novel that if the circumstances of an apparition 'be not self-evidently absurd, some weak minds, perhaps, might be induced to think them true or possible, and thereby be led into superstition'.[23] Anna Barbauld (née Aikin) agreed in her 'Critical Preface' to a later, 1810 edition of the book, that Reeve's quotidian horrors 'till lately, coincided with the belief, perhaps, of the generality of readers'; and repeating the aestheticist credo she and her brother had expounded in *Miscellaneous Pieces in Prose*, which had by now become critical orthodoxy, she states, 'at present we should require these appearances to be more artful and singular'.[24] A supernaturalism that was so easily reducible to naturalism raised goosebumps of apprehension by its blurring of the borders of reality; the tendency initiated by Reeve would later culminate in Ann Radcliffe's more problematic device of the 'explained supernatural'.

THE 1780s

The progress of the supernatural in the following decade was halting. When Clara Reeve lost the manuscript to her next ghost fiction, *Castle Connor, an Irish Story*, on the Ipswich to London coach in 1787, the setback is representative of the general state of anticlimax. There was no literary equivalent to Henry Fuseli's experiments with images of supernatural terror, culminating in *The Nightmare* (exhibited in 1782).[25] A. McDonald's *Vimonda* (1788), a quasi-Shakespearian Scottish tragedy, met with little encouragement; the *English Review* found the device of a real man impersonating a ghost 'peculiarly ludicrous'.[26] William Beckford's orientalist romance *Vathek* was anonymously published in 1786, and was, by contrast, well received by the reviewers. The convention of the ancient manuscript discovered and translated, employed again here, was by this stage so familiar that the critics simply ignored it. Instead, the improbabilities of Beckford's tale, as extreme as anything in *Otranto*, were accepted on the basis of their accurate evocation of Eastern beliefs and manners; a criterion derived from exemplary historicism. Acceptance was made all the easier by the addition of scholarly notes, which were universally praised for their erudition and cited at length in reviews. But *Vathek* was not popularly successful and had little effect on public taste or other Gothic fiction in the period.[27]

Walpole himself began to have second thoughts, and went so far as to recommend Dryden's *Fables* as an antidote to his own novel after Hannah More had mentioned the impression it had made on her protégée, the 'peasant' poet Ann Yearsley:

> What! if I should go a step further, dear Madam, and take the liberty of reproving you for putting into this poor woman's hands such a frantic thing as the *Castle of Otranto*? It was fit for nothing but the age in which it was written, an age in which much was known; that required only to be amused, nor cared whether its amusements were conformable to truth and the models of good sense; that could not be spoiled; was in no danger of being too credulous; and rather wanted to be brought back to imagination than to be led astray by it – but you will have made a hurly-burly in this poor woman's head, which it cannot develop and digest.[28]

Whether or not this posture of recantation is to be taken seriously, it points to the 1780s as a moment of division and promise. It was a stage at which *The Castle of Otranto*, through the lack of successors, could be seen itself as a relic of the past, yet there was undeniable evidence of the extraordinary attractions and power over the imagination of fantastic writing.

It may be that the very absence of further experiments was tending to relax critical opposition, preparing the way for the resurgence of terror fiction in the 1790s. This was a period when 'Gothic' literature was beginning in a limited way to be recognised as a distinct species, an independent division of taste, subtly undermining the assumptions of historicist thinking. 'Gothic' was becoming a specific image or atmosphere, an extension of consumer choice; and as the demand for Gothic increased, it would gradually come to matter less whether the text in question was historically authentic, or simply 'in the style of'. *Maria*, a novel from 1785 by Elizabeth Blower, indicates the latitude of contemporary fashions: Miss Hampden, anticipating a visit to Dunslough Castle, 'is impatient to enjoy the delightful horrors of Gothic galleries, winding avenues, gaping chimnies, and dreary vaults; and by way of enlivening the scene, she intends to take with her the tragedies of Eschylus, the poems of Ossian, Castle of Otranto, &c. &c... – Are you,' she asks the heroine of the story, 'a lover of this kind of sublimity?' There is something fortuitous in the printer's error that occasionally changes the name 'Maria' to 'Matilda', archetypal name of Gothic heroines. But within a few pages the passion for Gothic gives place to the vogue for Greek, and Maria is on her way to 'Wedgwood's Rooms' with her friends; she 'who had never before been there, was charmed with the classical taste, and Attic elegance that pervaded every thing she saw. – Lady Melmoth purchased a beautiful tea service, ornamented with curious bas-relief figures; and gave orders for a chimney piece for her library. Maria bought a bust of Pericles as a present for Mrs Tonto.'[29] The genuinely supernaturalist *Alan Fitz-Osbourne* (1787) by Anne Fuller, the partly humorous *Earl Strongbow* (1789) by James White, and a novel titled *The Spectre* (1789) by an anonymous author, where the apparition is revealed as a device, were among a handful of works that began to familiarise a wider public with the use of 'artificial terror' in prose fiction. But it was only with Ann Radcliffe that the remaining problems were overcome and popular success met and reinforced by critical acclaim, before the example of the German 'horror novel' began to undermine the enlightenment principles of critical legislation on the supernatural altogether.

III

The strange luxury of artificial terror

CHAPTER 6

Women, luxury and the sublime

That course of Reading must be unprofitable, which is confined to Novels; and this, I am apprehensive, is too much the case with your Sex. The Press daily teems with these publications, which are the trash to circulating Libraries. There are but few Novels, which have a tendency to give a right turn to the affections; or, at least, are calculated to improve the mind. A perusal of them, in rapid succession, is, in fact, a misemployment of time; as, in most Novels, there is a similarity in the incidents and characters; and these perhaps are unnatural, or seldom to be found in real life: so that young Women, who apply themselves to this sort of Reading, are liable to many errors, both in conduct and conversation, from the romantic notions they will thence imbibe. Novels are the last Books which they should read; instead of being almost the first.[1]

This passage offers a relatively sober rehearsal of a theme which resounded through the late eighteenth and early nineteenth centuries. It sketches the typical novel-reader as a member of 'your Sex', a young woman, the blankest *tabula rasa*, her mind a passive, soft, unresisting medium for external impressions, her affections absolutely malleable, able to be turned one way or another, for good or ill. The average novel is said to deal in 'unnatural' images, characters and incidents 'seldom to be found in real life'. By fitting her ideas to fictional standards the reader-as-receptor, by a mechanistic determination, is unfitted for her role in the world of the everyday.

The object of part III is to take up the stock connection of women and illusion and present ideas of sexual difference as a key factor in the development of a popular genre of supernatural fiction in the 1790s. This chapter relates the attacks on female novel-reading to issues already considered: criticism of modernity and consumer capitalism and the turn to an aesthetic theory of primitivism and the sublime. Chapter 7 will explore the particular impasse faced by women authors who wished to employ supernatural terror, and Ann

Radcliffe's narrative solution. Finally, in chapter 8, I will argue that the very force of the conventional distinction male/reality/history vs female/illusion/romance created a potential for subversion in Radcliffean Gothic fictions which supported the contemporary feminist challenge to the 'justice' of patriarchy.

The connection between female readers and improbable, unimproving fictions was well established by the 1790s, both in literary satire and in sober treatises on conduct and education. From the *Spectator* in the 1710s to Charlotte Lennox's *The Female Quixote* in 1752, the French genre of heroic romances came under attack for their giants and airborne chariots and epic feats of heroism and gallantry, considered capable of turning the heads of inexperienced misses and making them dissatisfied with dull reality. By the 1760s the attention of moralists had begun to turn to Richardson's sensationalising imitators, whose tales of seduction were unredeemed by Christian doctrine. Although there was no element of the marvellous in them, their heightened, romantic dialogue and depiction of passions ranging beyond rational control were felt to be a direct threat to the chastity of daughters and wives. In *The Rivals* (1775) Sheridan even-handedly mocked the novel-reader, in the form of Lydia Languish, and the novel-denouncer, represented by Sir Anthony Absolute: 'a circulating library in a town is as an evergreen tree of diabolical knowledge! It blossoms through the year! And depend upon it ... that they who are so fond of handling the leaves, will long for the fruit at last.'[2] However, it was not easy to exaggerate for the purposes of satire the already excessive virulence of the condemnations:

We consider the general run of Novels as utterly unfit for you. Instruction they convey none. They paint Scenes of Pleasure and Passion altogether improper for you to behold, even with the Mind's Eye. Their Descriptions are often loose and luscious in a High Degree; their representations of Love between the sexes are almost universally overstrained.[3]

A young woman, who employs her time in reading novels, will never find amusement in any other books. Her mind will be soon debauched by licentious descriptions, and lascivious images; and she will consequently remain the same insignificant creature through life; her mind will become a magazine of trifles and follies, or rather impure and wanton ideas.[4]

How far did reality bear out this picture of novel-addicted women? It would seem that the circular economy of the circulating library was itself in part the source of this confounding of books and female bodies, a confusion which asks to be read as a rhetorical rather than an actual event, a series of metonymic contaminations rather than a description of reality to be judged more or less accurate. The library books pass through many hands: held cheap by their temporary owners, they are soiled, marked and defaced, manhandled until they fall apart. It represents a prostitution of print, a commercial promiscuity, irresistably suggesting a parallel fate for the (*de jure*) female readers who devour and internalise the stories. Then again there was the plenitude of books, the image of the library as an inexhaustible fountain, always making available untried titles, fresh or newly released from the service of another reader. The unwearied tide of novelty, without beginning or end, was seen to introduce a similar compulsion into the physical being of its ultra-susceptible female customers, quickly making them addicts of fiction. Instead of remaining an amusement limited to clearly defined periods of leisure, the novel becomes an all-absorbing vocation. Readers become extensions of the library system, consume three, four, five volumes a day, every day: machines for reading. At the same time their habit is irregular, restless, distracted; library books are transient possessions, to be read in a hurry, surreptitiously. They are read in public places, disguised by false covers; or in private places, while doing, or failing to do, something else. They are connected with intimate moments of narcissism and self-abandonment: devoured in front of the mirror, while the hair is being dressed; or in bed, where the reader remains chained to the narrative until the early hours of the morning. Alternatively, the ever-changing kaleidoscope of the library that conceals a formulaic monotony is believed to encourage the still greater perversion of obsessive non-reading, not far from madness: a skimming and dipping technique which begins at the conclusion and allows a volume to be effectively gutted in minimum time, increasing the maximum rate of consumption. Finally, voracious consumption breeds further production. The library economy comes full circle when the readers become writers in turn, and devote not only all their time but all their energies and mental powers to the maintenance of the system. The long-held opinion of the vulnerability of women to possession by the written image, now exacerbated by an innovative means of distribution which extended access to print, was smoothly transcoded into the intelligible language of sexual threat.[5]

The rhetoric expressed and helped to spread the moral panic

connected with libraries and with novel-reading in general, a
fantasy of corruption far in excess of any influence the books might
realistically have had on their still-limited audience. The fantasy
hinged on the idea that women formed the principle audience for
novels and the most custom for libraries, but from the late
eighteenth century until the present day that assumption has been
the subject of debate.[6] In Clara Reeve's *The Progress of Romance*,
written in dialogue form, Horatio asserts that most fiction-readers
are women while Eustachia, the character who represents the
author's views, responds bluntly that this is 'not the case'; neither
offers any evidence.[7] From the beginning, persuasion or bald assertion has had to make up for the absence of facts and figures. Most
twentieth-century literary historians have been happy to accept the
common view of critics at the time. J. M. S. Tompkins states that
women 'were supposed to constitute three-quarters of the novel-
reading public' without mentioning her source or arguing the
point.[8] Ian Watt gives more weight to previously unsubstantiated
claims when he argues that 'a great increase in feminine leisure', the
result of a changing mode of economic production, provided the
expanded readership needed for the new type of fiction to flourish.[9]
Recent feminist histories of the novel which set out to show the
existence of an independent, women's literary tradition have had no
interest in questioning whether most readers were, in fact, women.

But since Reeve there have been a number of other challenges to
the common wisdom. Paul Kaufman gathered together all available
evidence – library catalogues and a list of subscribers for a circulating library in Bath, a rare and recent find – to suggest that the
stereotype was a male fabrication. Men outnumbered women as
patrons at the Bath library by up to 70 per cent in the 1790s, and
Kaufman insists that 'there is no reason to suppose it to be an
exception', while the more numerous catalogues of library stock
show a nationwide average percentage of fiction at only one-fifth of
the total, though amounts differed widely, from 5 per cent to 90 per
cent.[10] He does not speculate on the reason for the hitherto almost
universal 'misrepresentation' of library custom and merchandise in
the eighteenth century itself. Terry Lovell dismissed the image of the
leisured middle-class lady propagated by Watt and others as a
masculinist myth, but again without re-examining its textual sources.[11] Peter De Bolla went beyond the empirical dead-end to show
how gender categories functioned to hierarchise genres of writing

and practices of reading: poetry, say, and oral 'public' reading for men; the novel and silent solitary reading, with hints of illicit self-pleasuring, for women.[12] But his subsequent attempt to expose the destabilising tensions in this binary involves an uncharacteristically crude narrative of repression and disavowal: 'one detects a smokescreen: this raving attack on the women's reading scene, must, one suspects, be hiding the fact that men not only read and enjoyed these illicit texts, but that, at some level and in some fashion, they felt it of the utmost consequence that such textual forms remained the privileged, if illicit, and therefore often vociferously to be denied, territory of male reading'.[13] We are returned to the unproductive because ultimately undecidable question of who 'really' read the novels and borrowed from the libraries; the clause 'at some level and in some fashion' indicates an uneasy wish to avoid directly describing a written discourse (the conventional attacks on the novel) as a transparent symptom of a pre-constituted unconscious or as a mirror of a pre-given reality.

If the history of the debate reveals anything, it is that the hurry to use the condemnations of novel-reading as evidence of one thesis or the other has prevented them from being read in anything but a roughly descriptive or referential way. Their high rhetoric makes them extremely quotable, yet at the same time their repetitiveness has encouraged the illusion that they are 'already read', self-explanatory. The circumstantial evidence that women did form an increasingly important section of the reading public is convincing, and the suggestion that the attacks on female novel-reading contributed to a broader 'domestication' of femininity in the period also seems undeniable.[14] But my aim here will be to explore the neglected figurative dimension of this textual material. I want to show how the concern with changes in reading practice focuses the general issue of socio-historical change, while the concentration on the sex of the readers is part of a codification of gender with implications beyond the legislation of sexuality (though not exclusive of it).

The passage quoted at the beginning of the chapter, for instance, I initially glossed as the account of a dysfunction in the Johnsonian ideal of exemplary fiction: the female reader's mind is distorted by wrong images, it can be corrected by right ones. But we also need to notice how by focusing narrowly on the act of exchange between reader and written page, the critic is able to neglect other factors which he admits are causal, or contribute to the problem in some way, but which are less easy to define or legislate. In the background the press is 'teeming', as it always teems in descriptions of this kind, and the circulating libraries are dispersing the resulting 'trash'. How has the chief instrument for the diffusion of knowledge come to be misapplied in this way? Can it be stopped? The questions are unasked, and therefore no direct answer is called for. And what of the time that has been mis-employed? The alarming symptoms of addiction in the novel-reader, the desire and ability to read nearly identical narratives in quick succession, indicate new vistas of leisure which the traditional methods for the control and regulation of women's time have clearly failed to confront.

Here, the conventional rhetoric of the attacks can be seen to serve as a mechanism for absorbing conservative anxieties (I will try to name them more specifically shortly) about very general social tendencies and for reducing them to the scope of an individual woman's choice of reading. Another example shows this reductiveness at work in a more blatant manner. The author of an unsigned letter to the editor of the *Monthly Mirror*, headed 'Novel Reading a Cause of Female Depravity',[15] begins by deploring the trickle-down effect of fashion:

Had fashionable depravity been confined to the higher circles of life, I think I should hardly have troubled you with these my sentiments; I should have concluded it the offspring of effectually deprecating a vice which not the happy example of conjugal virtue held forth from the Throne could discountenance. But, like every other fashion, a little day [*sic*] hands it down to *the million*, and woman is now but another name for infamy.

It is only when the fashion reaches 'the middling orders of society' that it becomes a 'great calamity'. Without the downward mobility of leisure-reading, 'females in ordinary life would never have been so much the slaves of vice. The plain food, wholesome air, and exercise they enjoy, would have exempted them from the tyranny of lawless passions' as it had 'their virtuous grandmothers'. Now they are besotted with fine sentiment, vulnerable to the first lover who cunningly garnishes his *billets doux* with '*thous* and *thees* and *thys* and mellifluous compounds' and primed to seduce in turn their '"dearest friend's" husband' at the earliest opportunity ('Three instances, in as many years, have occurred in the little circle I move in'). '"And was novel-reading the cause of this?"' inquires some gentle fair one, who, deprived of such amusement could hardly exist

... I answer yes! It is in that school the poor deluded female imbibes erroneous principles ...' And the writer recommends a return to generous, liberal, refined thinking and the exertion of rational control over the passions, effectively excluding from consideration the purported first cause, the economy of fashion itself. The letter exhibits the pattern which can be found again and again: it sets up a problem at one level and offers to solve it on another; it paints the irresistible expansion of leisure, luxury, consumer choice, and seeks to eliminate the dreaded reality of change by replacing the picture with a struggle for the body and soul of woman, attainable by a personal act of will or the timely intervention of wise guardians.

From this perspective, the conflation of reading and female sexuality may be interpreted as a secondary construction, not fully meaningful in itself. It provided a codified and therefore distanced and acceptable means of handling the intractable subject of economic change and its social consequences. The issue of novel-reading (a representative by-product of consumerism at large) reduced the scope of the problem, and offered a language with which to 'narrate' it. Concern about the spread of leisure and luxury to the lower orders would be conveyed by a story about the corruption of a milliner or a lady's maid by reading fiction, as if the problem could only become discursively visible when charged with the sexual theme.[16]

This discursive technique is supported by a considerable genealogy. The linking of female sexuality with the eighteenth-century consumer revolution is, in effect, a variant of the long-standing link between women and luxury, which John Sekora has traced to classical Rome.[17] In Augustan England, civic humanism – the prevailing political discourse of the time, which described economics in terms inspired by the classical republican tradition – rearticulated this link in the context of capitalism. The civic humanist mapping of gender in the realm of the economic is not entirely congruent with the private/feminine vs public/masculine configuration that was to be a central feature of bourgeois hegemony in the following century. The latter ordering underlies the separation of the domestic sphere from the workplace and *polis*; gender categories here coincide with the discrete realms of activity of the two sexes. Civic humanism, while identifying 'private' with 'feminine', reveals its allegiance to aristocratic interests and values by classifying commerce, with mild disdain, as a private and hence 'feminine' activity.

Economic treatises throughout the eighteenth century reflect this gendering of the trading classes, and of trade in general. Contrary to our expectations, the pursuit of profit tends to be represented not as an aggressive, thrusting, 'masculine' activity, but as an innocent, gentle, civilising pastime, linked to the faculties of sensibility and sociability and typically gendered 'feminine' in opposition to the traditionally valorised aristocratic functions of public service and military leadership, gendered 'masculine'.[18]

Opponents of the monied interest naturally couched their abuse in gendered terms. Trade as such raised no objections and nor did its peaceful 'femininity' – on the contrary, the contribution made to Britain's international standing was applauded. But the transformative effect of trade on the fabric of the nation raised apocalyptic fears. What transfixed observers was not so much innovations in production and transportation, signs of the coming machine age, but instead the new potential for consumption: the disaccumulation of wealth on an unprecedented scale, a process not merely 'feminine', but actively, virulently emasculating. George Berkeley traces the short path from luxury to slavery by way of Isaiah's denunciation of the daughters of Zion for their 'tinkling Ornaments', 'Bonnets' and 'Mufflers'; the feminine love of fashion may seem 'a small offence . . . but is in truth the Source of great Corruptions' and spreads immorality through every section of society like an infection.[19] John Brown observes 'that the ruling Evils of our Age and Nation have arisen from the unheeded Consequences of our Trade and Wealth. That these have produced effeminate Manners, and occasioned Loss of Principle: That these have brought on a national Debility.'[20] Luxury represented the irrational play of passions, the unregulated and excessive progress of opulence, the erosion of hierarchy, the loss of an intelligible overview of the social and economic totality. Paternalist regulation from the top, the ideal of benign intervention by a 'wide Minister', was eclipsed by a state of economic anarchy in which private self-interest and pleasure-seeking ran riot, a state characterised synonymously as corrupt, regressive and feminine.

When Steele stated in the *Tatler* that 'The greatest happiness or misfortune of mankind depends upon the manner of educating and treating that sex', he was acknowledging the special status of Woman as index of the moral wellbeing of society as a whole.[21] As She is cherished or maltreated, contented or miserable, virtuous or

corrupt, so society must be judged. In the discourse of civic humanism Woman-as-luxury is implicitly constructed as the very form or
substance of modern society in its corrupting aspect: Man, the
subject, the soul of history, its consciousness and agent, faces this
image as a threat to (gender) identity. 'Effeminacy' is the conversion by which Man loses self-consciousness, self-determination,
rational control over his fate and the fate of the commonwealth,
loses the qualities in which masculinity and virtue are compounded,
and becomes passively, irresistibly merged with the drive towards
luxury that defines the modern. Until the last years of the century,
the civic humanist ideal of 'public man' monopolises the rhetorical
function of masculinity in its discourse on politics, society and
economics.

Civic humanism shares with bourgeois liberalism the use of
Woman as exemplar; but in the older discourse she signifies the
excesses of economic self-interest rather than the preservation of
those virtues excluded from the sphere of commercial competition.
Negative moral connotations apart, civic humanism was in fact a
better description of the structural importance of women as consumers within the capitalist order than the future cult of the house-
bound 'angel' would be. As such, its influence is found in sketches of
contemporary social life to the end of the century and after. We
could take as a relevant example S. J. Pratt's portrait of a lending
library, which strictly abides by the conventional gender division
(with class overtones) in the bookseller's discrimination of the 'folio
and quarto gentry', men who borrow only half-yearly, and 'what I
call my *consumers* – lasses, young and old, who run over a novel of
three, four or five volumes, faster than book-men can put them into
boards: three sets a day; morning vol. noon vol. and night vol. Pretty
caterpillars, as I call them, because they devour my leaves.'[22]

As early as the 1690s a counter-discourse emerged proclaiming
the usefulness of consumption as a stimulus to trade and production,
but it was generally condemned.[23] Mandeville's justification of
luxury drew on him the label of 'Antichrist'.[24] Civic humanist
priorities maintained their hold even in the work of the greatest
apologist for the new liberal economic order. In *Lectures on Justice*
Adam Smith laments the decline of the 'martial spirit' conducive to
a disinterested sense of public duty, as a bad effect of the growth of
commerce and the division of labour. 'By having their minds constantly employed on the art of luxury, [the bulk of the people] grow

effeminate and dastardly.' Later, the same anxiety concerning 'the disadvantages of a commercial spirit' is restated: 'The minds of men are contracted, and rendered incapable of elevation. Education is despised, or at least neglected, and the heroic spirit is almost utterly extinguished. To remedy these defects would be an object worthy of serious attention.'[25]

Plainly, Smith refers to the male population when he speaks of 'the bulk of the people'. Equally notable, following the discussion of the previous chapter, is the way the vocabulary he uses to describe the psychological consequences of commerce and luxury, of 'elevation' and 'contraction', recalls that of Burke and the Aikins in their discussions of the pleasures and benefits of terror. The convergence is clearest in Kant's equation of militarism and the sublime in the *Critique of Judgment*: while '[o]n the other hand, a prolonged peace favours the predominance of a mere commercial spirit, and with it a debasing self-interest, cowardice, and effeminacy, and tends to degrade the character of the nation'.[26] Recent commentaries on Burke's *Enquiry* have shown the gender hierarchy immanent in the distinction between the sublime and the beautiful.[27] In particular, Frances Ferguson has drawn attention to the dynamic character of the relation between the two terms, implicitly viewed from the perspective of the masculine subject in a quandary: the sublime, the principle of labour or exertion, arrives to remedy the excessive relaxation of the bodily and mental parts provoked by the beautiful, which had threatened to end in a resistless dissolution of identity.[28]

Is the sublime, then, the answer to Adam Smith's prayers, the solution to the defects of a commercial society? Like luxury, the 'encumbrance' that the sublime is designed to remove is a threat from within: body politic paralleling empirical body. But the parallelism is not consistent. The antithesis of luxury, a concept which can be defined as the mass effect of self-interested passions, is the disinterested public spirit best represented by military service, when love of self is suppressed to the extent that the individual is willing to die for the country's good. But in a peaceful mercantile state, organised on the principle of the division of labour, death in battle is an option open to few. It would seem that Burke acknowledges and accepts this essential, irreversible limitation when he displaces the issue by individualising it. The political language of luxury is translated into a psycho-empirical language of aesthetics, but the solution is found in the terms of the latter and cannot be retranslated. What

Burke offers is a private war without consequences. The sublime is a simulacrum of the external threat of violent death sufficient to arouse the strongest passions of self-preservation, while never requiring that these be surmounted in the name of public duty; it remains essentially a mind-game. Although it has the effect of catharsis and renewal, and confirmation of masculinity (here, the mental qualities that make men different from women), there is no bridge back to the sense of public spirit (such as Kant would attempt to provide, in criticism of Burke). It is a decisive alteration, an appeasement of individualist commercial values rather than an antidote to them, and the claim that it signifies a bourgeois appropriation of the political language of luxury must be judged correct, although, as I will argue, it came before its time.[29] Yet the differences should not be allowed to obscure continuity. Woman as negative term is a legacy passed from one political generation to the next, though for the first She comes to signify the quintessence of middle-class evils, and for the second those of the aristocracy.[30] The very change in the balance of socio-economic power was formulated as a 'crisis of masculinity', personal and/or national, and it was in response to a 'gender crisis' that the diagnosis was made and the cure prescribed.

Tales of supernatural terror, which the Aikins presented as the practice to Burke's theory, were crucially implicated in the play of social and economic ideas I have been describing. On the one hand, with their irrational plots and blatant appeal to the passions, they were the extreme violation of the tenet of fictional example, and therefore to be classed among the corrupting agencies of feminine luxury, intimately, physically identified with a reading subject constructed as feminine. On the other hand, within the legitimating discourse of the sublime, they were said to have the potential to cleanse the reading subject (constructed as masculine) of the effects of a luxurious society by a personally liberating extension of the powers of imagination. In the 1790s these two versions of the effectivity of ghost fictions were in the balance. Nowhere is this more apparent than in the work of Ann Radcliffe, whose trademark device of the 'explained supernatural' precisely withdrew with one hand what it offered with the other.

CHAPTER 7

The supernatural explained

A woman wishing to publish fiction in a supernatural vein needed to be prepared to negotiate. For reasons which have been suggested in the preceding chapter, her relations to both the code of literary decorum and the aesthetic of the sublime were likely to be mediated by an added dimension of gender associations. Clara Reeve's correction of Walpole's earlier imaginative excesses in *The Old English Baron* protected her from the almost automatic condemnation of the corrupting ways of female novelists, as much as from the disapproval attached to the supernatural itself. And at the same time as women writers were required with particular insistence to show their didactic credentials, it was especially difficult for them to attempt a narrative practice connected with the emergent discourse of the sublime, which could justify supernatural terrors on the alternative non-didactic grounds of psychological recuperation and aesthetic pleasure. As we have seen, this discourse was articulated in terms of gender, its subject masculine, its project actively anti-feminine. It may have been a sense of exclusion, or of some unspoken impropriety, which eventually led Anna Barbauld to attribute the fragmentary tale of terror 'Sir Bertrand' to her brother alone, although it had originally appeared under both their names,[1] and in Reeve's case resulted in a handling of spirits that was non-affective by design.

Certainly, in the course of the 1780s, it seems that the one woman writer who used a 'real' ghost to terrifying effect was Anne Fuller in *Alan Fitz-Osbourne* (1787), and she published anonymously. Ann Radcliffe's first novel, *The Castles of Athlin and Dunbayne* (1789), was also anonymous. But in her next, *A Sicilian Romance* (1790), she introduced the device she would become famous for: apparently supernatural occurrences are spine-chillingly evoked only to be explained away in the end as the product of natural causes. By the second edition of *The Romance of the Forest* (1791) her work is in every sense 'authorised': 'Ann Radcliffe' appeared on the title-page and the author was mentioned by name in the reviews which lavished praise on the *dénouement* by which 'every extraordinary appearance seems naturally to arise from causes, not very uncommon'.[2] This was a variety of imaginative fiction which the guardians of enlightenment felt they could wholly approve: 'By the aid of an inventive genius, much may still be done, even in this philosophical age, to fill the fancy with marvellous images, and to "quell the soul with grateful terrors".'[3] Progress and the taste for primitive superstition were reconciled. The eagerness of the critics' welcome gives the impression almost of relief, as if Radcliffe's innovation gave an opportunity to come to terms with the barbarians at the gates without surrendering the fort.

With *The Mysteries of Udolpho*, in 1794, the reviews again paid tribute to Radcliffe's achievement of the seemingly impossible:

Without introducing into her narrative any thing really supernatural, Mrs Radcliffe has contrived to produce as powerful an effect as if the invisible world had been obedient to her magic spell; the reader experiences in perfection the strange luxury of artificial terror, without being obliged for a moment to hoodwink his reason, or to yield to the weakness of superstitious credulity.[4]

In his enthusiasm the critic misrepresents matters slightly. The mysterious music, disembodied voices, shadowy figures and bumps in the night, before they are mundanely attributed to mad nuns, concealed fugitives and prisoners, or smugglers, are given their full affective weight. The impact of the narrative *depends* on the temporary 'hoodwinking' of reason; to experience 'the strange luxury of artificial terror' requires some sort of surrender to 'the weakness of superstitious credulity'. The 'strangeness' lies in the indeterminacy of aesthetic experience, voluntary and involuntary at once, just as terror must be real while it is felt, although the artificial mechanism that produced it remains clearly visible. The pleasures offered by this 'luxury', this fictional indulgence, also strike the enlightened reader as uncanny because of the way the course of the narration echoes the history of enlightenment itself. The reader progressively moves from the sense of mystery that encourages fearful, false ideas to full knowledge of the facts, intelligibility of causes, means and ends, and confirmation of the truth of reason: in other words, reliving the passage from gothic to modern times, a process here invested with a pleasurable blend of relaxation and control, licence and restraint.

Many novelists began to follow Radcliffe's lead including, during the 1790s, Charlotte Smith, Eliza Parsons, Eliza Fenwick, Isabella Kelly, Julia Maria Young, Elizabeth Bonhote, Mrs Carver, George Moore, Regina Maria Roche, Mrs Patrick, John Palmer, Jr, and Mary Meeke: the 'explained supernatural' became an identifiable school of writing. It is important to emphasise Radcliffe's initial success with this narrative technique, because it would very quickly give rise to a backlash which compromised her critical standing until recently. Her descriptive writing and command of suspense continued to be praised (with some complaint about repetition), but the enlightenment endings were eventually condemned as betrayals of the integrity of fiction, a treacherous refusal of the rights of the imagination to construct a world untouched by quotidian laws of probability. The revaluation took shape gradually. For the first suggestion of this kind we need to look to Coleridge's review of *Udolpho* and the remark that 'curiosity is raised oftener than it is gratified; or rather, it is raised so high that no adequate gratification can be given it; the interest is completely dissolved when once the adventure is finished, and the reader, when he is got to the end of the work, looks about in vain for the spell which had bound him so strongly to it'.[5] But by accepting that '*no* adequate gratification can be given' when clearly the 'adequate' resolution would be a supernatural one, Coleridge acknowledges the continuing authority of the enlightenment paradigm even as he complains against it. Reviews of *The Italian* (1796), the fourth and last of Radcliffe's novels published in her lifetime, complain at the way foreknowledge of the author's characteristic rationalising conclusion destroys the visionary effects which precede it. But it is more in the way of a technical and psychological observation than an outright principled challenge.[6]

It was Walter Scott who properly launched a critique of the 'explained supernatural' that was so persistent it could almost be called a campaign. He began in a review of an obscure novel by Dennis Jasper Murphy (better known as Charles Maturin), using it as a platform for explaining the new aesthetic imperative:

[W]e disapprove of the mode introduced by Mrs. Radcliffe and followed by Mr. Murphy and her other imitators, of winding up their story with a solution by which all the incidents appearing to partake of the mystic and the marvellous are resolved by very simple and natural causes . . . it is as if the machinist, when the pantomime was over, should turn his scenes, 'seamy side out', and expose the mechanical aids by which the delusions were accomplished ... There is a total and absolute disproportion of cause and effect [in the machinery of *Fatal Revenge*, by Murphy], which must disgust every reader much more than if he were left under the delusion of ascribing the whole to supernatural agency. This latter resource has indeed many disadvantages; some of which we shall briefly notice. But it is an admitted expedient; appeals to the belief of all ages but our own; and still produces, when well managed, some effect upon those who are most disposed to contemn its influence. We can therefore allow of supernatural agency to a certain extent and for an appropriate purpose, but we never can consent that the effect of such agency shall be finally attributed to natural causes totally inadequate to its production.[7]

This insistence on the autonomous coherence of fictional effects gathered impetus in Scott's introductions to the Ballantyne series of novel reprints. He digresses from a survey of Walpole's life and works to reiterate and expand on the objections to Radcliffe's practice; while in the discussion introductory to Radcliffe's own collected works many pages are given over to the subject and he quotes his own previous remarks and the unfavourable judgements of others at length.

Scott's criticism was authoritative and widely circulated, and it had two main consequences for the reception of Radcliffe's work. First, it confirmed and consolidated a general 'forgetting' of the reasons why the technique of the 'explained supernatural' had been devised in the first place. Thus, in the 'Memoir' prefixed to the posthumous edition of her novel *Gaston de Blondeville*, Thomas Talfourd can affect incomprehension at her 'extraordinary' decision to resolve 'superstitious apprehensions into mere physical causes'. 'She seems to have acted on a notion,' he adds, 'that some established canon of romance obliged her to reject real supernatural agency; for it is impossible to believe she would have adopted this harassing expedient if she had felt at liberty to obey the promptings of her own genius.'[8] The device, which originated out of the social definition of fiction itself, has been redefined as a regrettable personal lapse; a pusillanimous concession to obscure and obsolete prejudices.

A second and related consequence concerned the classification of Gothic as a distinct subgenre. Scott had unfavourably contrasted the Radcliffe method with the uninhibited supernaturalism of Walpole and Maturin. By making the criterion of the supernatural central to the aesthetic judgement of Gothic novels, he encouraged the development of an implicit gender hierarchy. Novels where spirits are not rationalised, the most famous example in the 1790s being *The Monk* by Matthew Lewis, are 'real' Gothic, while the class of the 'explained supernatural', largely authored by women, is a diminished, self-censoring version of the first.[9] Literary history provided a neat exemplification of the binary liberated/repressed in the succession of the couple Walpole/Reeve, by the couple Lewis/ Radcliffe. The analogy was strengthened by speculation that *The Italian* had been written as a moralising corrective to *The Monk*.

Whatever truth there is in the idea that Radcliffe, like Reeve, wrote in opposition to the gratuitous horrors of her male counterpart, there is a necessity underlying this gendered differentiation of Gothic modes which takes us back to the critique of commercial society. Scott's conception of an alternative, autonomous aesthetic 'logic' or 'reality' was ultimately founded on the discourse of the sublime, with its consolatory, remedial vision of art; *versus* rather than *in* society. Such a vision, as we have seen, predicated a masculine subject, as consumer and producer of elevated and elevating art. Its authority depended on the suppression of its own socially engaged origins in the pessimistic condemnation of modern luxury, which featured, by contrast, a feminine subject as a dangerous, degraded and degrading reader-cum-purveyor of imaginative fictions. The revaluation of supernatural fiction led by Scott necessarily entailed a sex change, as a mark of difference and transformation.

That said, it could be objected that Radcliffe herself introduced a 'real ghost' into her last romance *Gaston de Blondeville* (written in 1804 but not published until after her death) and prefaced it with a critical essay which supports the use of ghosts for dramatic effect.[10] However, this romance is a strange contradictory work which seems rather to demonstrate the continuing force of the old constraints on her writing than her embrace of aestheticism. The ghost is supplied only by breaking all the rules laid out in the theoretical section, meaning the loss of the techniques of suggestion which were the basis of her success in the earlier novels. Instead, the narrative is hedged about with distancing devices to prevent the reader from superstitious identification with the viewpoint of the characters. It is framed by an account of two modern-day travellers on a visit to Kenilworth Castle; the mood is more scholarly than dramatic and the novel finally closes on a tedious quibble over the date of an ancient manuscript. This manuscript contains the story of Gaston de Blon-deville and the ghost, which has been 'translated' for the benefit of the modern reader from Norman into ersatz medieval English, a stilted idiom ruling out atmospheric subtlety. The ghost itself is initially discovered in a crowd scene, without suspense, obscurity, doubt or any of the Shakespearian mood-setting accompaniments praised in the introductory dialogue. Psychological description is kept to a minimum, and we see the ghost mainly through the eyes of the unsympathetic Henry III.

The introductory dialogue on the sublime and the supernatural begins as a staged confrontation between a fervent Shakespeare enthusiast and a man whose speculations are said not to extend beyond the next dinner; a clash of sensibility and narrow pragmatism familiar from the novels. But as Mr Willoughton's raptures become increasingly overblown and Mr Simpson's remarks become increasingly perspicacious, the position of the author's sympathies becomes less clear. We can at least gather that Radcliffe had studied Burke's *Enquiry*, that she believed that obscurity was the most crucial characteristic of the sublime, since it forces the imagination to exert itself by reconstructing a partially perceived object, and that as a refinement on Burke she distinguished between effects of terror, where obscurity leaves room for pleasurable indecision, and horror, where the object is clearly visible and overwhelms the mental faculties (the 'ghost scene' from *Hamlet* and the 'banquet scene' from *Macbeth* are taken as contrasting examples). And so while the narrative practice of *Gaston de Blondeville* maintains a rationalist distance from superstition, the theory counsels the audience's willing submission to imaginary illusion; the antipathetic demands which Radcliffe managed for a short time to reconcile in the 'explained supernatural' here collapse into unyielding antinomy.

But to read the supernatural in Radcliffe through Scott, whose expectations are closer to our own, is in some ways misleading. There are dimensions of ghostliness in the work of Radcliffe and her followers that exceed and complicate the opposition of natural and supernatural, imitative and purely imaginary, presupposed by Romantic criticism of the 'explained supernatural'. The most obvious residue of the spiritual after all supposed apparitions have been cleared away is Providence. Thus *The Mysteries of Udolpho* closes: 'O! useful may it be to have shown, that, though the vicious can sometimes pour affliction upon the good, their power is transient and their punishment certain; and that innocence, though oppressed with injustice, shall, supported by patience, finally triumph over misfortune!'[11] The appeal to an 'invisible hand' was of course a common narrative strategy at the time, in both literary and non-literary writing: the paradoxes of existence, apparent conflicts between private and public interests, virtue and commerce, or more commonly, unmerited suffering and belief in a good and all-powerful God, were harmonised by the spectacle of a just dispensation of reward and punishment, a meaningful totality visible only in discourse. Didacticism, which I have suggested was an imperative especially felt by female writers of Gothic, was aided by use of a third-person omniscient narration which could lay down clear moral guidelines. This led to some conflict with the demands of suspense; when, in the infamous case of the Black Veil in *Udolpho*, the heroine faints on seeing the concealed object, the narration also loses consciousness and only recovers it to inform the reader of the sober truth hundreds of pages later. As Todorov has remarked, the ideal structure for the fantastic is a first-person narrative, where ignorance unites reader and narrator in egalitarian identity.[12] The Radcliffean mode of story-telling could be charged with bad faith, and was.

But in another way the lessons of Providence found an ideal vehicle in Gothic fictions where invisible agency constitutes a key mystery to be resolved. The narrative sees one metaphysical logic of causality, one form of pan-determinism, superstition, replaced by another, theodicy. The bizarre coincidences that are produced to explain the supernatural are not just a technical convenience, as Scott asserted, but evidence of a higher supernaturalism that ensures every 'accident' has its rightful place in the schema of Divine Justice. Genealogy, above all, is the hidden structuring principle of the plot that must finally be brought to light. Fortuitous contact with strangers or strange places gives rise to a multitude of blood connections. Thus in *The Romance of the Forest* Adeline is thrust on the protection of the La Mottes, fugitives from the law who, unknowingly, seek shelter in the very same ruined abbey where Adeline's father was held prisoner and murdered; the destitute M. La Motte attempts to rob a passing stranger who turns out to be the Marquis de Montalt, the owner of the abbey who is later identified as Adeline's uncle and her father's murderer; Adeline's would-be protector, Theodore Peyrou, an army officer subordinate to the

Marquis, is imprisoned on charges of desertion; Adeline escapes to Savoy, where she is thrown on the charity of the family of the pastor La Luc who happens to be the father of Theodore, in spite of the different surname; a M. Verneuil rescues Clara, daughter of La Luc, from accidental death in Savoy, reappears in Languedoc, is finally found to be a relation of Adeline's mother and marries Clara. In *Udolpho*, the family web is as intricate, or more so. Prosaic chance is discovered to be no less of an illusion than the suggestions of superstition; it is the other main casualty of the novels. The endings, far from being the confirmation of a common-sense, disenchanted reality, reveal the world to be a transparent medium of divinity; material existence is suffused by religion. *cf George*

Alongside this substitutive relation ('rational' religion for irrational folklore), there is the leakage of the supernatural as metaphor in natural descriptions. In *The Mysteries of Udolpho* Emily St Aubert's psyche is presented as a phantasmagoria of memory, living people 'haunt' the scenes of former happiness and are mistaken for ghosts, while the dead perpetually appear to the mind's eye and cast their shadow on current events. Terry Castle, who has written with great persuasiveness on this aspect of the novel, holds that '[t]he supernatural is not so much explained in *Udolpho* as it is displaced. It is diverted – rerouted, so to speak, into the realm of the everyday.'[13] She stresses the innovative quality of the neglected 'realist' sections of the book: *Udolpho* 'encapsulated new structures of feeling, a new model of human relations, a new phenomenology'. But it is worth adding that at the same time Radcliffe's writing is here often at its most deliberately derivative, willingly haunted by the example of the 'Graveyard School' of poets and the even older tradition of melancholy they drew on. It is when the heroine falls into reverie that the plot is most likely to be waylaid by a pastiche of Collins or the Wartons or a quotation from Gray, Thomson or Shakespeare: high culture authors invited like fairy godmothers to the christening of this popular culture form. The convergence of what Castle terms the 'spectralization of the other' and literary respectability (f. L. *respicere*, to look (back) at, regard) could be explored further.

Here, however, I am going to pause over a third instance of spectral excess, generated by the mechanism of the 'explained supernatural' itself. Walpole showed that fantasy could be made experientially 'real' for the reader by the employment of realist conventions of characterisation. With Radcliffe, reality is powerfully experienced as a fantasy which the reader is drawn into sharing. The dissolution of the fantasy raises certain questions. What conditions might lead a rational individual to perceive natural phenomena as if they were supernatural? (Radcliffe's heroines are invariably outspoken rationalists in their calmer moments.) Is there any class of phenomenon that especially lends itself to ontological errors? The first question will be dealt with in the next chapter. The second is easily answered. As every devotee of Gothic knows, smugglers or banditti and imprisoned wives or relations are the two most fertile sources of superstitious delusion. When supposed phantoms are detected so are systems of lawlessness and cruelty which secretly coexist with the 'natural' economies of legitimate profit-making, or of familial affection and duty. Roger Caillois called the fantastic 'an irruption of the inadmissible within the changeless everyday legality'.[14] This irruption will occur equally in the case of those so-called 'crimes against nature' concealed under the appearance of the fantastic. The supernatural seems to act here as a phenomenological symptom. Its truth is experiential. It attests to the existence of realities which cannot be admitted within the realm of the 'natural'.

Critics wanting to emphasise the escapist function of Gothic fiction have regularly claimed that the exotic settings naturalise and distance transgression; the criminal excesses which are native to the era of barbarism and to Roman Catholic southern Europe could, they say, be regarded with smugness by a bourgeois British audience. This may have been so but, given the importance of identification with the fantasising heroine in the mode of the 'explained supernatural', there is also the reverse possibility that such fictions might encourage an experience of estranged recognition, a capacity to see the everyday in another, less complacent, light. In other words, that they might cause readers, in particular young women, to apply 'illegitimate' methods of interpretation to reality just as contemporary opponents of romance feared.

CHAPTER 8

Like a heroine

'You must confess that novels are more true than histories, because historians often contradict each other, but novelists never do': the would-be heroine of E. S. Barrett's satire of romance fiction, *The Heroine*, goes on the the attack against the conventional depreciation of the 'feminine' novel in favour of 'masculine' history.[1] Gender is at the root of the matter when it is raised again in *Northanger Abbey*, for history, Catherine Morland observes, 'tells me nothing that does not either vex or weary me. The quarrels of popes and kings, with wars and pestilences in every page; the men all so good for nothing, and hardly any women at all, it is very dull.'[2] Both of these satires set out to show, in comic terms, what happens when an avid consumer of sensational novels fulfils at least part of James Beattie's gloomy prognosis:

Romances are a dangerous recreation ... and tend to corrupt the heart, and stimulate the passions. A habit of reading them breeds a dislike to history, and all the substantial parts of knowledge; withdraws the attention from nature and truth; and fills the mind with extravagant thoughts, and too often with criminal propensities.[3]

– and comes to read her own 'history' as if it were a sensational narrative.

Yet on the way to the satire's final rationalist confirmation of the divide between fact and fiction a curious alchemy takes place. Common sense, in temporarily assuming a fantastic disguise, finds it cannot so easily shake it off again. Thus Margaret Kirkham's feminist reading of *Northanger Abbey* discovers in it 'a major criticism of the assumptions associated with the schema of the burlesque novel in which a heroine learns that her romantic notions are all mistaken, and that the world of the everyday is better ordered than that of imagination'.[4] Catherine's Gothic imaginings about General Tilney and his late wife are partially borne out, for it emerges that Mrs

Tilney had been imprisoned by her marriage, that unhappiness had contributed to her death and that the General, in accordance with the laws of England and the customs of the time, does wield near-absolute power 'as an irrational tyrant' in the family. The reader discovers that the romance perspective, *pace The Heroine's* Cherubina, may be 'more true' than Henry Tilney's reassuring, Whig vision of historical progress ('Does our education prepare us for such atrocities? Do our laws connive at them?'). In attempting to cure it, by a dangerous mingling, satire itself catches the infection of fiction which Beattie feared.

During her early years as a writer, Mary Wollstonecraft wrote dozens of reviews of novels for the *Analytical Review*. The reviews for 1788 and 1789 attributed to her are conventionally dismissive, even exaggerating the usual show of condescension towards women writers and readers. In 1790 and 1791 novels by Helen Maria Williams and Elizabeth Inchbald, authors connected with radical circles, were given more sympathetic and serious treatment, but Williams's work is still praised only for its 'feminine sweetness', decorum and piety.[5] *Vindication of the Rights of Woman* (1792) offers an ambivalent opinion of the novel form's progressive potential with regard to women. While restating the rationalist valorisation of history over fiction, Wollstonecraft nevertheless insists that novel-reading is preferable to leaving 'a blank still a blank, because the mind must receive a degree of enlargement and obtain a little strength by a slight exertion of its thinking powers'.[6] Six years later the prologue of her novel *The Wrongs of Woman; or, Maria* requests the reader to consider the narrative as a 'history ... of woman'.[7] A conventional historical account of 'the partial laws and customs of society' relating to women has been rejected as inadequate.[8] In spite of her disclaimer regarding the use of '*stage-effect*', she has recourse in her fiction to the most melodramatic devices of the Gothic mode involving imprisonment, sexual tyranny and madness. In Gothic she finds the appropriate discursive form for her social critique of the rape of women's humanity.[9]

The change of sentiment that takes place between the writing of the *Vindication* and *The Wrongs of Woman* coincides with the rise of the Gothic heroine.[10] During the same space of time Ann Radcliffe's *The Mysteries of Udolpho*, apogee of Gothic fiction, had appeared and its success had resulted in a flood of imitations. On the basis of this success Radcliffe put into circulation the elements of a supernatural narrative-type structured around the subjectivity of the heroine, and thus distinct from the early romances of Horace Walpole and Clara Reeve and the more sensational strain of *Schauerroman*, available in translations from the German and later popularised by 'Monk' Lewis.[11] When Wollstonecraft remarks that in *The Wrongs of Woman* she had 'rather endeavoured to pourtray passions than manners', she echoes a distinction already made by Walpole and the Aikins between the tediously imitative breed of sentimental fiction and works which permit the imagination to take flight. When she appeals to the reader of *The Wrongs of Woman* to 'grant that my sketches are not the abortions of a distempered fancy' she assumes the logic of the 'explained supernatural', requiring the expansion of the framework of social reality to assimilate the 'improbable' yet experientially authentic products of the mind.[12]

THE MYSTERIES OF UDOLPHO AND THE LAW

Emily calmly said,
'I am not so ignorant, Signor, of the laws on this subject, as to be misled by the assertion of any person. The law, in the present instance, gives me the estates in question, and my own hand shall never betray my right.'
'I have been mistaken in my opinion of you, it appears', rejoined Montoni sternly. 'You speak boldly, and presumptuously, upon a subject which you do not understand. For once, I am willing to pardon the conceit of ignorance; the weakness of your sex, too, from which, it seems, you are not exempt, claims some allowance; but if you persist in this strain—you have everything to fear from my justice.'
'From your justice, signor,' rejoined Emily, 'I have nothing too fear – I have only to hope.'
Montoni looked at her with vexation, and seemed considering what to say ... 'Your credulity can punish only yourself; and I must pity the weakness of mind which leads you to so much suffering as you are compelling me to prepare for you.'
'You may find, perhaps, signor,' said Emily with mild dignity, 'that the strength of my mind is equal to the justice of my cause; and that I can endure with fortitude, when it is in resistance to oppression.'
'You speak like a heroine,' said Montoni contemptuously; 'we shall see whether you can suffer like one.'
Emily was silent, and he left the room.
Recollecting that it was for Valancourt's sake she had thus resisted, she now smiled complacently upon the threatened sufferings, and retired to the spot which her aunt had pointed out as the repository of the papers relative to the estates.[13]

Emily's assertion?
appears to represent a
challenge to Montoni's
patriarchal tyranny but
is
undermined
"heroine".

Prior to this clash between heroine and villain, *The Mysteries of Udolpho* carefully and lengthily establishes the conditions which have made the former vulnerable to disinheritance. After a blissful childhood Emily St Aubert loses her mother and father in quick succession. She is penniless and forced to go and live with her vain and foolish aunt, a rich widow. There she falls in love with and agrees to marry Valancourt, whom she had first met on a tour of the Pyrenees she made with her father. The aunt, after some opposition, permits the marriage and then vetoes it when she herself impulsively marries the mysterious and compelling Signor Montoni. The household moves to Venice. Emily is pressured to marry a man she dislikes, but before the ceremony there is an abrupt removal to Montoni's castle, Udolpho, in the Apennines. The castle is full of long dark passages, nameless fears and hints of ancestral wrongdoings. It emerges that Montoni is the chief of a band of *condottieri*. He has large gambling debts to pay off and threatens his wife in order to make her sign over some entailed estates to him. She refuses and he has her imprisoned. She dies of misery and neglect and bequeaths the estates to her niece.

The scene of confrontation just quoted occurs at this point in the story, at the moment when Emily is forced to stand alone against Montoni. Their battle of wills represents for Emily a rite of passage, a transition to a new status; the fact is acknowledged by Montoni when he sneers that she 'speaks like a heroine'. He means by this that her new resistance to his authority is excessive, irrational and romantic in the sense of illusory or fictional, because her view of reality has been distorted by reading romances and she had identified too closely with the language and behaviour of the female characters. The accusation is both vertiginous and routine. Vertiginous, because in the midst of this absorbing drama, it abruptly draws attention to the activity of romance-reading and the text's own illusory effects. What is Emily, after all, if not a heroine? What is the reader meant to infer when Montoni echoes the hackneyed complaints of critics of the novel and its female audience? Routine, because the same charge recurs in similar clashes in heroine-centred novels from Richardson's *Pamela* onwards. With ritual malice, an enemy jeeringly associates the main female character with romance-reading, accusing her of entertaining paranoid fantasies and of self-dramatisation, in order to undermine her opposition to corrupt or arbitrary authority.[14] When the heroine is vindicated, so too is the exemplary 'truth' of fiction.

This reflexive trope constitutes an indirect but cumulatively substantial vindication of the rights of illusion. But another part of Montoni's speech is even closer to home, that is to say, the specific narrative practice of the 'explained supernatural'. Emily is accused of 'weakness of mind' and 'credulity', words habitually applied by the third-person narrator to Emily's irrational fear of the supernatural. Emily's belief in her legal and moral rights is thus likened to belief in spirits. Montoni uses the sceptical language of reason to equate resistance to arbitrary power with superstition, thus legitimating his control over the interpretation of reality. 'Heroinism' becomes the name of a rival hermeneutics. It is initially projected as an illegitimate and irrational 'other' of authority, but finds justification in the outcome of the narrative. The powerless Emily eventually triumphs, while the figure of Montoni dwindles and vanishes from the storyline, confirming Emily's assessment of the relative strengths of virtue and violence over his.

But that conclusion is still a long way off. We are midway through the novel, Emily appears to be entirely in Montoni's power, and the next sequence of events demonstrates the 'truth' of superstition in a different, metaphorical way. Following the dispute, Emily returns to her chamber to dwell on her provisional victory. 'For a first time, she felt the full extent of her own superiority to Montoni, and despised the authority, which, till now, she had only feared.' Then suddenly 'a peal of laughter rose from the terrace, and, on going to the casement, she saw, with inexpressible surprise, three ladies, dressed in the gala habit of Venice, walking with several gentlemen below'.[15] In a rush all her sense of helplessness and fear returns as she attempts to divine the meaning of this apparition, extraordinary in the isolated fortress of Udolpho, and her shocked faculties lead her on to suppose the worst. These promenading men and women are a portent which exposes the absurdity of her former confidence. 'It was at this moment, when the scenes of the present and the future opened to her imagination, that the image of Valancourt failed in its influence, and her resolution shook with dread.'[16] In the event she is forced to sign away her property to her wicked uncle not because of any inability to suffer with fortitude, but because in a castle overrun with drunken mercenaries and Venetian courtesans she can no longer safeguard her privacy, and by extension her person, without *propriety* his protection.

While she remains at Udolpho, the sensations she derives from natural or supposedly supernatural phenomena are often indistinguishable. Both impress upon her the reality of her condition as a woman suffering the extremes of unlimited patriarchal control. Montoni places her in a room that cannot be locked from the inside, making her as vulnerable to intruders as she would be to spectres that can walk through walls; when Count Morano, her unsuccessful suitor from Venice, attempts to abduct her by night, 'terror . . . deprived her of the power of descrimination' and she at first interprets the 'mysterious' gliding figure as a ghost.[17] It is the rumours of Montoni's terrible misdeeds in the past that first raise the suggestion in her mind that Udolpho is haunted; and as his behaviour towards herself and her aunt continues to support this account, her susceptibility to 'ideal terrors' quite logically increases. As with General Tilney in *Northanger Abbey*, although the *narration* may deny the possibility that Montoni is really haunted by the female victims of his autocratic rule, everything in the *plot*, the presentation of his words and deeds, combines to insist that he ought to be.

The supernatural persists, unexplained, as the metaphysical coordinate of Emily's objective state. It signifies a consciousness of the actuality of women's subjection as a sex, an actuality unthinkable from within the velvet-gloved, paternalist version of patriarchy represented by La Vallée at the beginning of the story, a state of illusion which had permitted Emily to believe she had rights regardless of her sex. Now she is forced to recognise the extent to which her subjectivity – a fragile fabric of sensibility and virtue – is overborne by a determinism that is both economic and sexual, channelled through the inescapable bonds of kinship.[18] She is to serve as an instrument for the conveyance of property, whether by forfeit to a male relative-in-law whose status as guardian makes it impossible to resist his will, or as the merchandise of a profiteering marriage agreed between men. As a mere instrument, her qualifications for humanity – rationality, emotions – are superfluous; consciousness detached from effective agency is nothing more than a ghostly emanation, inwardly feeding and generating apparitions in its own image. The supernatural describes the experience of a woman defined by property laws, and the curious ambiguity of existing simultaneously as both a thing and a person in a twilight zone of being.

Montoni offers to disregard Emily's first show of defiance as a concession to 'the weakness of your sex'. But he soon demonstrates his knowledge that her sexual handicap is his trump card; the 'weakness' of the female sex is nothing other than the ideology of femininity, the code of propriety that underwrites a 'lady'. He has only to threaten to withdraw his protection and Emily is forced to concede. 'A man ... secure in his own good conduct, depends only on himself, and may brave the public opinion; but a woman, in behaving well, performs but half her duty; as what is thought of her, is as important to her as what she really is ... Opinion is the grave of virtue in a man; but its throne among women': Wollstonecraft quotes Rousseau.[19] There is nothing new in Radcliffe's use of propriety as a principle of terror. The already well-established novelistic tradition of 'virtue in distress' revolves around this double standard, alternately condoning and deprecating, pointing on the one hand to the throne on which the heroine will be installed at the end of her trials, and on the other hand to the grave where one false step might, however undeservedly, lead her. What *is* different in Radcliffe is the quality and intensity of the terror, the explicit allusions to the supernatural which alter her heroines' experience of a familiar scenario, eliciting new patterns of sympathetic recognition from the reader and raising awkward questions. Does the merging of moral and superstitious anxieties in the mind of Emily mean that a gentlewoman's attachment to appearances is a metaphysical delusion? Is her imagination, by social necessity, given over to superstition in this additional sense?

In Richardsonian romance propriety had always existed as a ubiquitous invisible presence, an imperative and a threat. Radcliffe offered a heightened mode of presentation. In *Udolpho* Montoni can be read as propriety personified in its most fateful aspect. Although he does not directly represent the prospect of sexual and social ruin himself, he can forward it and attach to it, by his haunted presence, the added horror of inexplicable circumstances. The impact of this model can be traced even in novels not strictly classified as Gothic, in which the stock predatory libertine assumes an almost superhuman aura, defamiliarising the civilised surroundings of assembly rooms and parlours. In Regina Maria Roche's *The Children of the Abbey* the lecherous Colonel Belgrave – grave of the beautiful? – materialises out of nowhere whenever Amanda is most vulnerable to the misconstruction of bystanders, plotting to destroy her reputation. The cancelling of the heroine's good name is not here, as in *Clarissa*, a mere by-product of seduction, but the preliminary to it. At a dance at the Pantheon, a fashionable London venue, Amanda appropriately reacts to the sight of Belgrave 'as if an evil genius had suddenly darted in her path'.[20] Two decades earlier, in *Evelina* Frances Burney had dealt with her heroine's embarrassment at the Pantheon with a humour outweighing the anguish. With the advent of the 'Female Gothic' the potential for terror in social intercourse was emphasised at the expense of satire, and painful contradiction is magnified in the confrontation of the young unmarried heroine adrift in the marriage market (in whom the moral value of the narrative is invested) and the values of propriety with its potential for abuse (nevertheless endorsed as the only possible reality for women). It seems likely, also, that the challenge of feminism in the 1790s helped to heighten sensitivity to sexual oppression, while diminishing the margin of consensus on which satire depends. There is the sense of a severe disenchantment with contemporary mores in Roche's novel, when towards the end, in a nightmarish sequence, the guiltless Amanda is stripped of the vital tokens of respectability and suffers a lightning fall through the levels of the English class system until she lands half dead in the gutter.[21]

Emily survives by turning the tables and learning to treat *herself* as a commodity. Pursuing the principle of synecdoche, part for a whole, Emily's humanity and the sum total of her actions are absorbed by her 'virtue', the need to preserve it and, what is more difficult still, the need to maintain its 'appearance' while preserving it, in the cause of her own economic viability: her 'property' in her self. (Here 'virtue' assumes its alternative meaning as the efficacy of *things* – as *use-value*, that is superscribed as *exchange-value*.) This is the pragmatic import of her father's warning against over-indulgent sensibility. By self-appraisal, the recognition of her exchange-value on the marriage market, she must learn to subordinate her will to the maintenance of herself as object. Of what use is her inheritance if her body is devalued? Although she needs a dowry to gain a husband, and 'afford that competency, by which she hoped to secure the comfort of their future lives',[22] the loss of respectability would debar her forever from the happiness of secure social status. Hence the often ridiculed scene in which the heroine, fleeing for her life from the castle, is especially troubled by her lack of a hat. But Radcliffe's dramatic instinct is perfectly accurate; what good is a life without the magic totems that guarantee social identity? If Emily emerges unscathed and triumphant, her exertions have by the end of the narrative left her paler and more pensive as though, by her strict adherence to it, the ideology of femininity had drained her of lifeblood, vampire-like. She has finished her task as entrepreneur of herself. She is in direct line of succession to Pamela, another literary paragon who turns propriety to profit, in effect managing her virginity as if it were a business.

By the close of *Udolpho* Emily St Aubert has received not one but two inheritances in providential recognition of her virtue; but it is worth looking further into this conventional 'happy ending' to establish the legal technicalities of the arrangement as far as they are shown in the story. Both the legacies derive from female heiresses, Mme Montoni and Laurentini di Udolpho, while the orthodox mode for the transmission of property, in sixteenth-century France and Italy as in eighteenth-century England, was through the male line. Wealthy women are in fact something of a feature in Radcliffe; as Kate Ellis has noted, the bride brings the money to almost every marriage mentioned in *The Romance of the Forest*. Adeline, like Emily, is loaded with riches before uniting herself with a poor soldier.[23] It is only in the case of Mme Montoni, however, that the wife is seen to keep her estate, the lands in Languedoc, independently of her husband; but her insistence on her legal rights precipitates her own death, since Montoni can control her movement and even imprison her (legal rights of a husband in eighteenth-century law). In the earlier novel M. La Motte and the Marquis de Montalt have unimpeded access to their wives' property, perhaps moveable property rather than land, and fritter it away on gambling and high living before turning to crime. When Emily defends her rights of inheritance against Montoni she does so 'for Valancourt's sake', and under English common law the sentiment is, strictly speaking, correct. There is a period, after her escape, when it is revealed that Valancourt spent the period of her captivity gambling and womanising in Paris and history looks set to repeat itself. Valancourt may be metamorphosing into a second Montoni, and Emily struggles to suppress her affection for him until explanations are offered which mitigate his wrongdoings and vindicate his good character.

The marriage of hero and heroine is to be exemplary, a utopian *rapprochement* to dispel preceding horrors. But this can be done only by blurring the outlines of the marriage settlement: the dispensation of economic power in the relationship. Instead of an official settlement we are given lovers' vows, which go no further than a vague commitment to live together religiously and charitably. Uncertainty is kept up until the final page, where Emily is glimpsed competently buying the old estate of her father and arranging for its upkeep and stewardship, but at the same time meekly begging Valancourt to allow her to resign the Udolpho estate to a needy relation. Valancourt, we are told, 'when she made the request, felt all the value of the compliment it conveyed'.[24] The import of the compliment, though it may have been clear to the contemporary reader, is cloudy today. Does it simply refer in some way to the matter of Valancourt's previous aid to the beneficiary, a M. Bonnac, and thereby acknowledge his sensibility? Or could it be the sign of a new matrimonial order in which patriarchal right, though supported by law, will always be managed with consummate chivalry?

In his celebrated *Commentaries on the Laws of England*, William Blackstone compared the law to 'an old Gothic castle, erected in the days of chivalry, but fitted up for a modern inhabitant'.[25] He was referring in particular to the old system of property laws developed under feudalism which was then in the process of being comfortably altered to suit the requirements of the now predominant 'commercial mode of property', above all 'to facilitate exchange and alienation'.[26] Blackstone reassured his readers that modernisation could be achieved by a 'series of minute contrivances', rather than a full-scale 'new-modelling' which might endanger the social infrastructure. The *Commentaries* as a whole, four volumes in folio, was the incarnation of legal rationalisation. It presented the system of law as a beautifully functional unity in which, as in the renovated Gothic castle, reason is integrated with organic tradition. Fixed and immutable principles are extracted from the haphazard accretions of time; a work of codification then attributed to a providential, natural order, beyond the reach of human criticism.[27] Enlightenment and theodicy combine to constitute the law as a closed economy, self-sufficient, impartial, abstracted from social relations. At the very moment that it was so assiduously lending its services to the establishment of capitalist hegemony, the law, as a discursive practice and increasingly as an institution, attained 'a "phantom-objectivity", an autonomy that seems so strictly rational and all-embracing as to conceal every trace of its fundamental nature: the relation between people'.[28]

All the same Blackstone was forced to confess that the law involved a number of 'fictions and circuities', which might 'shock the student'. He returns to this theme in a digression concerning laws dependent on the 'wisdom and will of the legislators': 'Thus our own common law has declared, that the goods of the wife do instantly upon marriage become the property and right of the husband; and our statute law has declared all monopolies a public offence: yet that right, and this offence, have no foundation in nature; but are merely created by the law, for the purposes of civil society.'[29] Medieval guild monopolies detrimental to free trade could be arbitrarily outlawed, while an ancient relic, coverture, was just as arbitrarily retained and adapted to the new economic structure.[30] But what shocks is not so much the news that the disentitlement of married women is *sui generis* rather than ordained by nature, as the pleasant fiction that 'the female sex' is a 'favourite . . . of the laws of England'[31] which Blackstone maintains in the face of his own bleak definition of the principle of coverture: 'By marriage, the husband and wife are one person in law; that is, the very being or legal existence of the woman is suspended during the marriage, or at least is incorporated and consolidated into that of the husband: under whose wing, protection, and *cover*, she performs every thing.'[32] Among the real consequences: the husband took control of the whole of his wife's property, past, present and future; he had sole rights over their children; a married woman could not enter into any legal agreement or lawsuit on her own behalf; she could not bring proceedings against her husband in common law; and since her 'very being' as a legal subject was suspended she no longer held property in her own person – Locke's minimum condition for civil rights. Ultimate justification for the doctrine could be sought in the New Testament text that husband and wife 'shall be one flesh'; so in law they became one, and the husband was that one. Consequently marriage meant in common law what has been called 'a kind of civil death' for women.[33]

But from the seventeenth century the law of equity was increasingly used to 'supply the defects and correct the injustices of common law' on the basis of an appeal to 'natural justice' rather than custom. It allowed flexibility in dealing with the mobile property which was assuming an ever-greater importance in a commercial economy; but it also enabled married women to hold separate property by means of formal transactions such as marriage settlements and wills. In historical terms this was a regressive attempt to prevent alienation of property from the blood kinship group by ensuring that it would pass through the daughter to her children, rather than being handed over to the son-in-law.[34] But it created the possibility that a woman might maintain her independence against the will of her husband.[35] Ann Radcliffe, by regularly endowing her female characters with inherited fortunes, foregrounds the ideological inconsistencies of the property laws relating to women of her time. In *Udolpho* Montoni forwards his claims under English common law to the estates of his wife: on marriage he has acquired a freehold interest, for life. After Mme Montoni dies without submitting to these claims, when Emily informs Montoni that she is 'not so ignorant ... of the laws on this subject, as to be misled by the assertion of any person', she refers to the 'natural justice' of equity which enabled her aunt to settle her estate on her next of kin without her husband's consent. The two different realities conflicting here are on a technical level these two perspectives in law.

The central Gothic indeterminacy illusion/reality enables legal metaphor to be represented as a lived experience. The 'civil death' required by common law is actualised in Mme Montoni's death. Elsewhere, married women reduced to 'ghosts' or the 'living dead' by law exist as supposed ghosts, notably in the story of Emily's other aunt, the Countess de Villefort, who died of poison administered by her adulterous husband and is rumoured to haunt Château-de-Blanc. In *A Sicilian Romance* the Marchioness of Mazzini is imprisoned, rumoured dead, for fifteen years in the south wing of the castle by order of her dissipated husband. When her daughters Julia and Emilia ask their governess whether a spirit could really be responsible for the mysterious noises and flashing lights, she responds 'such beings *may* exist'; certainly they may, for as the marchioness explains after her release, 'the marquis, you know, has not only power to imprison, but also the right of life and death in his own domain'.[36] The law itself engenders the supernatural; women are the ghosts in its machine.

Radcliffe employs the libertarian language of natural justice against the oppressive usages of custom, not because she was a radical, but because this was the shape that terror took for the projected reader, middle class and female: the point at which fantasy and reality met and mingled. Her writings, at least at the height of suspense, encourage reflection on the illusory nature of the law's 'phantom-objectivity', its interested, man-made nature, through a literal-minded representation of the law as haunted house. The metaphysical paraphernalia of an 'objectivist' system of justice is portrayed with objectivity in the terrifying phantasmagoria of Gothic fiction. 'Justice' is estranged from itself, retranslated into an unequal, repressive relation between people. Before the narrative reverts to a tidy dénouement there is a moment of illumination in which the unthinkable is felt to be real.

It is this moment that Wollstonecraft deliberately attempted to extend and activate as a means of political understanding. When the heroine of *The Wrongs of Woman* declares 'Marriage has bastilled me for life', the metaphor does not remain a figure of speech but is objectively realised in the plot.[37] Like the castle of Udolpho, the private lunatic asylum to which Maria is consigned by her husband is a Gothic ruin (why ruined? symbolic of the decadence of the legal powers they represent?). The next step from the charge of superstition levelled at Radcliffe's Emily is the charge of madness that is used to deprive Wollstonecraft's Maria of her freedom. She was 'imagining things' when she understood that her husband was planning to prostitute her to one of his creditors. There are obvious difficulties in converting 'Gothic' feminist critique into effective action, when it can be articulated only as a suspicion, an intimation, or, in classic Gothic mode, by the act of fainting, and when the enemy is reason itself. At the legal trial that belongs to the same tradition as Emily's confrontation with Montoni, Maria does not deny that she has taken a lover, and asks for a divorce and 'the liberty of enjoying, free from molestation, the fortune left to me by a relation'; after her husband's plot against her honour, she continues, she felt herself released from her marital bonds. The judge, in summing up,

alluded to 'the fallacy of letting women plead their feelings, as an excuse for the violation of the marriage-vow ... What virtuous woman thought of her feelings? – It was her duty to love and obey the man chosen by her parents and relations, who were qualified by their experience to judge better for her, than she could for herself. As to the charges brought against the husband, they were vague, supported by no witnesses, excepting that of imprisonment in a private mad-house. The proofs of an insanity in the family, might render that however a prudent measure; and indeed the conduct of the lady did not appear that of a person of sane mind.'[38]

Able only to argue her feelings, Maria is threatened with incarceration a second time. The 'potential' madwoman figured here, whose erratic conduct will be satisfactorily explained by the discovery of a hereditary taint, is the predecessor of the villainess of Victorian sensation fiction, for whom, D. A. Miller has observed, 'the very category of Madness' lies 'like a fate ... ever in wait to "cover" – account for and occlude – whatever behaviors, desires, or tendencies might be considered socially deviant, undesirable, or dangerous.'[39] Wollstonecraft's grimly humorous reflection on the social expediency of diagnosed insanity is a development of Radcliffe's earlier, more understated, yet equally ironic use of those charges of 'heroinism' (romantic distortion) and superstition (a typically feminine 'weakness of mind') placed in the mouth of her villain. The difference is that while Radcliffe was free to vindicate the feelings of her heroine in the providential happy ending, Wollstonecraft struggled to balance realism and hope and finally left the outcome of her narrative undecided.

ANACHRONISM AS SUBVERSION

Udolpho displayed in the form of romance the real contradictions and dangers which every gentlewoman of the period potentially faced. Above all it dramatised the fears of the women of the middle classes, whose social standing was most unstable, liable to upward and downward variation, and who were therefore necessarily the group most attentive to the taboos surrounding femininity. Wollstonecraft recognised the critical potential in the Radcliffean romance when she adopted its 'system of terror' for her political fiction *The Wrongs of Woman*, where she made explicit what was already immanent in the form. It was not coincidental that *Vindication of the Rights of Woman* had been addressed to middle-class women, the implied readers of Gothic romance. What Wollstonecraft calls the 'natural state' of middle-class women, their ability to experience in a conscious way the various demands made on the sex as contradictory, that which in addition allowed them to identify with the sufferings of the Gothic heroine, might also make them the bearers of critique. To realise contradiction as critique would be for the reader to become the heroine of her own life and apply to her own circumstances the lesson of how to 'suffer like a heroine'. The writers of the satires and condemnations of novel-reading women who confused fact and fiction inadvertently helped to create this opening for subversive reflection by the very strength of their protests. The novel form's power to disrupt orthodoxies was maintained by the critical opposition to it.

In the 1790s the idea seems to emerge, particularly among women authors, that romance, by its very inclusion of the marvellous or the apparently marvellous, can reveal the unpleasant truth about real life in a way impossible in the referential narratives of historians or realist novelists. Those twentieth-century commentators who have insisted that Gothic novels are escapist fictions set in the distant past ignore their steady progress to a present-day setting. *The Old English Baron* (1778) is set in the fifteenth century. Sophia Lee's *The Recess* (1785) sent ripples of unease through the community of critics by its mingling of Tudor history with the rhetorical distortions of romance: the period was considered too close for comfort.[40] Charlotte Smith pointedly titled her translations from a seventeenth-century French anthology of famous court cases *The Romance of Real Life* (1788). The book was offered both as a representation of 'the force and danger of the human passions' and as a compendium of 'authenticated fact', however improbable: both an amusement and a historical document.[41] A reviewer of Eliza Parson's *Castle of Wolfenbach* (1793) expressed his surprise at finding, in place of the expected 'tale of other times', 'a company of well-educated and well-bred people of fashion'.[42] Radcliffe's novels move nearer and nearer in time, from the sixteenth to the seventeenth to the eighteenth century. As for exotic locations, although Radcliffe may have favoured southern Europe, her followers generally set their novels in Britain – and it is in any case well known that anachronism regularly reduces the distance between the foreign scenes she herself never visited and Georgian England.

Fantasy came nowhere nearer to real life than in Charlotte Smith's passionately autobiographical introduction to *Marchmont* (1796), in which she justifies the *'egotism of which I have been accused'* and the mingling of 'fictitious sorrows' with her own. The identities of fictional heroine and female author are merged by her free admission of their shared experiences and sufferings, and she insists that the most fantastic character in the present work is the one most closely drawn from life – a loathsome attorney unequivocally dubbed 'Vampyre', a 'destructive monster, armed with the power of doing mischief and of robbing legally'.[43] But if supernatural fiction offered her the language in which to express her anger, it was equally the means by which her case could be tried and dismissed for lack of substantive evidence. It was only appropriate, after all, that Ann Radcliffe, the writer who had most vividly communicated the transient terrors of the 'explained supernatural', should be sent to end her life in a madhouse by the daydreams of the British reading public.[44]

IV

Magico-political tales

CHAPTER 9

The terrorist system

In the novels of Radcliffe and others of her school, supernatural suggestions are typically formed in the heroine's imagination like an imprint of the arbitrary excesses of patriarchy. They bring into effect a passing denaturalisation of 'natural' authority. But there are other moments when, instead of *manifesting* authority, invisible forces, concealed from the gaze of the tyrant, seem capable of eluding and thwarting him, forming a kind of alliance with the embattled heroine. In *The Mysteries of Udolpho* the dictates of Montoni are exposed to doubt and ridicule by a ghostly echoing voice.[1] Radcliffe reused the device for the Inquisition scenes of *The Italian*, in which an unknown and unseen interrogator interrupts the trial of the hero, and undermines the protocol of the court: ' "Who is come amongst us?" said the vicar general, in the voice of a person, who means to inspire in others the awe he himself suffers.'[2]

Invisibility and abstraction are natural weapons of resistance against the arbitrary power of state or sovereign. Thus, Montesquieu explains that bills of exchange, the first paper money, were the invention of the Jews, who were in constant danger of having their wealth confiscated by the ruling power.[3] In the course of time this ghost money served to transgress national boundaries, shifting the balance of economic power from royal house and the aristocratic caste, with their immobile landed inheritances, to the cosmopolitan trading classes. But, once dominant, the capitalist economy develops in turn its own bugbears: poachers, pirates, highwaymen, smugglers, invisible and unacknowledged agents of the growth and spread of luxury. In Gothic fictions, smugglers and bandits opportunistically inhabit spaces haunted by the rumoured crimes of patriarchy: the deserted wing of the castle, the ancestral crypt. Like spectres they are of necessity creatures of the night and they exploit this kinship by using popular superstition as a cover for their illegitimate activities.

On this basis, and with an eye to allegory, Charlotte Smith draws implicit comparisons between the various secret economies that subvert the personal empire of Mrs Rayland in *The Old Manor House*. 'In a great house there are among the servants as many cabals and as many schemes, as among the leaders of a great nation':[4] the naturally refined, though lowborn, Monimia is kept in thrall to her aunt, Mrs Rayland's corrupt housekeeper, through ignorance and superstitious fear, until her wellborn admirer Orlando contrives secret meetings in the library of the house and teaches her the beauty of reason; meanwhile the outwardly respectable butler and coachman are in league with a band of smugglers, whose activities in the cellar are concealed by the spreading of tales about Rayland phantoms. In the dead of night the two illicit economies, popular crime and cross-class enlightened love, literally collide and Orlando makes a pact with the picturesque villain Jonas Wilkins, listening sympathetically and with some fellow-feeling to accounts of his exploits on the wrong side of the law.[5] Unsurprisingly Smith was among the women novelists pilloried by Thomas Mathias for being 'now and then tainted with democracy', in the context of his dismissal of romances in general, and Gothic romances in particular.[6]

The link has often been made between the popular ghost fictions of the 1790s and the French Revolution, both by contemporaries and by twentieth-century critics; the coincidence of the outbreak of the Terror and the explosion of demand for terror fiction is too striking to ignore. I will be discussing the convergence of fictional and political narratives in chapter 10, but I want first to concentrate on the place of fictions of the supernatural in the less frequently considered 'reading revolution'. As we will see, the creeping democratisation of the republic of letters represented by the success of the popular novel was not unrelated to the threat of political democracy in the eyes of British anti-Jacobins. The extension of literacy and the commodification of literature, processes that had begun over a century before, somehow seemed to come to a head in the feverish 1790s, and find expression in the Gothic publishing phenomenon. If British anxieties regarding the subversion of state and status quo seem to cohere in contemporary fictions of mysterious and occult conspiracy, they were also stimulated at the time by the implications of the fashion for artificial fear itself: it was the unmistakable victory of popular demand and market forces over the legislation of writing from above.

Up to this point the progress of spectral representations had been slow and uncertain. I have outlined in the previous chapters the various blocks, both ideological and technical, which prevented the free commercial exploitation of improbable and sensational devices in fiction. How was it, then, that the fictional supernatural was at this moment able to break through or bypass long-standing resistances, and not only enter the commercial mainstream, but give rise to the most prodigious literary fashion that had yet been seen? No doubt the gradual turn towards an aesthetic justification of literary ghosts as a source of sublime experience, already discussed in connection with the 'explained supernatural', can provide part of the answer. But changes in methods of production and distribution were also crucial at this stage, and it is these I will emphasise, since they help us to share the picture of contemporaries of a phenomenon generated from below. These changes encouraged the growth of a demand-led industry which could afford to ignore attempts at moral regulation by the literary establishment. The 1790s represented a dramatic turnaround for novels in general, but above all for those novels which most flagrantly broke critical tenets – the improbable, the marvellous, the luridly sexual – and the prime mover was William Lane of the Minerva Press, on a par with Josiah Wedgwood as a pioneering entrepreneur, whose career can serve as introduction and evidence for an episode in publishing history which has been too little explored.

Lane, the son of a City poulterer, set up shop at No. 33 Leadenhall Street in 1775, and by 1784 had his own printing business.[7] A few years later he became co-proprietor of the *Star and Evening Advertiser*, the first London evening daily and one of the first predominantly trade newspapers; the owners used the *Star* to sell not only their own products, but offered a professional 'copy service' to other businesses. Lane's printing department was 'relaunched' in 1790 under the name of the Minerva Press. Advertisements were placed announcing to the public that business had 'commenced under general patronage', and that Minerva was 'now unrivalled in the public estimation, for Novels, Tales, Romances, Adventures'.

Manuscripts were invited from 'Ladies and Gentlemen' with the promise of excellent printing and perfect respectability; £500 had been placed with an eminent banker 'for the sole purpose of purchasing literary productions'. There was also an offer, for those wishing to engage in 'an employ both respectable and lucrative', of an instant library stocked from the Minerva warehouse containing anything from 100 to 5,000 volumes. This could be had at a few days' notice along with a catalogue for the subscribers and full instructions on 'how to plan, systemize, and conduct' a library.[8]

Lane revolutionised the techniques for retailing popular novels above all by building his own network of circulating libraries throughout the country specifically as outlets for the products of the Minerva Press. Where previously there had been libraries only in London and the principal spa and seaside resorts, now they sprang up in every provincial town as Lane 'persuaded shopkeepers of all kinds ... to give over a few of their shelves to the formation of a lending library; not only booksellers and bookbinders, but engravers and picture-framers, grocers, jewellers, confectioners, tobacconists, perfumers, ironmongers, all manner of shopkeepers might also become librarians'.[9] At the same time demand was stimulated by forms of publicity that bypassed the need for a mention in the review journals. Prospectuses of new publications were regularly issued, sometimes through the daily papers. In the *Morning Chronicle*, for instance, on 8 and 10 January 1793, fifty-one Minerva titles were announced. Another method was to advertise forthcoming or recently published books on the blank leaves at the end of novels in eye-catching layouts that resembled title pages, sometimes including, towards the end of the decade, enthusiastic extracts from reviews: another innovation. Occasional 'puffs' for Minerva books or Minerva libraries appeared in the very texts of the novels. Engraved frontispieces depicting the melodramatic climax of the story were designed to lure the browsing customer into buying or borrowing, at a time when illustrations were still rare in English fiction.

But perhaps the most canny and innovative selling point was the name 'Minerva Press' itself. This has been treated as a matter of course by literary historians, but it is difficult to find another instance in the eighteenth-century British book trade, perhaps in British trade in general, of a founder-owner choosing an 'image' for his business, in effect creating what we would call today a 'corporate identity'. The choice of the Goddess of Wisdom as emblem was clearly a good public relations gambit for a publisher with pretensions, as well as being a gracious compliment to the sex who would be expected to provide the most custom. A figure of the goddess in plumed helmet and grecian drapery leaning on a spear was placed in a niche over the door of the shop, and an engraved logo of the seated Minerva was stamped on customers' bills and the labels of library books. Lane's marketing policies tended to enhance the sense of a unified corporate style. Here, anonymous publication or pseudonyms were the rule, so that, like 'Mills and Boon', the name 'Minerva Press' guaranteed a dependable commodity to the regular consumer, regardless of individual authorship.[10] But in a few cases top-selling authors were publicised by name as part of a Minerva stable of writers, closer to the practice of modern fiction publishing companies at the middle or upper range of the market. A 1798 prospectus listed the works of ten 'particular and favourite Authors', all of them women, and including the Gothic specialists Regina Maria Roche, Eliza Parsons, Mary Meeke (who also published under the pseudonym Gabrielli), Isabella Kelly, Elizabeth Bonhote and Anna Maria McKenzie.

The birth of Minerva was instrumental in the decisive shift towards *popular* fiction in its modern form, aimed at a broad readership, commercially steamlined, with the profit motive uppermost. Lane, with full control over both production and retailing, could afford to ignore the dictums of official culture. Although in fact most of the novels he published were perfectly conventional sentimental or Gothic tales that paid the usual lip-service to Christian morals, the publication of a book like *Horrid Mysteries* – combining gruesome metaphysics with flamboyant eroticism – shows that they were not *necessarily* shaped by tactics of conciliation or evasion as the works of Walpole, Reeve or Radcliffe had been. Minerva forms the vital background for the appearance of the works of extreme sensationalism I will discuss in this chapter. Its example as a highly successful, independent, demand-led publishing house 'under general patronage' was undoubtably an inspiration to others, and the nationwide network of libraries must quickly have been exploited or rivalled by other booksellers. For the following generation of Romantic writers and critics Minerva's representative status made its name synonymous with 'trash'. Dorothy Blakey's brief summary of condemnations reads like a roll-call of nineteenth-century men of letters:

Carlyle, Charles Reade, Coleridge, Hazlitt, Scott, Charles Lamb and Thomas Love Peacock.[11] It is notable that the summary dispatch of Minerva as mere 'bad' writing, entertainment designed specifically for the undiscriminating masses, does not take place until after 1800, replacing earlier concern over the possibly corrupting influence of this type of fiction on the reading public at large. We should not assume that the broad mass of novel production in the 1790s was from the start in place, clearly grouped as what the Germans with precision call *Trivialliteratur*. Rather, we can see how the 'two nations' structure of cultural theory originates in response to the threatened departure of literary production from the model of social hierarchy.

The sense of market imperatives infiltrating and corrupting the republic of letters which had arisen in the 1720s returned with redoubled force in the last years of the century. At least Pope had had the reassurance of being able to *name* and *characterise* the parasitical hacks. The Grub Street of *The Dunciad* is still a village where there are no secrets. Now the trade seemed to resemble a chaos of shifting identities, mysterious reduplications or multiple repetitions, inscrutable acts of professional legerdemain. The vogue for supernatural fictions, simply because it was so plainly a response to an overwhelming demand, became a symbol for the general and ongoing commodification of literature. This unprecedented capacity of the market to absorb at great speed large amounts of a particular type of literary product, the 'terrorist' novel, shook old certainties. We could aptly say that the Gothic figures, after Burke's definition, a sublime of publishing whereby the reading public became something obscure and incalculable, its dimensions uncertain. With the tentacles of the bookselling industry now reaching into the previously untouched fastnesses of the provinces, the market for novels was made strange. Was there any limit to its appetite? How could the wishes of this prodigy be anticipated?

Although this coincidence of Gothic and the commercialisation of the book trade may have been a contingency, a mere accident of history – the free market economy might, after all, just as well have battened onto a craze for novels about hot-air balloons[12] or voyages to Australia – there *was* a more determinate link between the specific form of terror fiction and the experience of an expanded book market. This type of fiction, because of its connection with the discourse of the sublime and the concept of 'original genius', highlighted a new ambivalence in the category of the author. The theory of the sublime had it that nowhere was the quasi-divine power of imaginative creation more clearly seen than in writing which provokes pity and terror. But what happens to this model of authorial agency when terror becomes a banal assembly-line commodity? How can the claim to inspired origination, to *originality*, be sustained under pressure of repetition? What becomes of 'genius' and its uniqueness when the writer submits so readily to appeals for an encore within the corporate sales strategies of a Minerva Press? It could be objected that an evaluative distinction was made between poetry and prose fiction, but this is not apparent in Nathan Drake's emphatic restatement of the aesthetic of the sublime in connection with contemporary literature, *Literary Hours* (1798).[13] There is, then, a *frisson* of transgression when in the preface to *Midnight Weddings* Mary Meeke recommends aspiring novelists 'before planning a work, to consult their publisher as to how they may best satisfy the prevailing public taste'.[14]

The categories of 'high' and 'popular' culture, as I have suggested, were not yet available to defuse the contradiction; rather, it was out of this contradiction – not of course exclusive to Gothic but especially salient there – that the need for a categorial opposition was registered and eventually articulated. In the meantime a genre of fiction that appropriated to itself by regular citation the archetypes of sublime authorship, Shakespeare and Milton, was subjected, under commercial constraints, to tricks of the trade tending to occlude authorship. When demand threatened to outstrip supply old novels could be 'turned and retrimmed' to make new, with the additional advantage to the bookseller of a saving on copyright fees. Remainder sheets could be reissued under a new and more sensational title. Extracts from successful works could be recirculated in compilations: one of the 'pilfering practices' that Clara Reeve objected to because it undermined the economic and social position of authors.

The thematics of conspiracy which range between political and literary discourses in these years did not belong to official discourse alone; to an extraordinary degree suggestions of subversion, disguise, manipulation, criminality are the phenomenal attributes of a material practice: the specific mode of production of terror fiction. Just as the concrete economy of the circulating library had from the beginning summoned up images of sexual circulation, promiscuity, prostitution, as it were by a negative reflex action, so the industry in Gothic fictions of the latter part of the 1790s was bound to tropes of threat and paranoia, of the undermining or masking of identities, to the extent that the characteristic contents of the fictions appear as a natural extension of the framing melodrama of selling and buying. What follows is an outline phenomenology of ghost fictions as commodities.

Translation

To begin with, there was the sudden release into British circulation of translations from the German, which irresistibly connected a new phase of terror fiction with ideas of foreignness and invasion. The translation of French novels into English had long been the main-stay of hack writers and booksellers at times when the demand for sentiment threatened to outstrip native supply. The 1790s saw the belated discovery of a whole new field to exploit, the productions of the *Sturm und Drang* movement and the sensationalist *Schaurromane* – 'horror novels' – that came in their wake. For a readership accus-tomed to the school of Radcliffe the first encounter with this alien literature was eye-opening and disconcerting. Coleridge, while a student at Cambridge, recorded in a letter his emotions on reading the 'Storm and Stress' drama *The Robbers*, written in 1781 but only translated into English in 1792.

My God! Southey! Who is this Schiller? This Convulser of the Heart? Did he write his Tragedy amid the yelling of Fiends? – I should not like to [be] able to describe such Characters – I tremble like an Aspen Leaf – Upon my Soul, I write to you because I am frightened ... Why have we ever called Milton sublime?[15]

Here was a previously unknown source of a brand of aesthetic experience that surpassed in its violence even Milton, the national touchstone of sublimity. A generation of young writers, Coleridge, Wordsworth, Southey, Scott, De Quincey, applied themselves to the study of German in the hope that it would unlock the secret of genius, and made pilgrimages to the new literary Mecca on the Continent.[16]

The Robbers, as Coleridge observed in the notes to his ode addressed to the author of the play, 'introduces no supernatural beings', though the 'human beings agitate and astonish more than all the *goblin* rout – even of Shakespeare'.[17] *The Ghost-Seer*, by the same author, was first published in 1789 and part of it translated into English in 1795, when it instantly established a new Gothic narrative-type; if the Radcliffean narrative can be termed 'feminocentric supernaturalism', the narrative on the *Ghost-Seer* model instantiates a 'paranoiac supernaturalism', featuring a 'male chase' in which hunter and hunted systematically exchange roles.[18] Here, the simulation of the marvellous disguises and prepares for the revelation of a nightmare-like reality, a waking nightmare beyond a nightmare. The substance of everyday existence is honeycombed by invisible conspiracies, nothing can be taken for granted; friends, lovers, relations may be hired assassins; the outwardly normal order of things may be only a *mise-en-scène* contrived by unknown and malevolent puppet-masters.

Following Schiller came a string of translations authored by minor German writers,[19] and very quickly, of works by British writers modelled on or masquerading as German translations.[20] The impression of German ascendency in the writing of the supernatural was confirmed in 1796 by the publication of no less than five different translations of Gottfried August Bürger's ballad 'Lenore'.[21] The folklore tradition of the spectre-bridegroom that Bürger drew on would have been familiar to any English reader of Percy's *Reliques*,[22] but the driving, galloping rhythm of the stanza form, simulating the horseback ride of Lenore and her phantom lover, was experienced as something entirely new and astounding, fresh evidence of the unprecedented power of German writers employing the supernatural to play on the feelings of their audience. Form and narrative together build to a climactic marriage ceremony by the graveside, juxtaposing sex and death in a manner entirely unlike the decorous minuet of English sentimental Gothic, in which the love-plot politely gives way to the ghost-plot, and vice versa.

The response of the British reviewers was divided: on the one hand, they could complacently define extreme literary sensationalism, along with the Continental political disturbances evidently connected with them, as an inherently alien phenomenon, so that to an extent the uneasy speculation concerning the source and tendency of the Gothic mode was relaxed and detached assessment made possible; on the other hand, as the influx of foreign fictions grew and was joined by rumours of German-based conspiracies intent on world revolution, British wartime xenophobia spread to

the sphere of literature and gave rise to outright moral condemnation of imported products.[23] Matthew Lewis's education in
Germany and the obvious signs of German influence in *The Monk*
(1796) and his later writings offered evidence, if evidence were
needed, of the capacity of foreign ideas to pervert British minds and
morals.[24]

Imitation, plagiarism and misattribution

Translation was one short cut to boosting supply, recycling was
another. Reviews remarked the regular appearance of 'humble'
imitations of Radcliffe,[25] and of others in the Schiller mould. Writers
and booksellers were attempting to balance profitably the need for
both novelty and sameness with no comparable experience in the
past to guide them; the rage for Gothic could vanish as suddenly as it
had appeared, its origins were inscrutable and the only safe course
was to mine a proven formula, with minimal variations, until it was
exhausted.

The perceived tension between originality and imitation in commercialised Gothic fiction was another aspect of the contradiction,
already referred to, in the status of the Gothic novelist: creative
artist or pre-programmed automaton? 'Monk' Lewis was and has
remained the controversial exemplar of this contradiction, a role he
seemed almost to invite by his confession of a few *recherché* borrowings in the 'Advertisement' to *The Monk*.[26] The literati were provoked into a guessing-game of sources and influences and the
Monthly Review responded with enthusiasm:

This novel has a double plot. The outline of the monk Ambrosio's story was
suggested by that of the *Santon Barsisa*, in the Guardian: the form of
temptation is borrowed from the *Devil in Love* of Cazotte; and the catas-
trophe is taken from *The Sorcerer*. The adventures of Raymond and Agnes
are less obviously imitations; yet the forest-scene near Strasburgh brings to
mind an incident in Smollett's *Ferdinand Count Fathom*; the bleeding Nun is
described by the author as a popular tale of the Germans; and the convent
prison resembles the inflictions of Mrs Radcliffe.[27]

The hothouse productivity of the 1790s meant that the initial
reading of a Gothic novel was not unlikely to be the equivalent of
rereading half a dozen others. The repeated transmigration of a
limited number of conventions blurred the frontiers dividing one
text from another, revealed each text to be a fabric of other texts and

conflicted with the developing Romantic ideology of the organic work of art with impermeable limits.[28] But nevertheless the *Monthly Review* critic, perhaps to our surprise, declines to condemn Lewis for plagiarism (although he recognises condemnation as an option). Instead he produces an alternative to the sublime idea of artistic invention by reference to the neo-classical conception of ideal form, with its source in the legend of the Greek painter Zeuxis who composed a picture of Helen by copying the most flawless features of numerous women. Rather improbably this precedent is made a basis for praise of Lewis's gruesome creation, since the 'great art of writing consists in selecting what is most stimulant from the works of our predecessors, and in uniting the gathered beauties in a new whole, more interesting than the tributary models'.[29] But if the mirage is raised here of a criterion of aesthetic value that would have avoided the kneejerk dismissal of imitation, and thus the long critical neglect of the Gothic genre, it evaporates when, in a final reversal, the book is declared 'totally unfit for general circulation' – aesthetic judgement is overruled in the high court of morality.

The fact that Lewis in the end felt it necessary to 'clear his name' of charges of plagiarism (though not of immorality) is one more indication of the instability of the concept of authorship at this conjuncture; although his career was spent in a welter of translation, anthologising, parody and pastiche, he could not withstand the pressure to conform to increasingly hegemonic Romantic definitions of what was valid and valuable in literary production.[30] The Gothic phenomenon registers the imminent inauguration of author and work as 'a solid and fundamental unit',[31] a ground for knowledge and judgement, yet persistently violates this doxa-in-the-making with its high rate of anonymity, eye-catching pseudonyms and, from time to time, deliberate shuffling of proper names in the interests of publicity and improved sales.[32]

Pirating and chapbooks

The continuing disparity between the average worker's income and the price of books or even most library subscriptions meant the fashion for Gothic in the 1790s, though vast in eighteenth-century terms, was a limited affair by the standards of modern mass culture. The avoidance of copyright fee or full payment to authors by the various methods already mentioned could usually be expected to result in increased profit margins for the bookseller rather than lower prices. But Dublin, which lay outside the jurisdiction of copyright law, Scotland, and Newcastle, remained prolific sources of cheap editions of popular works,[33] and novels were routinely appropriated and serialised by literary periodicals which reached very large audiences.[34] In the last years of the decade a new cut-price form of fiction emerged in the shape of the old chapbooks, now known as 'bluebooks' on account of their generic blue paper covers. These were stitched pamphlets in the single size of 4 by 7 inches and generally found in two lengths of either thirty-six or seventy-two pages, to purchase at sixpence or a shilling respectively, or on loan from the smaller libraries for a penny or two at a time.[35] Anonymous hacks laboured to reduce multi-volume bestsellers, especially the 'shockers', to the length of a chapter or two. *The Italian* became *The Midnight Assassin: or, Confessions of the Monk Rinaldi* (1802) and *The Monk* became *Almagro and Claude; or Monastic Murder; Exemplified by the Dreadful Doom of an Unfortunate Nun* (1803).[36] The difficulties involved in condensing complex storylines are apparent in both these works: *Midnight Assassin* has the heroine discovered in an abrupt and unexplained swoon as a result of reckless cutting; the adapter of *The Monk* attempts only one half of the novel's double plot until, finding her or himself with four blank pages at the end, the second half is crammed in for good measure. But in spite of technical hitches the best chapbooks were successful enough to be pirated themselves. The chapbook format, which had earlier implemented the primitive commercialisation of traditional 'true stories' of the marvellous, now came full circle and brought commercially produced ghost stories from the town to the isolated country villages where the oral traditions of the supernatural had been strongest.

Dramatic adaptations, ballad spinoffs and phantasmagoria (magic lantern)

Apart from the chapbooks, stage versions of novels and the distribution of poems from the novels as broadside ballads were the means by which literary fashion could embrace a popular and even illiterate audience. James Boaden adapted several of the most famous Gothic novels for the theatre: Ann Radcliffe's *Romance of the Forest* as *Fountainville Forest* in 1794; *Herman of Unna* as *The Secret Tribunal* in 1795; *The Italian* as *The Italian Monk* in 1797; and *The*

Monk as *Aurelio and Miranda*, which played at Drury Lane from 29 December 1798, and in which Kemble and Sarah Siddons appeared in the leading roles. However, in the process the stories and characterisation were generally changed past recognition: the *Italian Monk* 'deviated from the romance, in reclaiming the character of Schedoni, and restoring him to domestic happiness: the scene of that monk's death, in the original, if successfully copied, might be too tragical for the stage'; in *Aurelio and Miranda* the she-devil Matilda becomes the virtuous Miranda and ends by marrying her monk – the show lasted six performances.[37] This convention of bowdlerisation implies a double standard of reception, depending on whether consumption takes place in public or in private and, by extension, we can suppose, on whether the class composition of the audience is more or less mixed. Qualms over the representation of heroic villains, which risked dividing sympathies, or the inclusion of supernatural elements, which were toned down or eliminated entirely, seem to have lasted longer in the theatrical context. When *The Castle Spectre*, a Gothic drama by 'Monk' Lewis, was presented at Drury Lane in 1797 it was regarded as a daring initiative; the first attempt to transfer to the stage the supernatural effects of modern romances.[38] But the grudging praise it won was not enough to save Harriet Lee's play of the following year, *The Mysterious Marriage or the Hermitage of Roselva*, from a critical roasting of the most reactionary kind: 'supernatural agency is the taste of a barbarous age, and ought to be banished from our theatres at once ... let ghosts and hobgoblins people the pages of a romance, but never let their forms be seen to glide across the stage'.[39]

The poetry from *The Monk* achieved independent fame, particularly the Bürgeresque ballad 'Alonzo the Brave and the Fair Imogine', like 'Lenore' a story of a mortal bride claimed by a spectre-bridegroom, and boasting an irresistible bouncing rhythm and imagery of unrivalled morbidity;

> The worms, They crept in, and the worms, They crept out,
> And sported his eyes and his temples about.

The poem was adapted within months as a 'Heroic Pantomime Ballet' which appears to have played at the Sadler's Wells Theatre for over a year. It also gave rise to numerous imitations and burlesques, the best of the latter being Lewis's own 'Giles Jollup the Grave and Brown Sally Green', which he included in the fourth edition of the novel.[40]

Yet another point of intersection between literary culture and popular entertainment was the phantasmagoria or magic lantern, which, however, only arrived in Britain from France in 1801.[41] The inventor Etienne-Gaspard Robertson had captivated French audiences with 'Gothic extravaganzas' involving the mechanical projection of a repertoire of images, including Henry Fuseli's *The Nightmare*, 'The Bleeding Nun' of *Monk* fame and a host of other celebrated phantoms out of Shakespeare, the Bible and classical mythology, along with eerie sound and lighting effects. But during the 1790s the British public only knew of the invention at second-hand, through descriptions like that in *The Ghost-Seer*.[42] Mary Wollstonecraft, who may have witnessed a performance during one of her visits to Paris, used it as a metaphor for memory in *The Wrongs of Woman; or, Maria*.[43] The early magic-lantern shows shared with novels employing the 'explained supernatural' an ambivalence towards popular superstitions and the exploitation of terror, an essential 'bad faith' which marked them as products of the transition of the spectral from truth to spectacle; they 'developed as mock exercises in scientific demystification, complete with preliminary lectures on the fallacy of ghost-belief and the various cheats perpetrated by conjurers and necromancers over the centuries' while in the following display '[e]verything was done, quite shamelessly, to intensify the supernatural effect'.[44]

Parodies and formulas

Although intense supernatural effects might work to stimulate terror once or several times, sooner or later the repetitious mechanism would become apparent and fear would turn to laughter. This natural fatality or planned obsolescence of Gothic fictions, which eventually turned them into parodies of themselves, also made them easy targets for satire.

The most obvious function of parody in works like Jane Austen's *Northanger Abbey* and William Beckford's *Modern Novel-Writing* (1796) and *Azemia* (1797) is as a method of control and prescription, the policing of fashion through ridicule. In Beckford's case the object of attack is very specifically the conventions of Radcliffe's 'explained supernatural'; *Azemia* contains, no doubt as a corrective, a very vivid tale of the real supernatural.[45] However, as a form of criticism the effect of parody is to complicate the distance separating object and commentary and make reception ambiguous, for blended with and offsetting the seriousness of the negative function is the positive pleasure of recognising the code, of being 'in the know', a response which may approach hedonistic celebration of the follies of the fashion system rather than ascetic rejection of them. As Robert Mayo has shown, the arrival of spoofs of the Gothic was not the signal for the immediate devaluation and decline of the mode; parody and its model coexisted for two decades before the popularity of the genre showed much sign of waning.[46]

Somewhat different in its tendency was the satirical Gothic formula or recipe:

> *Take* – An old castle, half of it ruinous.
> A long gallery, with a great many doors, some secret ones.
> Three murdered bodies, quite fresh.
> As many skeletons, in chests and presses.
> An old woman hanging by the neck; with her throat cut.
> Assassins and desperadoes, *'quant. suff.'*
> Noise, whispers, and groans, threescore at least.
> Mix them together, in the form of three volumes, to be taken
>   at any of the watering places before going to bed.[47]

The butt of humour here is the mindless cycle of reproduction already noted as a fixed feature in the demonology of novel-reading, whereby the addicted consumer becomes a cog in the fashion machine, internalising the code only to spew it out again in a novel of her own. The formula is therefore offered with sarcastic gallantry to 'female readers ... desirous of catching the season of terrors'; 'a few plain and simple rules, by observing which any man or maid, I mean, ladies' maid, may be able to compose from four to six uncommonly interesting volumes, that shall claim the admiration of all true believers in the marvellous'.[48] The breakdown of the Gothic narrative into a regular configuration of component parts was an effort towards demystifying its attractions, and provided yet more proof of the disparity between the theory of sublime literature and its cliché-ridden practice. It demonstrated also the extent to which the form of terror fiction, even apart from its supernatural content, departed from the ineffable rule of nature, that principle by which the value of the most under-theorised genre of the eighteenth century, the novel, was ultimately to be judged.[49] Yet at the same time, however dismissive the intention, Gothic was by such means constituted in critical discourse as an established and coherent literary type.

TOWARDS AESTHETIC SUPERNATURALISM

The year 1797 can be identified quite specifically as the year in which reviewers and critics began to put a name to the category of fiction we now call Gothic or the fantastic, although the name varied: 'modern Romance'; 'the *terrible* school'; 'the Terrorist System of Novel Writing'; 'Terrorist Novel Writing'; 'the *hobgoblin-romance*'.[50] Ghost fiction was coming to be acknowledged as a *genus* within the horizon of critical knowledge. It would cease to be dismissed as a personal fad of the author, or a temporary aberration which might disappear if it was firmly stamped on. Yet there was no consensus on the significance or tendency of the phenomenon; we could say that critical reception was characterised by uneven development. Some continued to uphold the Johnsonian ideal of the didactic novel, and to describe the taste for horrors as a 'second childishness' of the reading public, echoing the charges brought against *The Castle of Otranto* thirty years before.[51] But there was a general recognition that '*terror*' was '*the order of the day*', and that the tide could not be turned back.[52] With the craze for supernatural terror the realm of culture, fashion, consumption and luxury assumed new dimensions and, it appeared, could no longer be contained by reasoned legislation. A discordance gradually emerges between those who scrutinise fictions for signs of the times and go on to issue oracles of cosmic doom, and those for whom a novel is a novel, a pastime and nothing more, the only point at issue being whether a book is well written and entertaining or not.

The new pragmatism is expounded in a review of 1802:

It is a wise maxim in trade, which the booksellers have not disregarded, to proportion the supply of a commodity to the demand for it. The increase of circulating libraries within the last twenty years, has constituted an immense market for novels; but great as the demand is, we see no reason to apprehend a deficiency in the supply. Where so many tastes are to be consulted, and *de gustibus non disputandum*, the articles must be variously flavoured, and, therefore, variously compounded. If one appears insipid, and a second to be highly seasoned, we must not make wry faces, and be out of humour at this diversity; the chief duty that devolves on us, who are called upon to taste most of the commodities, will be to give open warning should any thing tainted, any thing unwholesome be exposed to sale; and this duty we will most scrupulously perform, if unhappily, it shall ever be required from us. On the other hand, it will give us pleasure to announce any thing of peculiar richness and fine quality; but on articles of ordinary goodness we shall not often give a very peremptory opinion.[53]

The exposition collapses the difference between aesthetic and physical taste that philosophers had laboured to establish throughout the previous century, enshrining in its place the heresy *de gustibus non disputandum*, 'each to his own taste'. Such a view would clearly represent an unqualified tolerance of the 'highly seasoned' representations of the supernatural in fiction, and thus the undoing of the enlightenment problematic that has been the subject of our investigation up to this point. Taste is privatised, singular, it cannot be enforced as a code of law, a principle of exclusion. The force of prohibition is lost, and with it the capacity of supernaturalist writing to scandalise, or to initiate a critique of the norms and practices of enlightenment reason, as I have speculated that it did in the cases of Walpole and Radcliffe.

It was in the spirit of optimism that the abolition of ghosts from fiction had been attempted. The reader would look into a novel as a mirror of the mind and discover there a mode of existence free of superstitious fears. Consequently we can detect a certain pessimism, or at least fatalism, inherent in the ecumenical overturning of the didactic model of fiction. In spite of the cheerfully officious tone of the critic quoted above, his underlying message is that this is a flawed world, that the republic of letters is in reality a Tower of Babel, and that the critic is invested with no more glorious purpose than to weed out a few of the most offensive literary specimens.

The rhetorical link made between women, luxury and novel-reading by moralists has already been noted. I argued that it entailed a strategic misrecognition of the growth of consumerism, such that anxieties aroused by unintelligible social change could be smoothed away by the monotonous repetition of strictures regarding the integrity of women's bodies, and the sense of helplessness in the face of unknown economic agencies dispelled by the traditional reassurances of patriarchal legislation. But what we see in the course of the 1790s is an increasing willingness to recognise that, for better or, more probably, for worse, consumerism is a fixture in modern society. This recognition turns to morbid fascination in the earliest attempts to identify and analyse the psychological patterns of hyper-consumption and, once again, novel-reading emerges as a crucial index of the wider scene.

The outstanding feature of the novel phenomenon was the

pattern of habit leading to addiction. Thomas Gisborne, in the
moralistic mode of the conduct book, predictably construes the
pattern as one of degeneration:

the perusal of one romance leads, with much more frequency than is the
case with respect to works of other kinds, to the speedy perusal of another.
Thus a habit is formed, perhaps of limited indulgence, but a habit that is
continually found more formidable and encroaching. The appetite
becomes too keen to be denied; and in proportion as it is more urgent,
grows less nice and select in its fare. What would formerly have given
offence, now gives none. The palate is vitiated or made dull. The produce
of the book-club, and the contents of the circulating library are devoured
with indiscriminate avidity. Hence the mind is secretly corrupted.[54]

Without denying the evidence of this pattern, some commentators
now began to place a new construction on it: it was justified
escapism, consolation for the unavoidable evils of life. Instead of
urging the reader to resist temptation, they were willing to excuse
'castle-building' as a harmless activity, or even to commend it.[55] As
so often, Walter Scott appears as a prominent advocate for the move
away from eighteenth-century structures of literary reception. In his
essay on Ann Radcliffe he remarks:

Perhaps the perusal of such works may, without injustice, be compared
with the use of opiates, baneful when habitually, and constantly resorted
to, but of the most blessed power in those moments of pain and of languor,
when the whole head is sore, and the whole heart sick. If those who rail
indiscriminately at this species of composition were to consider the quantity
of actual pleasure which it produces, and the much greater proportion of
real sorrow and distress which it alleviates, their philanthropy ought to
moderate their critical pride, or religious intolerance.[56]

In this period of transition from one dominant account of the uses of
fiction to another, what will be especially notable is the first, tentative introduction of class as an explanatory principle in discussions
of the development of the novel. We have seen how gender out-
weighed class in the early moral panics over the effects of fiction.[57]
Although Scott's formula anticipates the populist defence of mass-
produced romance fiction, there is no element of populism in it: he is
not singling out a specific social group as the likely market for this
kind of reading. But when Coleridge remarks in his review of
Udolpho that 'The love of poetry is a taste, curiosity is a kind of
appetite, and hurries headlong on, impatient for its complete gratification',[58] identifying the latter quality with Radcliffe's romance, we

find the outlines of a hierarchy that would rescue certain types of literature – those appealing to taste rather than appetite – from the mechanistic dualism of novelty and boredom determining the fate of the popular novel.

With Hugh Murray's *Morality of Fiction* of 1805 we can recognise a draft version of the sociological opposition high art/popular culture. Murray deals with the novel as a historical form, determined by the spread of literacy to the lower orders. Referring specifically to the variety of fiction that exploits improbability and inspires 'fantastic and visionary expectations' – as opposed to realistic, philosophical or ideally didactic works – he writes:

> The origin of this mode of writing is easily accounted for. The invention of printing, and consequent diffusion of books, has given birth to a multitude of readers, who seek only amusement, and wish to find it without trouble or thought. Works, thus conducted, supply them with one which is level to the lowest capacities. How well they are adapted to the taste of this description of readers appears plainly from the extraordinary avidity with which they are devoured.[59]

The classic circular logic of anti-populism – bad readers produce bad writing produce bad readers – is already in place, and there is also a reaching towards the fully-fledged cliché, 'lowest common denominator'.

The changes in reception associated with the popular novel, and above all with the Gothic novel, anticipate most closely the impact of the mechanical media in the twentieth century. Given the relation of Gothic and cinema through their shared kinship to the magic lantern, it is perhaps that much less of a surprise that Walter Benjamin in his essay 'The Work of Art in the Age of Mechanical Reproduction' seems to sum up the experience of fiction at the turn of the eighteenth century. 'The mass is a matrix from which all traditional behaviour towards works of art issues today in a new form. Quantity has been transmuted into quality. The greatly increased mass of participants has produced a change in the mode of participation.'[60] For contemporary observers were struck not only by the force of habit novels were capable of generating, but by the way this and other changes in the mode of consuming texts amounted to a revolution both physical and psychical, seeming to adapt mind and body to a new model of sensation.

First, there is the identification of distraction as a distinct style of receptivity. The reader of popular novels is 'too much occupied' to receive any 'deep impression'.[61] The act of consumption does not consist in a willed merging with the object of contemplation. Instead, the distracted mass audience *absorbs* the art object, osmotically, habitually. Is inattention the natural result of a commodity's lack of distinctive features, its near-perfect interchangeability? So a reviewer of *Castle Zittaw, A German Tale* suggests: 'Pope's satire on women might perhaps with more propriety be applied to the generality of modern novels – that they have no character at all – "Matter too soft a lasting mark to bear".'[62] The reader can enter the imaginary world of the novel as easily as walking into the street, and loiter or hurry at will – we remember, too, that the novels of the circulating library could be read indifferently backwards and forwards. Benjamin equates habit with tactile appropriation, the opposite of rapt concentration; it is a daily unthinking contact that in time breeds an offhand expertise. The earliest existing records of habitual reading we owe to the subsequent fame of the readers. For example, Thomas Medwin, describing his time at the preparatory school Sion House with his cousin Shelley, recalled the voracious consumption of Gothic bluebooks brought back to school after the holidays, and once these were exhausted, the sorties to the 'low' circulating library in the nearby town of Brentford in search of treasures by Ann Radcliffe or 'Rosa-Matilda' (Charlotte Dacre)[63] – similar scenes must have been repeated all over the country. Certainly it was much the same story with Thomas De Quincey, aged 17, confined to a quiet suburb of Liverpool after having run away from school, filling his days with visits to the three libraries in the town and painstakingly recording in his diary the cost and title of each volume borrowed – *The Italian* (3d. per vol.), *The Ghost-Seer* (4d.), *The Dagger* by Carl Grosse, *The Accusing Spirit*, *The Recess*, *Tales of Wonder*, *The Castles of Athlin and Dunbayne*, *Tales of Superstition and Chivalry*, *The Ghost-Seer* again (this time 6d.) – all of these and many others were read in the space of eight weeks, two or three at a time, dipped into throughout the day, sixty pages in the morning, a chapter in the afternoon, a volume and a half in the evening. Reading terror fiction was like eating and, most obviously, like sleeping: the same images ingested during the day were regurgitated in dreams at night. On the morning of Thursday, 5 May 1803, De Quincey jotted down the visions of the night before, among them 'a banquet or carousel of feodal magnificence – such (for instance) as in Schiller's Ghost-Seer, in ye middle of which a mysterious stranger should enter, on whose approach hangs fate and the dark roll of many woes'.[64] Correspondingly, conscious life becomes a waking dream; Coleridge uses the metaphor of the magic lantern to describe the 'kill-time' influence of circulating library merchandise on the mind of the reader, which

> furnishes for itself nothing but laziness and a little mawkish sensibility; while the whole *materiel* and imagery of the doze is supplied *ab extra* by a sort of mental *camera obscura* manufactured at the printing office, which *pro tempore* fixes, reflects and transmits the moving phantasms of one man's delirium, so as to people the barrenness of an hundred other brains afflicted with the same trance or suspension of all common sense and all definite purpose.[65]

It is clear enough that distraction, a kind of somnambulism of apperception, appeared as the reader's internal repetition of the thematic conventions of the Gothic novel itself. Either readers offered themselves up as projections of the dreams and visions contained in the text, or else narcissistically sought works in which to find the reflection of their experience.

The element of reduplication is even more explicit in a second and paradoxical aspect of the 'terrorist system' of novel-reading; on the one hand readers carelessly 'absorb' the texts, on the other, they are mentally tortured by them. It is with reference to terror fiction that the familiar trope 'on the rack of suspense' originates.[66] Here the circuitous adventures of hero or heroine, typical of the picaresque mode, are united with 'horrid' mystery, a veil suggestive of terrible but tantalising concealments. While the reader sympathetically 'doubles' for the central character, the author 'doubles' the role of the hero's or heroine's tormentors,

> those dreadful *unknown*, who, being acquainted with the most secret recesses of the human heart, know how to agonize its tenderest fibres, and how to lacerate its most sensible parts.[67]

Is it the anonymous or pseudonymous league of Gothic writers that is being described here? Or their cast of malevolent fiends? In fact it is the latter, but the possibility of confusion points to the essentially reflexive or abyssal nature of the genre in this period. From the beginning — Garrick's acting of Hamlet, *The Castle of Otranto* — fictions of supernatural terror had also served as guides to the aesthetic pleasures of supernatural terror. The lessons continue in the extreme works of the 1790s, where the audience learns to tolerate, then to love, ever-intensifying degrees of artificially stimulated fear. It is unnecessary to resort to explanations of the discovery of new psychological 'depths', except in so far as such spatial metaphors are encouraged as a reading-effect of the narratives themselves. Yet it would seem that the unprecedented quantities of morbid and fantastic literature produced in these years introduce a new relation of reader to literary text: addictive, irrational, masochistic, in sum, a posture of abjection. The consolations offered by the formula of the terror novel represent a sublimation. Anxieties could be assuaged by binding them to a narrative repeated over and over with only minor variations. Voluntary indulgence in the pleasures of terror grants an illusion of control; the reader is strangely placated by identification with a fictional character, the scope of whose sufferings and uncertainties can be held in the hand, or at most in three bound volumes. If the need to recover this passing reassurance was a cause and symptom of luxury, irrational modernity, then with time this prospect ceased to cause alarm. The consumer economy itself offered the imaginary means of a temporary overcoming.

Claims that the fantastic *per se* represented or continues to represent a literature of subversion need to be reconsidered in view of these definable post-1800 relations of production and consumption in Britain.[68] Radical potential is not inherent in a uniform content, a set of themes, or a formal structure; it concerns above all the event of the work, the determinate entry of a work into circulation and the systematic boundaries of the dialogue between reader and text. Subjective liberations may be made available by one narrative structure or another, but they are more than private, they are generically privatised; like the glass coffin in the fairy tale, the invisible relations through which uncanny, marvellous and fantastic fictions alike came to be read operated as an ultimate form of containment, although the contents might continue to appear lifelike. Walpole, Radcliffe, Wollstonecraft and William Godwin (whose work will be discussed in the next chapter) dealt with the incalculable when they experimentally introduced phantoms and phantasy into the novel form. At this moment is was possible for supernaturalism in the form of commodified fictions to collide with public cultural and economic hierarchies of value with disruptive force – these were conditions of open contradiction and confrontation; but the moment was almost instantly overtaken by a success which was also the compounding of a new orthodoxy in which calculation figured pre-eminently. Chapter 10 examines the point at which literary supernaturalism appeared to come closest to the themes of politics, even to the extent of identity, illustrating both the progress of the new reading contract and the remaining possibilities for critique before the revised terms had been fully established and agreed.

Conspiracy, subversion, supernaturalism

In his essay 'Reflections on the Novel' the Marquis de Sade famously connects the rise of supernatural fiction with the events of the French Revolution:

This genre was the inevitable product of the revolutionary shocks with which the whole of Europe resounded. For those who were acquainted with all the ills that are brought upon men by the wicked, the romantic novel was becoming somewhat difficult to write, and merely monotonous to read: there was nobody left who had not experienced more misfortunes in four or five years than could be depicted in a century by literature's most famous novelists: it was necessary to call upon hell for aid in order to arouse interest, and to find in the land of fantasies what was common knowledge from historical observations of man in this iron age. But this way of writing presented so many inconveniencies [sic]! The author of *The Monk* failed to avoid them no less than did Mrs Radcliffe; either of these two alternatives was unavoidable; either to explain away all the magic elements, and from then on to be interesting no longer, or never raise the curtain, and there you are in the most horrible unreality.[1]

The passage is of interest not only for its insistence on a direct political–fictional correspondence, but for the ironic juxtaposition of 'revolutionary shocks' with the novel-reader's jaded tastes and clamour for ever-new products, a device which suggests de Sade shares the contemporary intimation that the emergence of a mass political movement might have something to do with the expanding demand-led publishing industry discussed in the previous chapter. This is a subject to which I will return. De Sade also speaks of the difficulty of convincingly employing magical elements in a novel, and I want to consider an alternative solution which he disregards, that is, a third type of supernaturalist plot which avoided the 'inconveniences' he observes in Radcliffe's 'explained supernatural' and Lewis's out-and-out irrationalism, and which seemed for a time to transcend the division of fact and fiction itself: its objective was

156

the demystification of metaphysical appearances, but only in order to leave the reader in the most horrible reality.

Schiller's *The Ghost-Seer*, translated into English in 1795, was a paradigm text, not only thematically and formally, but in its contemporary setting and explicit reference to topical political events. It is related in the form of an anecdote by one Count O–, a German, who is eye-witness to the adventures of his friend, the Prince of W–, which begin during a sojourn in Venice. The Prince is shadowed by a mysterious Armenian, who appears to be connected in some way both with the Prince's prospects for inheriting the throne of his native principality and with the Venetian Inquisition. The Prince's fascination with the occult is excited by a series of uncanny events, culminating in a séance at which the apparitionist is exposed as a fraud by the seeming appearance of a real ghost, and soon after is arrested by the Venetian police. The Armenian is implicated, and the supernatural aura surrounding him is increased by the confession of the false apparitionist, who says he has seen examples of his power before. But at this point the Prince comes to suspect that the apparitionist, the Armenian and the police are all in league for reasons he is unable to guess. The first-person account ends here, and the rest is summarised by the translator: in spite of his suspicions, when the Count leaves him to return home, the Prince is irrevocably drawn into a web. The Armenian is revealed to be an agent of the Holy Inquisition, with a commission to convert the Prince to Catholicism and place him on the throne of his Protestant province, where he will enforce the mass conversion of the people. The Prince is seduced by a female agent and, his will broken, joins the scheme to murder the present ruler of the province. When this fails he is poisoned by his fellow plotters to avoid discovery and dies 'in the bitterest agonies of contrition and remorse'.[2]

The tale had immediate relevance to contemporary events, and not merely in an allegorical or poetic way. The translator explains:

> It appeared at a time when the sect of the *Illuminated*, as it is called, was beginning to extend itself very rapidly in Germany. These people, it is well known, were accustomed to seduce the ignorant and the superstitious, by extravagant and incredible tales of supernatural powers and appearances. This story being calculated in some measure, to expose these miraculous accounts would, of course, be received with avidity.[3]

The reference was to the secret society of the Illuminati, which had been founded in 1776 by a professor at the University of Ingolstadt,

Adam Weishaupt, with the aim of spreading radical perfectionist doctrines, and had been twice abolished by the Bavarian government without success. But this was perhaps the first public mention of the society in Britain, and it appears to have meant very little to the critic in the *Monthly Review*, who instead dwelt on the idea of an anti-Protestant plot, more familiar to English sensibilities and equally topical. In 1773 the Jesuits had been suspended by the Pope, and many priests had taken refuge in Protestant Prussia. In 1778 the Spanish Inquisition was re-established with full powers. These two events stimulated rumours of a resurgence of militant Catholicism, operating through secret channels, which *The Ghost-Seer* explicitly related to:

The extraordinary popularity of this tale in Germany was much favoured by the allusions which it contained to those machinations of the mystics at Berlin, of which some mention occurs in the fifty-second and other letters of the Secret Memoirs of Mirabeau. This singular sect, which dispersed with assiduity the writings of Swedenborg, and the leaders of which laid claim to supernatural illuminations and even to intercourse with departed spirits, was supposed to be under the management of certain ex-jesuits; who aspired, through their known influence over persons of the first consequence in Berlin, to re-establish catholicism in Prussia; for which event the diffusion of superstitious books had a natural tendency to prepare the multitude.[4]

In this account the danger of subversion is reassuringly situated abroad and in the past. But two years later, in 1797, came John Robison's startling *Proofs of a Conspiracy Against All the Religions and Governments of Europe, Carried on in the Secret Meetings of Free Masons, Illuminati, and Reading Societies*, with the news that 'this detestable Association exists, and its emissaries are busy among ourselves'.[5] The aims of the secret society Robison described were primarily political and anti-religious, but there was the same involvement of the outlawed Jesuits, the same claims to privileged enlightenment, and the same front of occultism. But now its field of operations had extended to Great Britain. The imagination of the reading public was well prepared to encompass this threat by German terror fiction, a literary commodity which followed migratory routes identical to those of the alleged terrorist agents themselves.[6] The components of the narrative were already in place; Robison's story, and that of the Abbé Barruel which followed, had the truth-effect of a recollection.

The key element of the narrative was the double bluff. The scene of the séance from *The Ghost-Seer* is exemplary. The false ghost, produced by a mechanical apparatus, is the front for a second false ghost; but even after the second exposure a mystery remains to entice the victim: the question 'Why?' The first ghost has as natural referent a financial swindle, but what is the referent of the second ghost? The sequential structure of the plot creates the promise of a deep truth; the Prince, in spite of his own rational dismissal of the Armenian's spectral ploy, is led to his destruction by the appeal of an enigma that is the means of entrapment. The veil is the metonym of that desire to know the unknowable. In Robison's account the Illuminati are seen infiltrating the Freemasons and exploiting the spurious Masonic mysteries to construct a still more alluring inner mystery, which ultimately conceals nothing but naked ambition and opportunism. The novice would pass through grades of initiation and would have contact only with a senior initiate, who would supervise a programme of study leading towards the secret doctrines of the Order, though further secrets always remained in reserve. The initiation ceremonies, involving terrible vows, blood, hooded figures, were designed in the interests of intensified mystery rather than progressive elucidation. Robison's main fear was that British liberals might be taken in by the philanthropic veneer of the conspirators' plans. He stressed that even the most elevated initiates were mere instruments for the eleutherarchs' aim of world domination.

An air of occult mystery is achieved through the blurring of identities. 'Natural' forms of selfhood and identification are submitted to estrangement. The first half of *The Ghost-Seer* is set at the time of carnival, when masks become the norm. It is an indication of the new ideological significance of nationalist passions aroused by the revolutionary wars that the first and most fundamental erosion of selfhood in the narrative is the erosion of national identity: guarantee of origin and authenticity. For opponents of the Revolution, cosmopolitanism was intrinsically suspect, becoming almost synonymous with republicanism and atheism. Hence the symbolic fascination of Venice, a favourite resort of foreigners and a bridge between East and West. The Prince's decision to live in Venice incognito is but one example of the deracination endemic to fashionable Venetian society. The city of the story is peopled almost entirely by foreigners: a Spaniard and a Frenchman at a coffeehouse, 'an English lord ... several merchants from Leghorn, A German

Prelate, a French abbé', and several Swiss at the pleasure-house on the Brenta where the séance takes place. The Armenian, whose race serves as his name, nevertheless disguises himself with perfect success as a Russian officer, and the false apparitionist, when questioned about this mysterious individual by the Prince, plays up the internationalism:

> he is nothing of what he appears to be. There are few conditions or countries, of which he has not worn the mask. No person knows who he is, whence he comes, or whither he goes. That he has been for a long time in Egypt, as many pretend, and that he has brought from thence, out of a catacomb, his occult sciences, I will neither affirm not deny. Here we only know him by the name of the *Incomprehensible* ... There are several creditable persons who remember having seen him, each at the same time, in different parts of the globe.[7]

The Armenian, the Wandering Jew of German folklore and the conjurors, occultists and pseudo-scientists who roamed the Continent in the second half of the century were characters out of more or less the same script – and so too were the Illuminati agents and propagandists who were said to have formed secret networks connecting the whole of Europe to the headquarters of the organisation in Munich. After his arrest in Rome by the Papal Inquisition in 1789, the celebrated alchemist Cagliostro confessed to having made a pact with Baron Knigge, the coadjutor of the Illuminist Order, to recruit in France on a commission basis.[8] The mythology of secret societies extended backwards in time to encompass the traditions of the assassins, the Rosicrucians, the Knights Templar and the medieval system of secret tribunals allegedly promoted by the Holy Roman Empire (this last, the subject of *Herman of Unna*): all with codes of obedience in direct conflict with the 'natural' claims of the homeland, and often with the aim of actively subverting national sovereignty. Like God, the conspirator is anywhere and everywhere, a universal presence with an all-seeing eye and an invisible hand.

A second erosion of personal identity was through the renouncing of family ties. The outlaw creed is most clearly stated in Grosse's *Horrid Mysteries*:

> If you will become a deserving member of our community you must dissolve all bonds whereby men bind themselves to men. Our property is only to be found in the world at large. Murder your father, poniard a beloved sister, and we shall receive you with open arms. When human society expels you, when the laws prosecute you, when the state execrates

you, then you shall be welcome to us. However, our society rejects the tear of humanity.[9]

As with cosmopolitanism, the promise of initiation is that of becoming, whether more or less, *other* than human as humanity is customarily defined. The ultimate overcoming of familial obligations is regicide, murder of the political and symbolic father of the nation. The reward for liberating the self from the bonds of convention will be '*universal dominion*', a quasi-divine power over the totality, the claim to 'call the great world *your property*'.[10] The hero and unwilling initiate Don Carlos swoons at the sublimity of the concept.

The French cult of Republican Rome, with its illustrative sacrifices of private affection to public duty[11] gave the hint to the opposition; John Robison's smear tactics focused on the relations of the leaders of the secret order with women, their indoctrination of daughters with libertarian ideals and their adulterous betrayal of wives. The system of secret denunciation founded by the Inquisition and imitated by the Committee of Public Safety turned every family member into a spy on every other (Cagliostro was denounced for heresy by his wife). Equally shocking, unnatural and fascinating was the purported wholesale rejection of marriage by the secret revolutionists in favour of a communality of women more in keeping with the doctrinal communality of property. In conspiracy fictions women are natural spies and *agents provocateurs*; frequently veiled, they reinforce by sexual metaphor the formal principle that secrecy is the basis of seduction.[12] Biondetta of *Le Diable amoureux* and Matilda in *The Monk*, instruments of the devil's plot, are types mid-way between the she-devil of Christian legend and the secular *femme fatale* of Romanticism. In structural terms their function is identical to that of the seductress of the Prince in *The Ghost-Seer*, or that of Rosalia in *Horrid Mysteries*, who temporarily succeeds in winning over Don Carlos to the aims of the Society through her natural enchantments.

Perhaps the most powerful formal enactment of the break in social ties comes at a point early in *Horrid Mysteries*, two chapters into the first volume, where the chief narrator, Carlos, whose voice has been accepted from the opening lines as the guarantee of truth and sincerity amid the (already) multiple confusions of the plot, is questioned by his life-long friend Count S–: 'For God's sake! who are you?'[13] The reader is instantly faced by an abyss in authority, the equivalent in the dimension of communication and knowledge to the cliff over which Francisca will be thrown by cloaked executioners for unfathomable reasons. And just as Francisca will return from the scene of her destruction inexplicably alive and well at a later stage, so the reader's trust in the competence and goodwill of the narration will involuntarily revive only to be destroyed again and again. The line dividing life and death, natural and supernatural, truth and delusion, is crossed and recrossed so many times that the reader is only prevented from rebelling because, as Michael Sadleir has put it, the 'sheer opulence of language [crushes] him into gibbering acquiescence'.[14] Carlos's wife Elmira dies three times before she is finally laid to rest; his guardian spirit Amanuel is revealed first as his wife's dead brother, then as a living Confederate agent, then as Carlos's uncle and head of the Confederacy in disguise.

With the chaotic example of *Horrid Mysteries* before us it is perhaps a little hard to credit J. M. Roberts's assertion that the mythology of the secret societies was 'an attempt to impose same sort of order on the bewildering variety of changes which suddenly showered upon Europe with the Revolution and its aftermath'.[15] Nevertheless this view has been taken up and elaborated by Ronald Paulson in an influential article 'Gothic Fiction and the French Revolution': 'The assumption of individual agency (as opposed to the more popular modern explanations of social and economic determinism) is ... evident in the allegorizations of revolution as the actions of a single man'.[16] Certainly, conspiracy theory might be seen as taking individualist ideology to its outer limits, the point at which it reverses into its opposite: extraordinary autonomy is attributed to the leaders, credited with the superhuman powers of omniscience, omnipresence and omnipotence, while their subordinates and victims are by contrast abject, powerless, less than human. But why should the identification of the vast ramifications of revolution with 'the actions of a single man' have been considered relatively reassuring and empowering as counter-revolutionary propaganda, when the emotions it was most likely to induce were paralysed awe, hopeless fatalism? In the opening lines of Grosse's novel Carlos speaks of the impossibility of escaping the 'invisible web' that surrounds him, acknowledging the '*Superior Power*' that exposes any sense of personal autonomy as a future illusion: 'Every action of my life seems to me to have been computed and arranged in their dreadful archives before I was born.'[17] If this sounds uncannily like the definition of providence, that is surely no accident; the force of the myth of secret societies lay in its assimilation of theories of human agency to traditional theories of divine or infernal agency: for the head conspirator read a vengeful God or the treacherous Devil.

The Illuminati scare shows the lengths to which the opponents of revolution were prepared to go in order to deny the evidence that the common people, by their own will, had taken up arms against the established authorities. They were prepared to reverse the course of enlightenment, to laboriously knit together the events of the present with the superstitions of the past, they were prepared to cast doubt on the coherence of treasured institutions, which according to their story could be swept away like sandcastles by the machinations of a handful of plotters. They were even willing to risk the general diffusion of fatalism and inertia, which suggests that rather than representing an alternative to modernist theories of social and economic determinism (as Paulson argues), their account of historical change was in a sense a prelude to them. The French Revolution, in this account, was not a spontaneous, popular outburst of protest against the *ancien régime*, it was rather the plot of fiendishly clever intellectuals and their dupes, the liberal aristocrats. The scenes of mob violence from *The Monk* which Paulson cites are a rare item in conspiracy fictions. In general, the only permitted model of mass participation was abject consumerism, a modernised version of superstitious enthralment. Books and reading assumed a key importance in the conspiracy theories of Robison and particularly of Barruel, for whom the French *philosophes* were the chief villains. Thomas Mathias gave this view its strongest expression: 'LITERATURE, *well or ill conducted*, IS THE GREAT ENGINE, *by which all civilized states must ultimately be supported or overthrown.*'[18] It was a licence to ignore the role of grassroots political association and direct activism in favour of coming to terms with a lesser terror: the entry of the mob into literate culture and the arousal of its passions by the consumption of books.

Terror fiction was a writing that both thematised and profited by the creation of irresistible mysteries. In their content Gothic novels allegorise their own effects. *The Ghost-Seer* was considered by its author and dealt with by reviewers as a work of demystification, an enlightenment cure to political and religious enchantment, yet its own powers of attraction lay in the irrational delights of scenes of the marvellous and the supernatural; as de Sade observed, to explain away the magic was 'from then on to be interesting no longer'. Implicitly, the psychopathology of reading Gothic matched the psychopathology of revolutionary conspiracy. The homology was explicit in Mathias's influential attack on *The Monk* in the anonymously published satirical poem with prose commentary, *The Pursuits of Literature*. The 'very poetical descriptions of castles and abbies' in Lewis's novel, the 'diablerie and nonsense fitted only to frighten children in the nursery', were the lure which gave the story its unparalleled capacity to corrupt the morals of the nation.[19] The fact that peasants and shepherds now read *The Rights of Man* and the realm of politics was becoming infested with '*unsexed* female writers' was judged by Mathias a mere side-show next to the threat posed by this novel. 'Is this a time to poison the waters of our land in their springs and fountains? Are we to add incitement to incitement, and corruption to corruption, till there neither is, nor can be, a return to virtuous action and to regulated life?'[20] With this allusion to a venerable anti-Semitic conspiracy theory, Mathias amplifies his accusations of obscenity and blasphemy. His threats of possible legal action led Lewis to remove the offending scenes from the fourth edition, although his publisher took precautions to meet the subsequently increased demand for uncensored copies. The controversy gave the book a vertiginous slant; the subversion of morality and social institutions, which was its subject, was now publicly announced to be its end; the fate of Ambrosio, a figure of authority unmasked, seemed to foreshadow the discomfiture of M. G. Lewis, Member of Parliament. The *coup de grâce* was the counter-accusation by defenders of the novel that the author of *The Pursuits of Literature*, by refusing to reveal his name, imitated the terrorist tactics of the Inquisition. The confused overlappings of the content of *The Monk*, its reception and alleged effects, and rumours of actual political plots created an indeterminacy over allegiances and identities which in turn favoured an indiscriminate paranoia. How could the political loyalties and tendencies of a work like *Horrid Mysteries* be deciphered, a roller-coaster ride of serial dénouements which has the Confederacy at one moment denounced, at the next vindicated, which finally numbs the reader to everything but the thrill of 180 degree turns? If terror fiction was implicated in the plot, whose side was it on? Conservatism had no monopoly on ghost-mongering.

It had, in fact, proved remarkably difficult for the representatives of reaction in Britain to harness the iconography of conspiracy and

6. James Gillray, *Smelling out a Rat*, 1790

7. James Gillray, *Tom Paine's Nightly Pest*, 1792

invisible persecution to their cause before the arrival of foreign conspiracy narratives, fictional and 'factual', came to their aid. Problems can be seen at the very outset of the anti-Jacobin campaign in James Gillray's print *Smelling out a Rat* (1790; fig. 6). Subtitled *The Atheistical-Revolutionist disturbed in his Midnight Calculations*, the image is ostensibly pro-Burke and anti-republican, yet the figure of Dr Richard Price hardly appears sinister beside the at once monstrous and absurd caricature of Burke, an Inquisitorial apparition, bearing crown and cross and with a nose like a giant accusing finger. A similar reversal operates in *Tom Paine's Nightly Pest* (1792; fig. 7). Again, Gillray's supernaturalist rhetoric irresistably attaches itself to figures of state authority rather than to the supposed threat, radicalism. The nightmare apparition of faceless judges with trailing lists of illegible accusations, backed by pillory, prison chains and gallows, is far more disturbing than the diminutive republican devil disappearing out of the window above Paine's sleeping head.[21]

For more than a century the state publicists had laboured to associate superstition and deception with arbitrary rule and unwarranted privilege, whether of church or secular government, and this provided a rhetoric which could be directed against foreign despotism or help to check royal prerogative or the influence of religious dissenters at home. By contrast, the government of Great Britain was understood to be founded on reason, its guiding principle the disinterested protection of the freedom of the individual, over and above the right to own property; a principle witnessed, for example, in the legal safeguards against arbitrary arrest and imprisonment without trial, and in the generous allowances for freedom of speech and publication. But the rhetoric backfired when the Cabinet felt the need to impose emergency measures in response to the events in France. The self-declared constitutional protector of the rights of the individual began to assume the characteristics of its demonised other, the secret state, and saw the ideal of the 'free-born Englishman' it had cultivated in the past used to challenge its authority. Erstwhile liberal parliamentarians, chief among them Edmund Burke, applied themselves to the task of rationally justifying the need for irrational prejudices of rank and religion as a vital adhesive for social order.

In *Political Justice*, William Godwin was able to extend his sympathies far enough to imagine the perplexity of a 'champion of political imposture', like Burke, having to fulfil 'the two opposite purposes of prolonging the deception, and proving that it is necessary to deceive'.[22] Godwin himself can admit of no circumstances in which superstition and deception are to be preferred to rational debate and explanation as a method of rule, however benevolent the intention. Whereas rule by reason is inherently egalitarian, rule by mystery naturally creates two classes, tyrants and slaves, and since it is founded on the bubble of illusion, and bubbles can burst, it suffers from chronic instability. The multitude 'are kept in perpetual vibration, between rebellious discontent, and infatuated credulity. Sometimes they suppose their governors to be the messengers and favourites of heaven, a supernatural order of beings; and sometimes they suspect them to be a combination of usurpers to rob and oppress them.'[23]

Godwin's decision to write the novel *Caleb Williams* in the 'terrorist' mode was not based only on his desire to communicate his ideas to the widest possible audience; the question of whether or not imaginary systems are a political necessity was central to the Revolution debate, and in support of the radical case, the novel illustrates the perilous oscillation between awe-filled reverence and paranoid hatred outlined in *Political Justice*. With his Calvinist background Godwin already had a close acquaintance with the language of hellfire and damnation, but as part of his preparation for writing the book he refreshed his memory with a reading of the popular treatise *God's Revenge Against Murder*, from which he drew in the depiction of Caleb's rancorous master, Falkland, adopting from it the idea of the all-seeing eye of an invisible avenging deity. From the first pages of his account Caleb relates how, when angered, Falkland's voice 'seemed supernaturally tremendous', and later how he 'assumed an expression as of supernatural barbarity'. As if to emphasise the artificiality of the impression, Falkland is also said to habitually recline on the edge of a precipice in apparent mimicry of Danger in Collins's 'Ode to Fear' who 'throws him on the ridgy steep / Of some loose hanging rock to sleep'. As much as Caleb, he is in thrall to the sense of his own power: 'At this moment you are enclosed with the snares of my vengeance, unseen by you, and at the instant that you flatter yourself you are already beyond their reach, they will close upon you. You might as well think of escaping from the power of the omnipresent God, as from mine!' This 'super-human power' is objectively exercised through the organs of the law, weighted in favour of great property-holders and against the common working man. It makes a mockery of Caleb's patriotic boast of independence: 'I am an Englishman; and it is the privilege of an Englishman to be sole judge and master of his own actions.' Caleb is imprisoned for robbery on the word of his employer in spite of his protests of innocence, and is chained and kept in solitary confinement without trial. Reverence and abjection gives way to bitter rebelliousness. A fellow servant who visits Caleb in prison discovers British justice to be 'all a flam': 'Things are done under our very noses, and we know nothing of the matter; and a parcel of fellows with grave faces swear to us that such things never happen but in France, and other countries the like of that.' After escaping, Caleb briefly joins a band of robbers, who delude themselves by claiming for their own reign of terror over the surrounding community the virtue of justice they deny exists in the society which persecutes them: 'We, who are thieves without a licence, are at open war with another set of men, who are thieves according to law.' The rebellious slave forms himself in the image of his master; Caleb comes to nurse the same egotistical passions of hatred and revenge as Falkland. Godwin's revised second ending to the novel has been considered problematic in relation to his political programme, but in one important respect it offers a perfectly apt resolution. In this final courtroom confrontation the veil of illusion is removed from Caleb's eyes and he sees with a shock that Falkland is not the preternatural being of his waking dreams, but a decrepit old man on the point of death; all his 'fine-spun reasonings' of justified retaliation 'vanished before the object that was now presented to me'.[24] This crucial moment of demystification shows that the master–slave relationship based on imagination and passion is not an eternal condition of human nature, but a mental prison that can be overcome, although the realisation comes too late to save Caleb from a lifetime of remorse.

Godwin's warnings of the threat of self-mystifying tyranny at home were quickly reinforced by the turn of events. The stock iniquities of terror fiction were not reserved for the past, or for a foreign country, let alone for the pages of a book. Writing to her friend Mrs Montagu, Elizabeth Carter had agreed that *Herman of Unna* was 'very dull', but she was fascinated by the idea of 'that most horrid institution' the secret tribunal. 'Is it not strange that any people should for so many ages, from Charlemagne to Maximilian, have supported a tyranny from which no one could be safe, by any precaution, and every man was liable to be stabbed by his best friend?'[25] Carter's astonishment is turned to irony for, in 1794, habeas corpus was suspended in Britain and a Committee of Secrecy established for the interrogation of suspected political activists detained under arbitrary arrest.[26] The treason trials of the same year gave the defendants and their supporters the opportunity to accuse the government of anti-constitutional behaviour and the resort to irrational mystery and threat.[27] The trials ended triumphantly for the radicals in acquittal by the jury, but it was only the signal for a more forceful clampdown on political societies and publications. In 1795 the Two Acts, popularly known as the 'Gagging' Acts, effectively outlawed association and made it 'a treasonable offence to incite the people by speech or writing to hatred or contempt of King, Constitution or Government'.[28] Here the government apparently adopted as policy the occultist machinery the radicals had accused it of employing surreptitiously. E. P. Thompson observed that the aim of the acts was not so much to coerce as to terrorise the opposition into submission with an illusion of ruthless omniscience:

It has been argued that the bark of the Two Acts was worse than their bite. The death penalty was never exacted under their provision. Although Habeas Corpus remained suspended for eight years, it seems that only a few score were detained for any period without trial. It was, of course, the bark which Pitt wanted: fear, spies, watchful magistrates with undefined powers, the occasional example.[29]

As the intensifying mysteries of British rule were supplemented by the mysteries of the rumoured international republican conspiracy, the incoherence of *Horrid Mysteries* may well have come to seem not only plausible but accurate, just as the passivity of its bewildered hero may have appeared a useful model for survival in this everyday hall of mirrors. The Marquis de Sade described a situation in which the writers of fiction were compelled to turn to effects of the supernatural in order to outdo the secular terrors that had become a commonplace reality. But, as he added, fictive appeals to hell could only equal the revolutionary shocks which resounded throughout Europe, not surpass them; the novelists would merely 'find in the land of fantasies what was common knowledge from historical observations of man in this iron age'. Their efforts to keep pace with history in pursuit of a readership would inevitably end in failure, for when the fantastic becomes a resource in the service of politics, more limited fictions, however true to life they may be, soon become tame and hackneyed and are overtaken by the cycle of fashion.

Afterword

The 1790s saw a process whereby, as Gothic fiction moved towards the political, politics moved towards a Gothic aesthetic. Godwin's *Caleb Williams* represents the terrorist genre at the peak of its potential as a means of conscious intervention in the political events of the day. Yet, just like any Minerva Press bestseller, the work was duly adapted as an anodyne stage play; and his next novel of ideas, *St. Leon: A Tale of the Sixteenth Century* (1799), with an even more pronounced element of the marvellous, elicited not a court order but a parody, *St Godwin*, which overlooked the radical doctrines to focus entirely on the tangles of Godwin's private life and the idiosyncrasies of his prose style.[1] Meanwhile the French Revolution was being written, and consumed by a paranoid British public, like a gripping romance translated from the German. A few years later and the conspiracy narrative, once conceived of as the substance of history, is being classified simply as a sophistication of a basic Gothic fiction type, the 'explained supernatural'.[2]

It was in the late 1790s that Coleridge and Wordsworth conceived their plan for *Lyrical Ballads*, a plan which Coleridge would later explain in terms particularly interesting for the present investigation. The collection was to consist of two sorts of poem:

it was agreed that my endeavours should be directed to persons and characters supernatural, or at least romantic; yet so as to transfer from our inward nature a human interest and a semblance of truth sufficient to procure for these shadows of imagination that willing suspension of disbelief for the moment, which constitutes poetic faith. Mr Wordsworth, on the other hand, was to propose to himself as his object to give the charm of novelty to things of every day, and to excite a feeling analogous to the supernatural, by awakening the mind's attention from the lethargy of custom and direction it to the loveliness and the wonders of the world before us.[3]

It is striking how closely Coleridge's task accords with that of Walpole, announced in the second preface of *The Castle of Otranto*: to naturalise the circumstances of supernatural creations in order to engage the emotions of the reader to the utmost. Wordsworth, on the other hand, is to attempt an effect which approximates the technique of Ann Radcliffe's 'explained supernatural', 'supernaturalising' and thus defamiliarising common reality.

Is this a case of eighteenth-century supernaturalism setting the agenda for the new project of Romanticism? If so, there are clearly problems. Coleridge's side of the arrangement has become too easy, too lacking in productive resistance. There can be none of the sense of a subversion of expectations, an altering of the horizon of the literary, that accompanied Walpole's innovation; by now readers were well accustomed to lending their 'poetic faith' to any sensational potboiler they might happen to pick up. Could this have been a factor in Coleridge's writer's block? He would eventually contribute only four poems to the first edition, against Wordsworth's twenty-three. Wordsworth, initially, appeared to have undertaken a far more radical challenge. What Radcliffe had done for middle-class women – revealing, however fleetingly, the true conditions of irrationality and oppression governing their existence – he might take into a wholly new area and apply to the lives of labouring people. But while this political possibility remains visible in the finished poems, the Preface to the second edition of the collection confirmed that Wordsworth's principal commitment was to transform the consciousness of a readership distinct from the class he wrote about. He practises a refined, formalised, 'natural' supernaturalism, designed to inspire elated wonder, rather than the revelatory horror of recognition. How could it be otherwise? Elitism was the price an author must pay for autonomy from the demand-led tyranny of the marketplace. Shelley's autobiographical 'Hymn to Intellectual Beauty' shows the aesthetic sublimation of the popular taste for terror, when the boy who 'sought for ghosts' is met instead by a transcendental apprehension of the natural that is the mark of his literary calling.

The best supernatural fiction of the Romantic period, works by James Hogg, Mary Shelley and Charles Maturin, engage in complex ways with contemporary social realities, as recent critical studies have been able to show.[4] Yet the formal strategies of their narratives, the diaries, letters, 'Chinese box' involutions, betray as unmistakably as the manifestos of the poets the determinate alienation of art from social agency.

It is for Thomas Love Peacock in his satirical novel *Nightmare Abbey* to provide the epitaph for eighteenth-century progress towards a fictional supernatural. Shelley, Coleridge, Southey and Byron are all indicted for their part in the transition from an enlightenment literature of engagement to a phantasmatic, solipsistic literature of evasion. The vast unknowns of the political are put aside in favour of the more manageable enigma of fashion, as the Coleridgean Mr Flosky muses on the processes of the culture industry which, in time, will substitute the Byronic hero for the walking spectre as the object of collective desire:

It is very certain, and much to be rejoiced at, that our literature is hag-ridden. Tea has shattered our nerves; late dinners make us slaves of indigestion; the French Revolution has made us shrink from the name of philosophy, and has destroyed, in the more refined part of the community (of which number I am one), all enthusiasm for political liberty. That part of the *reading public* which shuns the solid food of reason for the light diet of fiction, requires a perpetual adhibition of *sauce piquante* to the palate of its depraved imagination. It lived upon ghosts, goblins and skeletons (I and my friend Mr Sackbut served up a few of the best), till even the devil himself, though magnified to the size of Mount Athos, became too base, common, and popular, for its surfeited appetite.[5]

There is truth in this verdict, but the comedy is perhaps too bleak and absolute to stand as a final word. It is only by recovering the history of lost possibilities, what might have been, that we can shake the naturalness of what is.

Notes

INTRODUCTION

1 For the concept of 'effective history', a translation of the German
  Wirkungsgeschichte, see H.-G. Gadamer, *Truth and Method*, rev. trans.
  J. Weinsheimer and D. G. Marshall (New York, Seabury Press, 1989).
2 From Horace, *The Art of Poetry*, 1. 188.
3 *Spectator*, no. 12 (14 March 1711), D. F. Bond (ed.), *The Spectator*, 5
  vols. (Oxford University Press, 1965), 1, pp. 53–4.
4 J. Thomson, *The Seasons*, ed. J. Sambrook (Oxford, Clarendon Press,
  1981), p. 232.
5 Roger Lonsdale (ed.), *The Poems of Gray, Collins and Goldsmith* (London,
  Longmans, 1969), p. 504.
6 See notably N. McKendrick *et al.*, *The Birth of a Consumer Society: The
  Commercialization of Eighteenth-Century England*, 1982 (London, Hutchison, 1983); Colin Campbell, *The Romantic Ethic and the Spirit of Modern
  Consumerism*, 1987 (Oxford, Basil Blackwell, 1989), which lays particular emphasis on the novel in the spread of an 'ethic' of hedonistic
  consumption; and L. Lowenthal and M. Fiske, 'The Debate Over Art
  and Popular Culture in Eighteenth Century England', *Common Frontiers
  of the Social Sciences*, ed. M. Komorovsky (New York, The Free Press,
  1957), pp. 33–112.
7 J. G. A. Pocock, *The Machiavellian Moment: Florentine Republican Thought
  and the Atlantic Tradition* (Princeton University Press, 1975), p. 426.
8 See Pocock, *Machiavellian Moment, passim.*; S. Copley (ed.), *Literature and
  the Social Order in Eighteenth-Century England* (London, Croom Helm,
  1984), esp. pp. 3–7; J. Barrell, *The Political Theory of Painting from
  Reynolds to Hazlitt* (New Haven, Yale University Press, 1986), esp.
  pp. 3–10.
9 See D. Dabydeen, *Hogarth, Walpole and Commercial Britain* (London,
  Hansib, 1987), pp. 15–34.
10 B. Mandeville, *The Fable of the Bees*, ed. and introd. P. Harth
  (Harmondsworth, Penguin, 1970).
11 E. Burke, 'Thoughts and Details on Scarcity', *The Works of the Right
  Honourable Edmund Burke*, introd. R. W. Rafferty, vol. VI (Oxford

University Press, 1907), pp. 3–32, p. 22; J. Tucker, *The Elements of Commerce and Theory of Taxes* (Bristol?, 1755), p. 41.

12 J. Barrell and H. Guest, 'The Uses of Contradiction: Pope's "Epistle to Bathurst"', in J. Barrell, *Poetry, Language and Politics* (Manchester University Press, 1988), pp. 79–99, p. 83.

13 Smith, *The Theory of the Moral Sentiments*, ed. D. D. Raphael and A. L. Macfie (Oxford University Press, 1976), pp. 184–5 (v.i.10–11); cf. Smith, *An Inquiry into the Nature and Causes of the Wealth of Nations*, ed. R. H. Campbell, A. S. Skinner and W. B. Todd, 2 vols. (Oxford University Press, 1976), where the trope arises in connection with capitalist investment in industry: 1, p. 456 (iv.ii.9).

14 F. Moretti, 'Dialectic of Fear', *Signs Taken For Wonders: Essays in the Sociology of Literary Forms*, trans. S. Fischer *et al.* (London, Verso, 1983), pp. 83–108, p. 108.

15 T. Adorno, 'Free Time', in *The Culture Industry: Selected Essays on Mass Culture*, ed. J. M. Bernstein (London, Routledge, 1991), p. 168.

16 T. Adorno, *In Search of Wagner*, trans. R. Livingstone (London, New Left Books, 1981), pp. 95–6.

I THE CASE OF THE COCK LANE GHOST

1 For a full account see D. Grant, *The Cock Lane Ghost* (London, Macmillan, 1965); also 'Elizabeth Parsons' in *Dictionary of National Biography*.

2 Cit. Grant, *Cock Lane Ghost*, p. 71.

3 C. Churchill, *The Ghost*, *The Poetical Works of Charles Churchill*, ed. D. Grant (Oxford University Press, 1956), pp. 63–191, p. 101 (Bk. II, lines 807–8).

4 Hogarth's double target is the traditional association of Catholicism with the manipulative encouragement of superstition, and the current efforts of the Methodists to win converts by publicising miracles, like the Cock Lane ghost. In the revised print, a clergyman expounds the text 'I speak as a fool', his wig flying off to reveal a monk's tonsure and a harlequin's suit revealed under his gown (see below, p. 37 for harlequin). He holds out images of a witch on a broomstick and a devil. Above him, a *putto* bears notice 'To St. Money-trap'. Below, at the foot of the pulpit, there is a thermometer of enthusiasm on a scale from suicidal madness to ecstatic madness, decorated by emblems of the 'Drummer of Tedworth' (a seventeenth-century forerunner of the Cock Lane ghost whose story was parodied in Addison's *The Drummer*), of Fanny bearing a hammer and of Elizabeth Parsons in bed. It rests on copies of Wesley's *Sermons* and Glanvill's *On Witches*. In front of the choir Mary Tofts gives birth to a litter of rabbits and a youth vomits pins, reference to a number of well-known cases in the previous century when innocent women were charged as witches by accusers feigning

elaborate symptoms of enchantment. For more discussion of this iconography see pp. 27–31.

5 Cit. Grant, *Cock Lane Ghost*, p. 84.

6 J. Addison, *The Drummer*, *The Miscellaneous Works of Joseph Addison*, ed.
A. C. Guthkelch, vol. I (London, Bell, 1914), pp. 423–90, p. 443.

7 *The Plays of David Garrick*, ed. H. W. Pericord and F. C. Bergmann,
vol. I (Carbondale and Edwardsville, Southern Illinois University
Press, 1980), p. 251.

8 J. Boswell, *The Life of Samuel Johnson*, ed. G. Birkbeck Hill, rev. and enl.
edn ed. L. F. Powell, 6 vols. (Oxford, Clarendon Press, 1934), III,
p. 298.

9 For other examples of an interest in the 'testability' of the paranormal,
see Johnson on the story of Lord Lyttelton's ghost, Boswell, *Life*, IV,
p. 298; and Boswell on second sight: 'To entertain a visionary notion
that one sees a distant or future event, may be called *superstition*; but on
the correspondence of the fact or event with such an impression on the
fancy, though certainly very wonderful, *if proved*, has no more connection with superstition, than magnetism or electricity.' S. Johnson and
J. Boswell, *Johnson's Journey to the Western Islands of Scotland and Boswell's
Journal of a Tour to the Hebrides with Samuel Johnson, L.L.D.*, ed. R. W.
Chapman (Oxford University Press, 1924), p. 424.

10 There is unfortunately no space here to describe the Reformation
controversy over the nature of spirits, which produced the first appar-
ition narratives. In any case, the battle against the atheists tended to
obscure the terms of the earlier debate between Protestants and Catho-
lics, discussed in K. Thomas, *Religion and the Decline of Magic*
(Harmondsworth, Penguin, 1971), pp. 702–5; J. Dover Wilson, *What
Happens in Hamlet* (Cambridge University Press, 1935), ch. 3; R. H.
West, *The Invisible World: A Study of Pneumatology in Elizabethan Drama*
(University of Georgia Press, 1939); E. E. Stoll, 'The Objectivity of
Ghosts in Shakespeare', *PMLA*, 22, 2 (1907) (n.s., 15, 2), pp. 201–33;
Lewes Lavater, *Of Ghostes and Spirites Walking by Nyght*, 1572 (Oxford
University Press, 1929), ed., J. Dover Wilson and M. Yardley, Intro-
duction and Appendix.

11 The Cambridge divine Ralph Cudworth, cit. J. Tulloch, *Rational
Theology and Christian Philosophy in the Seventeenth Century*, 2nd edn, 2 vols.
(Edinburgh, 1874) II, p. 260. Cf. Joseph Glanvill, in *Saducismus
Triumphatus* (1681), who numbered among the crucial bastions against
free-thinking, 'Particularly the distinction of the soul from the Body,
the being of spirits, and a future life are assertions extremely despised
and opposed by men of this sort, and if we lose those articles, all religion
comes to nothing', cit. Grant, *Cock Lane Ghost*, p. 60. Defoe's writings on
apparitions take a stand against this widespread revisionism. In *The
Political History of the Devil* (1726) and *Essay on the History and Reality of
Apparitions* (1735) he maintains the impossibility of the dead returning

to earth, and advises that the origin of a spirit, whether from Heaven or Hell, may be judged by the character of its errand: see R. M. Baine, *Daniel Defoe and the Supernatural* (Athens, Georgia, University of Georgia Press, 1968).

12 See Moody E. Prior, 'Joseph Glanvill, Witchcraft, and Seventeenth-Century Science', *Modern Philology* 30 (1932), pp. 167–93.

13 J. Glanvill, *Saducismus Triumphatus: Or, Full and Plain Evidence Concerning Witches and Apparitions* (1689) (Gainesville, Florida, Scholars' Facsimiles and Reprints, 1966), intro. C. O. Parsons, p. 448.

14 R. Baxter, *The Certainty of the World of Spirits* (London, 1691), preface, n.p.

15 McKeon, *The Origins of the English Novel 1600–1740* (London, Century Hutchison, 1988), p. 87.

16 Cit. McKeon, *Origins*, p. 85.

17 D. Hume, 'Of Miracles', *Essays Moral, Political, and Literary*, ed. T. H. Green and T. H. Grose, vol. II (London, 1875), pp. 88–108, p. 92.

18 See pp. 2–5.

19 For instance the 'Advertisement' to George Sinclair's *Satans Invisible World Discovered*, cit. C. O. Parsons, 'Ghost-Stories Before Defoe', *Notes and Queries*, 201 (July 1956), p. 295.

20 See D. L. Patey, *Probability and Literary Form: Philosophic Theory and Literary Practice in the Augustan Age* (Cambridge University Press, 1984), ch. 1, 'From Rhetoric to Science'.

21 S. Johnson, *The History of Rasselas, Prince of Abissinia*, ed. and intro. J. P. Hardy (Oxford University Press, 1988), p. 76.

22 Bond (ed.), *Spectator*, I, pp. 453–6. Addison refers to Locke's *Essay Concerning Human Understanding*, ch. 33, 'Of the Association of Ideas'.✳

23 Bond (ed.), *Spectator*, I, p. 480.

24 Glanvill, *Saducismus Triumphatus*, p. x.

25 Glanvill, *Saducismus Triumphatus*, p. 16.

26 Glanvill, *Saducismus Triumphatus*, p. xiii.

27 C. O. Parsons, 'Ghost-Stories', pp. 294–5. For a sampling of early sensationalist accounts of the supernatural, with minimal pretensions to moral instruction, see I. M. Westcott, ed., *Seventeenth-Century Tales of the Supernatural*, Augustan Reprint Soc. no. 74 (Los Angeles, University of California, 1958).

28 See D. Defoe *et al.*, *Accounts of the Apparition of Mrs Veal*, intro. Manuel Schonhorn, Augustan Reprint Soc. no. 115 (Los Angeles, University of California Press, 1965), and J. Sutherland, 'The Relation of Defoe's Fiction to his Non-Fictional Writings', in *Imagined Worlds, Essays on Some English Novels and Novelists in Honour of John Butt*, ed. M. Mack and I. Gregor (London, Methuen, 1968), pp. 37–50; for a discussion of the varying accounts, see pp. 45–8.

29 C. Drelincourt, *The Christian's Defence Against the Fears of Death*, 5th edn (London, 1706), p. 9. See Boswell, *Life*, II, Appendix B, p. 493, on the

publishing history of 'Drelincourt on Death' and 'Defoe's *True Relation*'.
30 Hume, 'Of Miracles', p. 95.
31 (29 Jan. 1762), Walpole, *The Yale Edition of Horace Walpole's Correspondence*, vol. x, ed. W. S. Lewis (New Haven, Yale University Press, 1937–83), pp. 5–7.
32 Grant, *Cock Lane Ghost*, p. 45. Hogarth depicted the Tofts incident at the time under the title 'Cuniculani, or The Wise Men of Godliman in Consultation' (1726), in a print that applies the metaphor of farce to lampoon the credulity of the clergymen involved; see Dabydeen, *Hogarth*, p. 59.
33 Foote did in fact create a comic Interlude entitled *Lectures in Oratory*, featuring the ghost as the defendant in an imaginary court of law, see Grant, *Cock Lane Ghost*, pp. 89–90.
34 Cit. Thomas Wright, *Caricature History of the Georges* (London, Chatto & Windus (1867?)), p. 231.
35 To Bentley (18 May 1754), Walpole, *Correspondence*, vol. xxxv, p. 175.
36 See Grant, *Cock Lane Ghost*, pp. 47–53.
37 Another example was the occasion in 1750 when, after a prophesied earthquake in London had come to nothing, lists naming the 'quality' who had fled the city along with the superstitious masses circulated in public for weeks afterwards. See Wright, *Caricature History of the Georges*, pp. 233–5; T. D. Kendrick, *The Lisbon Earthquake* (London, Methuen, 1956), ch. 1.
38 Churchill, *Poetical Works*, Bk. ii, lines 241–2.
39 Cit. Grant, *Cock Lane Ghost*, p. 98.

2 PRODUCING ENTHUSIASTIC TERROR

1 Addison, *Miscellaneous Works*, i, p. 428.
2 On earlier examples of 'pretended ghost' dramas, see K. M. Briggs, *The Anatomy of Puck: An Examination of Fairy Beliefs among Shakespeare's Contemporaries and Successors* (London, Routledge & Kegan Paul, 1959), p. 145; West, *Invisible World*, p. 58; R. A. Zimbardo, *A Mirror to Nature: Transformations in Drama and Aesthetics, 1660–1732* (Lexington, University of Kentucky Press, 1986), pp. 157–9.
3 Bond (ed.), *Spectator*, i, p. 186.
4 *The Works of John Dryden*, ed. J. T. Swedenberg, Jr *et al.* (Berkeley, University of California Press, 1978), p. 12.
5 H. T. Swedenberg finds a surprising amount of critical support for supernatural machinery in the late seventeenth and early eighteenth centuries, but this is because he does not distinguish between the use of allegorised figures and personifications, which was relatively acceptable, and the inclusion of apparitions of the dead, which was not: 'Fable, Action, Unity and Supernatural Machinery in English Epic Theory, 1650–1800', *Englische Studien*, 73 (1938), pp. 39–48.

6 J. Dennis, 'The Grounds of Criticism in Poetry' (1704), *The Critical Works of John Dennis*, ed. E. N. Hooker, 2 vols. (Baltimore, Johns Hopkins University Press, 1939), I, p. 361.

7 See Patey, *Probability*, Appendix B, 'John Dennis and Christian Marvels', pp. 274–80.

8 Aristotle, *Aristotle's Art of Poetry. Translated from the Original Greek, according to Mr. Theodore Galston's Edition. Together With Mr. D'Acier's Notes Translated from the French* (London, 1705), p. 162. Cf. J. Dennis, 'The Usefulness of the Stage' (1698), *Critical Works*, I, p. 152; where 'the purgation that Aristotle mentions' is cited as a defence and justification against Jeremy Collier's charge that the theatre excites immoral and profane passions. Dryden's inclusion of devils in *King Arthur* is referred to as a case in point, p. 185.

9 See notably P. De Bolla, *The Discourse of the Sublime* (Oxford, Basil Blackwell, 1989); cf. T. Weiskel, *The Romantic Sublime: Studies in the Structure and Psychology of Transcendence* (Baltimore and London, Johns Hopkins University Press, 1976).

10 See, however, Addison's later series of papers 'On the Pleasures of the Imagination', Bond (ed.), *Spectator*, nos. 412–21, where examples of the effect of the terrible or wonderful are drawn from 'primary sources' in nature, or 'secondary sources' in art, predominently literary (note that no. 419 is on 'the fairy way of writing').

11 *Prompter* no. 100 (1735), n.p.

12 See M. Summers, *The History of Witchcraft and Demonology*, 1926 (London and Boston, Routledge & Kegan Paul, 1973), ch. 7, 'The Witch in Dramatic Literature', on the move towards farce in post-Restoration productions of *Doctor Faustus*, *Macbeth* and Thomas Shadwell's *The Lancashire Witches* (1681), an adaptation of *The Late Lancashire Witches* (1634) by Heywood and Brome which was based on a contemporary witch trial: esp. pp. 282–304.

13 *Gentleman's Magazine* 23 (1752), pp. 52–3.

14 A. Pope, *The Poems of Alexander Pope*, ed. J. Butt (London, Methuen, 1963), p. 416.

15 Cit. Cecil Price, *Theatre in the Age of Garrick* (Oxford, Basil Blackwell, 1973), pp. 75–6.

16 Cit. Price, *Theatre*, p. 75. In Germany in the same period Harlequin became the subject of a far more developed critical debate. Mikhail Bakhtin describes how the demand of the classicists for the character's expulsion from 'the serious and respectable stage' was countered by Lessing, among others. 'Beyond the narrow scope of this dispute there was a wider problem of principle: could manifestations such as the grotesque, which did not respond to the demands of the sublime, be considered art?' He finds in an essay by Justus Moser, entitled 'Harlequin, or the Defense of the Grotesque-Comic' (1761), the outlines of an aesthetic of the Romantic Grotesque which came to fruition with

Schlegel and Jean Paul; *Rabelais and His World*, trans. H. Iswolsky, 1968 (Bloomington, Ill., Indiana University Press, 1984), p. 37.

17 *Prompter*, no. 100 (24 Oct. 1735), n.p.

18 D. Diderot, *The Paradox of Acting*, trans. W. H. Pollack (New York, Hill & Wang, 1957), pp. 32–3.

19 G. C. Lichtenberg, *Lichtenberg's Visits to England as Described in His Letters and Diaries*, trans. and nn. M. L. Mare and W. H. Quarrell (Oxford, Clarendon Press, 1938), pp. 9–11. Lichtenberg recorded his impressions of England for a periodical at home, and included the account of Garrick's performance of *Hamlet* in his first instalment (1776), having seen the production three times. Any regular theatre-goer would have been able to describe it in equal detail. *Hamlet* was the second most frequently repeated tragedy, after *Romeo and Juliet*, at the two patent theatres between 1747 and 1776, and rose to become the fifth most frequently performed play of any genre at the London theatres between 1775 and 1800; see Price, *Theatre*, pp. 143, 112.

20 *An Essay on the Character of Hamlet As Performed by Mr. Henderson at the Theatre-Royal in the Hay-Market*, 2nd edn (London, 1777), n.p.

21 Although the ghost's costume may have been unaccustomed, in *Hamlet* Garrick wore a black court-suit in the modern style. There was little attempt at historical accuracy in eighteenth-century theatre costumes; the supernatural elements in Shakespeare productions were not on the whole distanced by historicism. On the other hand the criticism was made that modern dress actually hindered emotional response by violating the rules of propriety. The *St. James's Chronicle* for 30 Oct. 1773 complained to Garrick that in *Macbeth* he looked too much like a 'modern fine gentleman, so that when you came among the Witches in the Fourth [*sic*] Act, you looked like a Beau, who had unfortunately slipped his Foot and tumbled into a Night Cellar, where a Parcel of Old Women were boiling Tripe for their Supper'. Cf. Aaron Hill: 'the generality, being led by the *eye* can conceive nothing extraordinary, where they see nothing uncommon'. Cit. Price, *Theatre*, p. 59.

22 H. Fielding, *The History of Tom Jones*, ed. R. P. C. Mutter (Harmondsworth, Penguin, 1966), p. 757.

23 H. Fielding, *Joseph Andrews and Shamela*, ed. and introd. D. Brooks-Davies (Oxford University Press, 1970), p. 34.

24 Johnson and Boswell, *Johnson's Journey*, p. 183.

25 Cit. Price, *Theatre*, p. 18.

26 Price, *Theatre*, p. 20.

27 Aaron Hill, *Essay on the Art of Acting* (1746), cit. G. Taylor, '"The Just Delineation of the Passions": Theories of Acting in the Age of Garrick', *Essays on the Eighteenth-Century English Stage*, ed. K. Richards and P. Thomson (London, Methuen, 1972), p. 64.

28 Diderot, *Paradox of Acting*.

29 See De Bolla, *Discourse of the Sublime*, ch. 6, 'Of the Gesture of the Orator: the Speaking Subject'.

30 See Taylor, 'Just Delineation of the Passions,' pp. 60–1.

31 Cit. Taylor, 'Just Delineation of the Passions', p. 54.

32 J. Burgh, *The Art of Speaking*, 2nd edn with additions (Dublin, 1763), pp. 25–6. The description was valued highly enough to be plagiarised: Taylor quotes the same passage word for word from John Walker's *Elements of Elocution* (1781), 'Just Delineation of the Passions', p. 70.

33 Cf. Boswell, *London Journal 1762–1763*, ed. F. A. Pottle (London, Heinemann, 1950), 28 December 1762, where he records a dispute at the home of Thomas Sheridan in which the rhetorician and retired player states 'that an actor ought to forget himself and the audience entirely, and be quite the real character; and that for his part, he was so much so that he remembered nothing at all but the character'; while a Captain Maud counters, with Boswell's approval, that an actor, to play well, ought to remain 'master of himself', p. 109.

34 The rhetorical classification of the passions was one offshoot of empiricist philosophical enquiry into the processes of the mind. Another, it should be noted, was the developing medical discourse on the passions, gradually replacing the traditional theory of the humours. On the place of fear in the medical theory of the Enlightenment, see A. Luyendijk-Elshout, 'Of Masks and Mills: The Enlightened Doctor and His Frightened Patient', *The Languages of the Psyche*, ed. G. S. Rousseau (Los Angeles, University of California Press, 1990), pp. 186–230. The article is regrettably piecemeal, but it shows the wealth of material available. Particularly interesting are the case histories which record methods for deliberately provoking terror in a patient suffering from nervous diseases, as a form of shock therapy (see pp. 222–5). It could be argued that one of the achievements of Burke's *Enquiry into . . . the Sublime and the Beautiful* was to assimilate the aesthetic and the medical valuations of the passion of terror: in his system, fear is both a source of imaginative inspiration and physical therapy.

35 Lonsdale (ed.), *Poems of Gray, Collins and Goldsmith*, p. 418.

36 'One who successfully invokes nature is one to whom nature might, in its turn speak. He makes himself poet, visionary. Thus, invocation is a figure of vocation. This is obvious when one thinks how often invocations seek pity or assistance for projects and situations specifically related to the poetic vocation . . . [the] voice calls in order to be calling, to dramatize its calling, to summon images of its power so as to establish its identity as poetical and prophetic voice'; J. Culler, 'Apostrophe', *The Pursuit of Signs* (London, Routledge & Kegan Paul, 1981), p. 142.

37 G. A. Stevens, *The Adventures of a Speculist* (1788), ii. 131; cit. Price, *Theatre*, p. 16.

3 THE ADVANTAGES OF HISTORY

1 *Monthly Review*, 32 (Feb. 1765), pp. 97–9.
2 *Monthly Review*, 32 (May 1765), p. 394.
3 For a full definition of the term, see H. R. Jauss, 'Literary History as a Challenge of Literary Theory', *Toward an Aesthetic of Reception*, trans. T. Bahti (University of Minnesota Press; Brighton, Harvester Press, 1982), pp. 3–45.
4 *Critical Review*, 19 (Jan. 1765), pp. 50–1; my emphasis.
5 [Macpherson], *The Works of Ossian*, I, 3rd edn, 2 vols. (London, Becket and Dehondt, 1815), pp. xxii–xxiii.
6 H. Blair, 'A Critical Dissertation of the Poems of Ossian', commentary, [MacPherson], *Ossian*, II, pp. 310–443, pp. 340–1.
7 Aristotle, Horace, Longinus, *Classical Literary Criticism*, trans. T. S. Dorsch (Harmondsworth, Penguin, 1965), p. 157.
8 Johnson collaborated with William Lauder, who alleged in his *Essay on Milton's Use and Imitation of the Moderns in His Paradise Lost* (1749) that the poem was a mass of plagiarisms from neo-Latin writers. When Lauder's attack was itself shown to be fraudulent Johnson wrote or dictated a confession for him to sign. Fredric Bogel discusses this and other instances of Johnson's complex attitude to authorship and forgery in his essay 'Johnson and the Role of Authority', though he does not touch on his involvement in the Ossian and Rowley controversies: *The New Eighteenth Century*, ed. F. Nussbaum and L. Brown (New York and London, Methuen, 1987), pp. 189–209.
9 Boswell, *Life*, III, p. 50.
10 Boswell, *Life*, IV, p. 183; II, p. 126; I, p. 396.
11 S. Johnson, *Yale Edition of the Works of Samuel Johnson*, ed. W. J. Bate and A. B. Strauss, 16 vols. (New Haven and London, Yale University Press, 1969), III, p. 19.
12 *Critical Review*, 13 (1762), pp. 252–7.
13 In the second edition of *Otranto*, only the second preface was printed, therefore assuming a knowledge of the first. From the third edition in 1766 onwards the two prefaces were printed together, as they are in modern editions today.
14 H. Walpole, *The Castle of Otranto* (Oxford University Press, 1964), p. 3.
15 Walpole, *Otranto*, pp. 3–4.
16 Walpole, *Otranto*, p. 5.
17 Walpole, *Otranto*, p. 7. Walpole explains in a letter to de Beaumont that he is sated with sentimentalism and finds Richardson 'insupportable': 'I thought the *nodus* was become *dignus vindice*, that a god, at least a ghost, was absolutely necessary to frighten us out of too much sense': *Correspondence*, XXXVIII, p. 380.
18 *Monthly Review*, 32, p. 394.
19 See R. W. Babcock, *The Genesis of Shakespeare Idolatry 1766–1799: A Study*

of English Criticism of the Late Eighteenth Century (New York, Russell & Russell, 1964), ch. 8, 'The Reaction Against Voltaire', pp. 90–110.

20 E. Montagu, *An Essay on the Writings and Genius of Shakespear*, Eighteenth-Century Shakespeare Criticism 12, gen. ed. A. Freeman, facsimile of 1769 edn (London, Frank Cass, 1970), esp. pp. 133–69, 'Of Praeternatural Beings'. Montagu takes up Hurd's argument on the close connection of superstition and poetic expression. Without suggesting that Shakespeare himself held superstitious beliefs, she claims he 'saw how useful the popular superstitions had been to the ancient poets: he felt that they were necessary to poetry itself', p. 135. In response to classical scholars for whom 'the ghost of Hamlet is an object of contempt and ridicule' she demonstrates by textual comparison of Aeschylus' *The Persians* and *Hamlet* the superior effects of terror and pity created in the latter. The anachronistic traces of vulgar opinion adhering to the supernatural in high art are less repulsive if they belong to a deep-rooted national tradition, when memories of nurse's tales permit recognition and 'give reins to imagination . . . as spectators . . . willingly give themselves up to pleasing delusion', p. 158. For this reason, the disappearance of the ghost in *Hamlet* at cock's crow adds to the 'pleasing delusion', while the efforts to lure the ghost of Darius with milk and honey in *The Persians* can only appear ridiculous to a modern British audience, since it is not among their native folk beliefs.

21 Walpole *Otranto*, p. 8.

22 Walpole would later produce a more extreme restatement of the primacy of novelty, at the same time distancing himself from it by placing it in the mouth of another 'artful priest', Benedict in *The Mysterious Mother*: he fulminates against

> *reason* – curses light
> On the proud talent! 'twill at last undo us.
> When men are gorged with each absurdity
> Their subtle wits can frame, or we adopt;
> For very novelty they will fly to sense,
> And we shall fall before that idol, fashion.
> (*Mysterious Mother*, IV.i)

The Castle of Otranto and The Mysterious Mother, introd. M. Summers (London, Constable & Co., 1924), p. 212.

23 O. Goldsmith, *An Enquiry into the Present State of Polite Learning in Europe* (1759), *Collected Works of Oliver Goldsmith*, ed. A. Friedman (Oxford, Clarendon Press, 1966), I, pp. 253–341, p. 315.

24 See Jauss, 'Literary History', p. 25, where 'culinary or entertainment art' is given as a gloss for the German critical category of *Unterhaltungskunst*, which in the sphere of literature describes books which bypass reflection, knowledge and judgement and aim solely at emotional stimulation, effect for effect's sake. The elitist assumptions of

this definition are in accordance with the inherent anti-populism of attempts by eighteenth-century theorists to separate the concept of taste from its bodily etymology. Cf. Campbell, *Romantic Ethic*, pp. 154–60 and Lowenthal and Fiske, 'Debate over Art and Popular Culture'.

25 See above, Introduction, p. 12.

4 BACK TO THE FUTURE

1 The first citation of 'gothic' in this sense in the *Oxford English Dictionary*: '1695 Dryden *Du Fresnoy's Art Paint.* 93 All that has nothing of the Ancient gust is call'd a barborous [*sic*] or Gothique manner.'

2 R. Hurd, *Letters on Chivalry and Romance* (1762), ed. and intro. H. Trowbridge, The Augustan Reprint Society, publication no. 101–2, 1st edn facsimile (Los Angeles, University of California Press, 1963). Hurd acknowledged his use of material from Ste-Palaye, *Mémoires*, and had possibly read Jean Chapelain, *De la Lecture des Vieux Romans* (1650), p. iii.

3 Wellek sees Hurd's arguments as already taking effect in the same year in the second edition of *Observations on the Fairie Queene of Spenser* (1754) by Thomas Warton, where, Warton states, it is 'absurd to think of judging either Ariosto or Spenser by precepts which they did not attend to', *The Rise of English Literary History* (New York, McGraw-Hill, 1966), pp. 167–8.

4 Hurd, *Letters*, pp. 28–9.

5 T. Spence, *A Supplement to the History of Robinson Crusoe*, new edn (Newcastle, 1782), p. 12, cit. Olivia Smith, *The Politics of Language 1791–1819* (Oxford, Clarendon Press, 1984), pp. 101–2.

6 But see Walpole's later explicit use of fantasy to figure contemporary realities in *The Works of Horatio Walpole*, 9 vols. (vols. I–V, ed. R. Berry) (London, 1798–1825), II, pp. 93–102. Here a fiction of the discovery of a race of giants in Patagonia allowed Walpole to vent his anti-colonial and anti-slave-trade opinions with a satire of the various discourses of 'civilisation': 'Naturalists, politicians, divines, and writers of romance, have a new field opened to them'; literary primitivism comes in for the same treatment: 'Oh! if we could come at an heroic poem penned by a giant!', and the essay concludes, 'I hope we shall go calmly and systematically to work: that we shall not exterminate these poor monsters till we are fully acquainted with their history, laws, opinions, police, & c.'. See P. Sabor (ed.), *Horace Walpole: The Critical Heritage* (London, Routledge & Kegan Paul, 1987), pp. 107–10, for contemporary reviews.

7 Walpole, *Otranto*, p. 8.

8 Cf. Anna Barbauld's preface to *The Old English Baron*, where the affect of the novel is seen as dependent on inexperience: 'we foresee the

conclusion before we have read 20 pages: but this is not the case with the young and unpracticed reader', *The British Novelists*, vol. xxii (London, 1810), p. ii.

9 Walpole, *Otranto*, pp. 15–16.

10 For the civic humanist conception of 'real' property, employed throughout this chapter, see Pocock, *Machiavellian Moment*, e.g. pp. 450, 463–4.

11 Cit. R. W. Ketton-Cremer, *Horace Walpole*, 3rd edn (London, Methuen, 1964), p. 127.

12 M. Summers, Introduction to Walpole, *The Castle of Otranto and The Mysterious Mother* (London, Constable and Co., 1924), pp. xix–xxi.

13 Walpole, *Otranto*, p. 110.

14 Walpole, *Otranto*, p. 30.

15 Robert Walpole gained power in the wake of the South Sea Bubble in 1724, and promised strong, paternalist government. But it was not long before his policies made his name synonymous with the machinations of the stock market. Just as the *Monthly Review* accused Horace Walpole of being a purveyor of 'false tales', his father was pilloried by Swift for his provision of 'false news', the stock-in-trade of the low stock-jobber (see p. 53). There is a particular aptness in this coincidence. Robert Walpole was held personally responsible by Swift and his fellow 'Wits' for putting a stop to political patronage of literature; for ejecting writers from their dignified station in the world of public affairs and instrumenting their 'Grub Street' proletarianisation at the hands of greedy booksellers. (A generation later Horace Walpole would offer a new affront to the self-importance of the literary establishment, with a work that flouted critical proprieties and made a blatant appeal to the consuming passions that drove a commercialised, demand-led book trade.) The decay of literature was just one more instance of the universal circulation of debased coinage under the management of 'Old Corruption', as the prime minister was named by his opponents. His regime was one in which, it was widely asserted, the reward of true merit was replaced by bribery, nepotism and a disturbing upward mobility, and the interests of the landed aristocracy and gentry, identified as the true interest of the nation as a whole, were ignored in favour of the narrow self-interest of the City money-merchants. In spite of Robert Walpole's gentry background, his extravagant style of living and building of a huge new mansion at Houghton in Norfolk seemed to support the labels of *'parvenu'* and 'embezzler' applied to him by enemies.

16 E. Burke, 'A Letter to a Noble Lord' (1796), *Burke, Paine, Godwin, and the Revolution Controversy*, ed. Marilyn Butler (Cambridge University Press, 1984), pp. 49–59.

17 H. Walpole, 'Account of My Conduct Relative to the Places I Hold under Government and Towards Ministers' (1782), *Works*, ii, pp. 363–70, p. 365.

18 See, for instance, the remarks on his 'useless hoard of trinkets' in a review of his collected works, *The Ladies Monthly Magazine*, I (July 1798), p. 64.

19 Cf. Walpole to Conway, 8 June 1747: 'It is a little plaything-house that I got out of Mrs Chevenix's shop', *Correspondence*, XXXVII, p. 269.

20 McKeon, *Origins*, p. 154.

21 H. Home, *Sketches of the History of Man*, 2 vols. (Edinburgh and London, 1774), II, pp. 481–3; K. Marx, *Early Writings*, trans. R. Livingstone and G. Benton (Harmondsworth, Penguin, 1975), p. 340.

22 See, on the preference of the middle class for partible inheritance over primogeniture, L. Davidoff and C. Hall, *Family Fortunes: Men and Women of the English Middle Class, 1780–1850* (London, Hutchinson, 1987), pp. 205–7.

23 Walpole, *Otranto*, p. 17.

24 W. Hazlitt, *Lectures on the English Comic Writers*, in *The Complete Works of William Hazlitt*, ed. P. P. Howe, vol. VI (London, J. M. Dent, 1931), pp. 5–168, p. 127. Cf. John Dunlop's equally critical remarks in *The History of Fiction*, 2nd edn (1816), iii, 470–2, cit. Sabor (ed.), *Horace Walpole*, pp. 99–100.

25 Although some years later Walpole, in a flippant mood, would dismiss William Warburton's comparison of *Otranto* with the work of 'any of the best Dramatic Writers', capable of effecting 'the full purpose of the *ancient Tragedy*, that is, *to purge the passions by pity and terror*'; cit. Sabor (ed.), *Horace Walpole*, pp. 74–5.

26 H. Walpole, *Correspondence*, XIV, p. 137; XXXVIII, p. 380; XXXV, p. 575.

27 A. Vincent-Buffault, *The History of Tears* (London, Macmillan, 1991), p. 10, cf. p. 6. Cf. also R. Darnton, 'Readers Respond to Rousseau: The Fabrication of Romantic Sensibility', *The Great Cat Massacre* (Harmondsworth, Penguin, 1984), pp. 209–81; H. R. Jauss, 'Rousseau's Nouvelle Heloise and Goethe's Werther within the Shift of Horizons from the French Enlightenment to German Idealism', *Question and Answer*, trans. M. Hays (Minneapolis, University of Minnesota Press, 1982), pp. 148–96.

28 'Madame de la Fayette led the way to novels in the present mode. She was the first who introduced sentiments instead of wonderful adventures, and amiable men instead of bloody heroes. In substituting distresses for prodigies, she made a discovery that persons of taste and feeling are more attached by compassion than by wonder', Home, *Sketches*, I, p. 107.

5 THE VALUE OF THE SUPERNATURAL IN A COMMERCIAL SOCIETY

1 [William Hutchison], *The Hermitage; A British Story* (York, 1772), preface, np.

2 J. and A. L. Aikin, 'On the Pleasure Derived From Objects of Terror; with Sir Bertrand, A Fragment', *Miscellaneous Pieces, in Prose* (London, 1773), pp. 119–37, p. 125.

3 Aikin and Aikin, 'On Romances, An Imitation', *Miscellaneous Pieces*, pp. 39–46, p. 46.

4 E. Burke, *Enquiry*, esp. pt. 4, sec. VI, 'How Pain can be a Source of Delight', and pt. 4, sec. VII, 'Exercise Necessary for the Finer Organs'.

5 Burke, *Enquiry*, p. 136.

6 Walpole, *Otranto*, p. 4.

7 Aikin and Aikin, 'An Enquiry Into Those Kinds of Distress Which Excite Agreeable Sensations', *Miscellaneous Pieces*, pp. 190–214.

8 J. Ralph, *The Case for Authors by Profession or Trade* (London, 1758), p. 21.

9 Ralph, *Case for Authors*, pp. 71–2.

10 K. Marx, *Grundrisse*, trans. with foreword by M. Nicolaus (London, Allan Lane–Penguin, 1973), pp. 90–1.

11 Reeve, *Old English Baron*, pp. 3–6.

12 Reeve, *Old English Baron*, p. 5.

13 The impression of irrefutable common sense is reinforced by the no doubt conscious echo of the 'wonderful long Chapter concerning the Marvellous' from *Tom Jones*, in which the narrator proposes that authors introduce the supernatural, if at all, 'like arsenic, and other dangerous drugs in physic, to be used with the utmost caution', and even then to bear in mind the risk of raising an unintended 'horse-laugh in the reader', Fielding, *Tom Jones*, p. 362.

14 Reeve, *Old English Baron*, p. 100.

15 Reeve, *Old English Baron*, p. 124.

16 J. M. S. Tompkins, *The Popular Novel in England 1770–1800* (London, Constable & Co., 1932), pp. 229–30.

17 Ralph, *Case for Authors*, pp. 6–9.

18 See J. P. Klancher, *The Making of English Reading Audiences 1790–1832* (University of Wisconsin Press, 1987), on the periodical as a 'paradigm of audience-making' (p. 3).

19 J. Lackington, *Memoirs of the Forty-Five First Years of the Life of James Lackington* (London, Lackington, Allen & Co., 1803), p. 255.

20 *A Series of Genuine Letters between Henry and Frances* (1757), cit. A. Adburgham, *Women in Print: Writing Women and Women's Magazines* (London, George Allen & Unwin, 1972), p. 164.

21 Adburgham, *Women in Print*, p. 110.

22 C. Reeve, *The Progress of Romance*, 2 vols. (Colchester, 1785), II, p. 6.

23 *Gentleman's Magazine*, 48 (July 1778), pp. 325–6.

24 Barbauld, 'Preface', *The Old English Baron*, 1810 edn, p. ii.

25 Henry Fuseli (1741–1825), an expatriate Swiss, specialised in extravagantly imaginative paintings illustrating Shakespeare and Milton. *The Nightmare* was his first London success; see N. Powell, *Fuseli: The Nightmare* (London, Allen Lane, 1973).

26 *English Review*, 12 (1788), pp. 286–91.
27 See, on the contemporary reception of the novel, F. M. Mahmoud (ed.), *William Beckford of Fonthill, 1760–1844* (Port Washington, New York, Kennikat, 1972), pp. 63–121, esp. pp. 98–101.
28 To H. More (13 Nov. 1784), *Correspondence*, XXXI, pp. 220–1.
29 [E. Blower], *Maria: A Novel*, 2 vols. (London, 1785), I, pp. 87–8; pp. 109–10.

6 WOMEN, LUXURY AND THE SUBLIME

1 John Burton, *Lectures on Female Education and Manners*, 2 vols. (London, 1793), I, p. 188.
2 R. B. Sheridan, *The School for Scandal and Other Plays*, ed. E. Rump (London, Penguin, 1988), p. 50.
3 J. Fordyce, *Sermons to Young Women*, 3rd edn (London, 1766), cit. De Bolla, *Discourse of the Sublime*, pp. 272–3.
4 Joseph Robertson, *An Essay on the Education of Young Ladies* (London, 1798), pp. 44–5.
5 Cf. Cowper's summing up of the sexual–textual crisis in *The Progress of Error*:

> Ye pimps, who, under virtue's fair pretence,
> Steal to the closet of young innocence,
> And teach her, inexperienced yet and green,
> To scribble as you scribble, at fifteen;
> Who kindling a combustion of desire,
> With some cold moral think to quench the fire,
> Though all your engineering proves in vain,
> The dribbling stream ne'er puts it out again;
> Oh! that a verse had power, and could command
> Far, far away these flesh-flies of the land,
> Who fasten without mercy on the fair,
> And suck, and leave a craving maggot there.   (315–26)
> *The Poetical Works of William Cowper*, ed. H. S. Milford,
> 4th edn (Oxford University Press, 1934)

John Tinnon Taylor, *Early Opposition to the English Novel* (New York, King's Crown Press, 1943), ch. 2, and De Bolla, *Discourse of the Sublime*, pp. 252–78, survey the discourse of condemnation. Tony Tanner investigates the moral symbolism of the circulating library in one literary text, the novel *Sandition*, in *Jane Austen* (London, Macmillan, 1986), pp. 272–3.
6 With the decrease in anonymous publication towards the end of the century it is easier to prove that women novelists (as opposed to women novel-readers) were in the majority, though even here the issue is complicated by contemporary claims that male hacks

regularly wrote under female pseudonyms in the hope they would get a
kinder reception from the critics: see Tompkins, *Popular Novel*, pp. 120–2.

7 Reeve, *Progress of Romance*, II, pp. 80–1.

8 Tompkins, *Popular Novel*, p. 120.

9 Ian Watt, *The Rise of the Novel* (London, Chatto & Windus, 1957),
pp. 45–9, 194–7.

10 P. Kaufman, *Libraries and Their Users* (London, Library Association,
1969), pp. 223–8. During the final revision stage of my work, Marilyn
Butler alerted me to the more recent investigation of booksellers'
records by Jan Fergus, leading to different conclusions from those of
Kaufman: for instance, she was able to argue on empirical grounds that
the majority of readers of Minerva Press books were women of the lower
middle class: 'Women Readers of Fiction and the Marketplace in the
Midlands, 1746–1800', paper delivered at UCLA, Spring 1991
(unpublished).

11 T. Lovell, *Consuming Fiction* (London, Verso, 1987), p. 36.

12 De Bolla, *Discourse of the Sublime*, pp. 230–78.

13 De Bolla, *Discourse of the Sublime*, p. 273; cf. p. 271 where Kaufman is
cited for empirical support.

14 See, for instance, on conduct books and the periodical press aimed at
women readers, M. Poovey, *The Proper Lady and the Woman Writer*
(University of Chicago Press, 1984), ch. 2.

15 *Monthly Mirror*, 4 (Nov. 1797), pp. 277–9.

16 On working-class reading as a relative non-issue until the 1790s, see
R. D. Altick, *The English Common Reader: A Social History of the Mass
Reading Public, 1800–1900* (University of Chicago Press, 1957), pp. 30–5,
65–6.

17 John Sekora heads his historical survey of 'luxury' with a list of the
polarities which define it as a discrete moral and political discourse, a
catalogue illustrating the intersection of gender and class, among other
values; these include town/country, feminine/masculine, innovative/
traditional, immoderate/temperate, irrational/wise, corrupt/virtuous,
mob/men of substance, 'they'/'we'. 'Luxury' is loosely summarised by
Sekora as 'anything unneeded', a mobile category with a wide and
unstable range of association indicated by the Latin roots of the word
luxus, 'sensuality, splendour, pomp', and the derivative, *luxuria*, 'riot,
excess, extravagance' – meanings which suggest both the conspicuous
display of wealth that confirms hierarchy, and the threat of excess and
subversion of hierarchy from within. From the earliest times this trou-
bling instability appears to have been contained by increasingly sexual-
ising and thereby depoliticising 'luxury', a tendency taken furthest in
the middle ages, when the various types of greed it covered, financial,
political, etc., were narrowed to lust, sexual greed alone. In this period
luxuria was almost invariably emblematised as a woman; interestingly,
images of luxury in cathedrals and churches were among the few

allowed to stand during the English Reformation. By the eighteenth century 'luxury' had become detached from sexuality in the descriptive sense, yet a section of *Humphry Clinker* discussed by Sekora shows how Smollet's use of the discourse retains women as an emblem of luxury, notably in the case of those 'shovel-headed sharks', middle-class women. The story of Mr Baynard, a country gentleman of good family financially ruined by his bourgeois, socially ambitious wife, becomes steadily more representative, as first two or three similar cases are discovered in the neighbourhood, and then it is estimated by the narrator that 'nineteen out of twenty, who are ruined by extravagance, fall a sacrifice to the pride of silly women', until in the scheme of the novel as a whole it becomes an allegory of the general decline of the nation. Women are used as shorthand for the economic, social and cultural effects which the rising middle classes have supposedly brought in their wake. *Luxury: The Concept in Western Thought, Eden to Smollett* (Baltimore and London, Johns Hopkins University Press, 1977), pp. ix, 23, 28, 44–5, 47, 261–2.

18 See A. O. Hirschman, *The Passions and the Interests: Political Arguments for Capitalism Before Its Triumph* (Princeton University Press, 1977), pp. 56–63, on money-making as innocent and *doux*, and as a calm passion; cf. pp. 58–9, on the idea that (like beauty in the scheme of Burke's *Enquiry*) the innocuousness of money-making invites contempt.

19 G. Berkeley, *An Essay towards Preventing the Ruin of Great Britain* (1721), in S. Copley (ed.), *Literature and the Social Order*, pp. 91–2.

20 J. Brown, *An Estimate of the Manners and Principles of the Time* (1957), in Copley (ed.), *Literature and the Social Order*, p. 96.

21 No. 141 (4 March 1710), D. F. Bond (ed.), *The Tatler*, 3 vols. (Oxford University Press, 1987), II, pp. 306–7.

22 Courtney Melmouth [S. J. Pratt], *Family Secrets*, 5 vols. (London, 1797), I, pp. 388–9; in the *Oxford English Dictionary* the earliest cited usage of 'consumer' in the neutral economic sense of 'using up exchange value' rather than the moral definition 'wastes, squanders or destroys' is 1745. In her youth the novelist Mary Russell Mitford kept a record of her library borrowings: the representative list for January 1806, which includes the Gothic titles *Vincenza*, *The Castles of Athlin and Dunbayne*, *Amazement*, and *Midnight Weddings*, amounts to a total of fifty-five volumes in thirty-one days which, excluding Sundays, would mean a rate of consumption of at least two volumes a day – not very far from the bookseller's estimate; A. G. Lestrange (ed.), *The Life of Mary Russell Mitford*, 3 vols. (London, 1870), I, pp. 30–1.

23 See N. McKendrick *et al.*, *The Birth of a Consumer Society: The Commercialization of Eighteenth-Century England* (London, Hutchinson, 1983), pp. 13–19.

24 See Mandeville, *Fable of the Bees*, p. 8.

25 Adam Smith, *Lectures on Justice, Police, Revenue and Arms*, ed. E. Cannon, 1896 (New York, A. M. Kelley, 1964), pp. 42–3, 259.

26 I. Kant, *The Critique of Judgement*, trans. J. C. Meredith (Oxford, Clarendon Press, 1952), p. 113. The German *Weichlichkeit* is properly translated as 'softness'; by substituting 'effeminacy', Meredith merely makes explicit the clearly implied gender opposition.

27 See Frances Ferguson, 'The Sublime of Edmund Burke, or the Bathos of Experience', *Glyph*, Johns Hopkins Textual Studies, 8 (1981), pp. 62–78; Anne K. Mellor, *Romanticism and Gender* (London and New York, Routledge, 1993), pp. 85–106; Vivien Jones (ed.), *Women in the Eighteenth Century: Constructions of Femininity* (London, Routledge, 1990), pp. 2–6.

28 Ferguson, 'Sublime', p. 76.

29 I see the fruition of Burke's project in normalisation of aesthetic autonomy and 'privatised' literary practice around the turn of the century; see my chapters 7, 9 and 10. On the bourgeois 'appropriation' of the rhetoric of luxury see Tom Furniss, 'Edmund Burke: Bourgeois Revolutionary in a Radical Crisis', *Socialism and the Limits of Liberalism*, ed. Peter Osborne (London and New York, Verso, 1991), pp. 15–50. Adam Smith, in spite of his earlier acceptance of the civic humanist gendering of commerce, experimented in *The Wealth of Nations* with the rhetorical 'feminisation' of the aristocracy, most notably in the chapter, 'How the Commerce of the Towns Contributed to the Improvement of the Country,' with its derisive account of how the great feudal lords became hapless consumers, steadily trading in the cost of maintaining their private armies for the new and alluring manufactures of the towns, and so unwittingly helping to undermine their own power. Yet at the same time the parable displays a continuing tension between the discourse of liberalism, which laid a positive value on consumption, and the civic humanist ethic, which judges consumer behaviour irrational, regressive, less than manly: Smith, *Wealth of Nations*, I, pp. 411–27 (III.iv).

30 Naturally the threatened spread of luxury to the labouring masses was another continuity, a fear shared by the aristocracy and middle classes (a) because it would bring the economy grinding to a halt, (b) because it would encourage the lower orders to covet the property of their betters; yet these, to our eyes, far better-founded causes for concern did not attain the symbolic charge of gender anxieties.

7 THE SUPERNATURAL EXPLAINED

1 See Tompkins, *Popular Novel*, p. 221.

2 *Critical Review*, 2nd ser. 4 (April 1792), p. 459.

3 *Monthly Review*, ns 8 (May 1792), pp. 82–7.

4 *Monthly Review* (William Enfield), ns 15 (Nov. 1794), p. 280.

5 *Critical Review*, 2nd ser. 11 (Aug. 1794), pp. 361–72.

6 *Analytical Review*, 25 (1797), pp. 516–20; *English Review*, 28 (1797),

pp. 574–9; *Monthly Review*, ns 22 (Mar. 1797), pp. 282–4 (attrib. Arthur Aikin); *Critical Review*, 2nd ser. 23 (June 1798), pp. 166–9 (attrib. Coleridge).

7 [Sir Walter Scott], *Quarterly Review*, 3 (May 1810), p. 344.

8 A. Radcliffe, *Gaston de Blondeville*, 4 vols., with 'Memoir of the Author', by [T. Talfourd] (London, 1826), vol. I, pp. 1–132, p. 115.

9 See M. Summers, *The Gothic Quest*, 1938 (London, Fortune Press, 1968), which presents M. G. Lewis as the culminating genius of the genre. Also F. Garber: 'Lewis took the next great step forward after Mrs. Radcliffe, a step inconceivable without her work but which went as far beyond her as she had gone beyond Walpole and Clara Reeve', A. Radcliffe, *The Italian*, ed. and introd. F. Garber, (Oxford University Press, 1981), p. xii.

10 The latter was extracted from the published novel and printed separately under the title 'On the Supernatural in Poetry' in the *New Monthly Magazine*, 16 (1826), pp. 145–52.

11 A. Radcliffe, *The Mysteries of Udolpho*, ed. and introd. B. Dobrée, explanatory notes by F. Garber (Oxford University Press, 1970), p. 672.

12 T. Todorov, *The Fantastic*, trans. R. Howard, 1973 (Ithaca, New York, Cornell University Press, 1975), pp. 83–6.

13 T. Castle, 'The Spectralization of the Other in *The Mysteries of Udolpho*', *The New Eighteenth Century*, ed. Felicity Nussbaum and Laura Brown (New York and London, Methuen, 1987), pp. 231–53, p. 236.

14 Cit. Todorov, *The Fantastic*, p. 26.

8 LIKE A HEROINE

1 E. Stannard Barrett, *The Heroine, or Adventures of Cherubina*, 2nd edn (London, 1814), p. 78.

2 J. Austen, *Northanger Abbey, Lady Susan, The Watsons, and Sandition*, ed. J. Davie (Oxford University Press, 1971), p. 84.

3 J. Beattie, 'On Fable and Romance', *Dissertations Moral and Political* (London and Edinburgh, 1783), pp. 573–4.

4 M. Kirkham, *Jane Austen, Feminism and Fiction* (New York, Methuen, 1986), p. 89.

5 See M. Wollstonecraft, *The Works of Mary Wollstonecraft*, eds. J. Todd and M. Butler, 7 vols. (London, William Pickering, 1989), VII, pp. 251–3, 369–70; also R. M. Wardle, 'Mary Wollstonecraft, Analytical Reviewer', *PMLA*, 62 (1947), pp. 1000–7.

6 M. Wollstonecraft, *Vindication of the Rights of Woman*, ed. and intro. M. Brody (Harmondsworth, Penguin, 1985), pp. 306–7.

7 M. Wollstonecraft, *The Wrongs of Woman; or Maria*, ed. and intro. G. Kelly (Oxford University Press, 1976), p. 73.

8 Gary Kelly has suggested that the novel was the second volume promised in the *Vindication*, a work which would look closely at 'the laws relative to women', Wollstonecraft, *Wrongs of Woman*, p. 156 n. 1.

9 Cf. the use of Gothic conventions by a friend and fellow radical, Eliza Fenwick, in *Secresy, or The Ruin on the Rock*, 1795 (London, Pandora Press–Unwin Hyman, 1989).

10 Radcliffe and Wollstonecraft achieved celebrity in the same instant: there are long articles on the *Vindication* and on *The Romance of the Forest* in the same volume of the *Monthly Review*, ns 8, and in a single number of the *Critical Review*, 2nd ser. 4 (Apr. 1792). See the short but very favourable review of *The Italian* attributed to Wollstonecraft, *Works*, VII, pp. 484–5.

11 See M. Foucault, 'What Is an Author?', trans. J. V. Harari, *The Foucault Reader*, ed. P. Rabinow (Harmondsworth, Penguin, 1986), pp. 101–20. Foucault uses Radcliffe as an example of the way a novelist's 'author function' can exceed the limits of their own work: 'Ann Radcliffe's texts opened the way for a certain number of resemblances and analogies which have their model or principle in her work. The latter contains characteristic signs, figures, relationships, and structures which could be reused by others', p. 114.

12 Wollstonecraft, *Wrongs of Woman*, p. 73.

13 Radcliffe, *Udolpho*, pp. 380–1.

14 See. J. Austen, *Love and Freindship* (*sic*), *The Works of Jane Austen*, ed. R. W. Chapman, vol. VI (Oxford University Press, 1963), p. 81, for a satirical father–son version of the same scenario.

15 Radcliffe, *Udolpho*, pp. 381–2.

16 Radcliffe, *Udolpho*, p. 384.

17 Radcliffe, *Udolpho*, p. 261.

18 Some interpretations have drawn attention to the importance of economic factors in the unravelling of the plot. 'Money ...', Mary Poovey states in 'Ideology and *The Mysteries of Udolpho*', 'lurks behind every turn of *The Mysteries* plot': *Criticism*, 21 (Fall, 1979), pp. 307–30, p. 323. Ellen Moers pioneered the view that property takes precedence over 'true love' among the themes of what she called the 'Female Gothic': *Literary Women*, 1963 (London, Women's Press, 1978), p. 136. Janet Todd has found in all of Radcliffe's works an unstated equation of sexual and financial threat 'but it is not really an equal association; perhaps it might better be said that the economic is sexualised', *The Sign of Angellica: Women, Writing and Fiction, 1660–1800* (London, Virago, 1989), p. 262. Each suggests that fiction provided an apt if heightened representation of the real condition of women: 'Fear is an appropriate response in a world where women have property or at least the opportunity of transmitting it, but where they have little power to control it', Todd, *Sign of Angellica*, p. 262.

19 Wollstonecraft, *Vindication*, p. 242.

20 R. M. Roche, *The Children of the Abbey*, 2nd edn, 4 vols. (London, 1797), II, pp. 190.

21 The same radical dualism – throne or grave – appeared with exemplary force in Wollstonecraft's own life story after the publication of William Godwin's incautious *Memoirs of the Author of 'The Rights of Woman'* (1798). A champion of feminine propriety like the Revd R. Polewhele was able to write, 'I cannot but think, that the Hand of Providence is visible, in her life, her death, and in the Memoirs themselves. As she was given up to her "heart's lusts", and let "to follow her own imagination", that the fallacy of her doctrines and the effects of an irreligious conduct might be manifested to the world; and as she died a death that strongly marked the distinction of the sexes, by pointing out the destiny of women, and the diseases to which they are liable; so her husband was permitted, in writing her Memoirs, to labour under a temporary infatuation, that every incident might be seen without a gloss – every fact exposed without an apology', *The Unsex'd Females* (np, 1798) [pp. 29–30].

22 Radcliffe, *Udolpho*, p. 379.

23 Kate F. Ellis, *The Contested Castle: Gothic Novels and the Subversion of Domestic Ideology* (Urbana, University of Illinois Press, 1989), p. 122.

24 Radcliffe, *Udolpho*, p. 672.

25 W. Blackstone, *Commentaries on the Laws of England* (1765), 4 vols., 15th edn, with notes and additions by E. Christian (London, 1809), III, p. 268.

26 Blackstone, *Commentaries*, III, p. 268.

27 See D. J. Boorstin, *The Mysterious Science of the Law. An Essay on Blackstone's COMMENTARIES* (Boston, Beacon Press, 1958).

28 G. Lukács, *History and Class Consciousness: Studies in Marxist Dialectics*, trans. R. Livingstone (London, Merlin Press, 1971), p. 83.

29 Blackstone, *Commentaries*, I, p. 55.

30 See C. Pateman, *The Sexual Contract* (Cambridge, Polity Press, 1988), on the survival of patriarchy in what has traditionally been seen by historians as the post-patriarchal 'civil world of contract' of the eighteenth century and after.

31 Blackstone, *Commentaries*, I, p. 445.

32 Blackstone, *Commentaries*, I, p. 441.

33 Davidoff and Hall, *Family Fortunes*, p. 200.

34 See J. O'Faolain and L. Martines, *Not in God's Image: Women in History* (London, Virago, 1979), pp. 240–1.

35 It may have been partly for this reason that the middle classes seem to have abided by the principle of coverture in their inheritance arrangements: see Davidoff and Hall, *Family Fortunes*, pp. 209–11. Though trusts in equity were sometimes used to endow married daughters, sons-in-law were frequently named among the trustees. 'The idea of "provision" for women as dependants derived from aristocratic

arrangements, but took new forms within middle-class property. The provision was made in such a way that male trustees had access to the women's capital to use in the pursuit of their own economic interests' (p. 209).

36 A. Radcliffe, *A Sicilian Romance*, ed. A. Milbank (Oxford University Press, 1993), pp. 36, 180. This, Radcliffe's second novel, appeared the year after the death, aged 93, of a real-life Gothic heroine, whose career was, as the saying goes, 'stranger than fiction'. Lady Cathcart was imprisoned in a castle for twenty years by her fourth husband, an impoverished Irish landowner, in an attempt to make her reveal the hiding-place of the titles to her estate. Maguire was within his rights and her friends in England were powerless to help her. Finally she relented, but the story goes that in trying to force the sliding panel which concealed the deeds with a large jackknife Maguire cut himself and died of lockjaw within a few days. 'Perhaps no more striking instance of retributive justice can be found on record.' See *Gentleman's Magazine*, 59 (Aug. 1789), pp. 766–7; M. Edgeworth, *Castle Rackrent*, ed. and introd. G. Watson (Oxford University Press, 1980), pp. 29–30; Edward Ford, *Tewin Water, or The Story of Lady Cathcart* (Enfield, 1876).

37 Wollstonecraft, *Wrongs of Woman*, pp. 154–5.

38 Wollstonecraft, *Wrongs of Woman*, pp. 198–9.

39 D. A. Miller, '*Cage aux folles*: Sensation and Gender in Wilkie Collins's *The Woman in White*', in *The Novel and the Police* (Berkeley, University of California Press, 1988), pp. 146–91, p. 169.

40 See, for example, Richard Graves, Critical Preface, *Plexippus* (London, 1790), pp. xi–xii. Ernest Baker made Lee's novel the basis for a revisionist genealogy of Gothic, citing the influence of the French writers Baculard D'Arnaud and Abbé Prevost, whose *Cleveland* featured the fictive bastard son of Oliver Cromwell, as *The Recess* did the 'secret children' of Mary, Queen of Scots, E. Baker, *The Novel of Sentiment and the Gothic Romance*, vol. v of *The History of the English Novel* (London, Witherby, 1934), p. 179. See Jane Spencer, *The Rise of the Woman Novelist* (Oxford, Basil Blackwell, 1986), for a detailed feminist reading of the opposition history/romance in the novel. Spencer comes close to the questions raised in the present chapter when she asks, 'Why should women in general, and hence women writers, not subscribe to realism?', but her answer, that romance 'offered escape from male-dominated reality through a fantasy of female power' ignores the full consequences of inversion, and with it the implication that patriarchy is itself a form of fiction: pp. 183–4.

41 C. Smith, *The Romance of Real Life*, 3 vols. (London, 1788), I, p. vi.

42 *British Critic*, 3 (1794), p. 199.

43 C. Smith, *Marchmont: A Novel* (London, Sampson Low, 1796), 4 vols., I, pp. vi–xv. See Wollstonecraft's review, *Works*, VII, pp. 485–6.

44 The rumour that Ann Radcliffe had gone mad by 'the excessive use of

her imagination in representing extravagant and violent scenes' was widely credited: see C. F. McIntyre, *Ann Radcliffe in Relation to Her Time*, Yale Studies in English 62 (Yale University Press, 1920), pp. 19–20. It seemed to offer an explanation for her prolonged silence after the publication of *The Italian*. The *Monthly Review* circulated the story in their issue of July 1826, but printed an apology and correction after the posthumous appearance of *Gaston de Blondeville* (1826) complete with a doctor's report confirming her sanity at the time of death.

9 THE TERRORIST SYSTEM

1 Later the voice is found to belong to M. Dupont, a prisoner in the castle who has discovered a secret passage running under the conference chamber: Radcliffe, *Udolpho*, pp. 288–91, 394–5.

2 Radcliffe, *The Italian*, p. 316.

3 C. S. Montesquieu, *The Spirit of the Laws*, trans. T. Nugent, 2 vols. (New York, Hafner Press, 1949), I, p. 365.

4 C. Smith, *The Old Manor House*, ed. A. H. Ehrenpreis, intro. J. Phillips Stanton, rev. edn (Oxford University Press, 1989), p. 52.

5 Smith, *Old Manor House*, p. 131. On the widespread popular support for smugglers, see E. J. Hobsbawm, *Bandits* (Harmondsworth, Penguin, 1972), p. 40: professional smugglers were idealised as popular heroes in the eighteenth century, when the 'trade was never considered criminal by anybody except governments'. There was considerable sympathy from the liberal middle class, who blamed the hypocrisy of the luxurious ruling class; see, for instance, Elizabeth Carter, who lived at Deal, a centre for smuggling, and knew personally those involved: 'Never will there be any effectual or equitable law passed against smuggling, unless the legislators can settle some means of punishing, in an exemplary manner, the buyers': *Letters from Mrs Elizabeth Carter to Mrs Montague Between the Years 1755 and 1800*, 3 vols. (London, 1817), III, p. 213. But cf. Radcliffe's far less sympathetic portrayal of pirates and bandits in *Udolpho*.

6 [T. Mathias], *The Pursuits of Literature. A Satirical Poem in Four Dialogues*, 12th edn (London, 1803), dial. 1, line 90n., p. 56. The 'mighty magician of THE MYSTERIES OF UDOLPHO' is cleared of this charge.

7 The following account is largely based on D. Blakey, *The Minerva Press 1790–1820* (London, The Bibliographical Society at Oxford University Press, 1939).

8 Cit. Blakey, *Minerva Press*, pp. 16–18.

9 Adburgham, *Women in Print*, p. 164.

10 'As the profession of novelist became less discreditable, writers were more ready to acknowledge their works; but in 1800 anonymous books still formed about half the annual output of the Minerva, and twenty years later the proportion was almost as large'; the convention 'by A

Lady' was 'by far the most common item in the Minerva list of
pseudonyms': see Blakey, *Minerva Press*, pp. 48, 51.

11 Blakey, *Minerva Press*, pp. 1–3.

12 See *Balloon; Or Aerostatic Spy* (1789), listed by Montague Summers in *A
Gothic Bibliography*, (New York, Russell & Russell, 1964).

13 N. Drake, *Literary Hours, Or Sketches Critical and Narrative*, 2 vols.,
facsimile of 2nd rev. edn, 1800 (New York, Garland Publishing, 1970);
see particularly the essays 'On the Government of the Imagination' and
'On Gothic Superstition' in vol. I, and 'On Objects of Terror', vol. II.

14 Cit. *Dictionary of National Biography*. Cf. an exchange 'lately heard' by
the editor of the journal:

BOOKSELLER: My dear Web, spin me out a couple of vols.
WRITER: Gay or grave, Sir.
BOOKSELLER: Tears, tears, Mr. Web – misses must cry or its nothing
– write for the white handkerchief, dear Web, an' you love me ...
(*Flowers of Literature*, 2 (1802), p. 107)

15 S. T. Coleridge, *Collected Letters of Samuel Taylor Coleridge*, ed. E. L.
Griggs, 6 vols. (Oxford, Clarendon Press, 1956–1971), I, p. 122.

16 See F. W. Stokoe, *German Influence on the English Romantic Period, 1788–
1818* (Cambridge University Press, 1926).

17 S. T. Coleridge, *Poetical Works*, ed. E. H. Coleridge (Oxford University
Press, 1969), p. 73.

18 See E. K. Sedgwick's brief but suggestive remarks on this subject, *The
Coherence of Gothic Conventions* (New York, Methuen, 1986), pp. vi–xi.

19 The following list of terror fiction in translation has been compiled from
a number of sources, but is unlikely to be complete: *Herman of Unna* by
Benedicte Naubert (aka Professor Cramer) and *The Necromancer: or The
Tale of the Black Forest* by Lawrence Flammenberg, translated by Peter
Teuthold, appeared in 1794, the year before Daniel Boileau's rendering
of the first half of *Der Geisterseher*; *The Victim of Magical Delusion; or the
Mystery of the Revolution of P------l: a Magico-Political Tale, Founded on
Historical Facts* (1795) by Cajetan Tschink, translated by Peter Will;
The Sorcerer (1795) by Veit Weber, translated by Robert Hirsch; and
two versions of Carl Grosse's *Der Genius* in 1796, *The Genius; or the
Mysterious Adventures of Don Carlos de Grandez* and *Horrid Mysteries*,
translated by Joseph Trapp and Peter Will respectively. Alongside this
German influx came a sole French work, *Le Diable amoureux* by Jacques
Cazotte, which was possibly the first to employ a theme of occult or
invisible persecution and, it is probably safe to say, is the earliest
example of the literary fantastic as defined by Todorov, wherein the
choice between a natural or supernatural interpretation of events
remains undecidable to the end. It was originally published in 1773,
five years before the second English Gothic novel *The Old English Baron*,
but arrived in England at roughly the same moment as the German

novels and failed to make much of an impact (but see speculation concerning its influence on *The Monk* below, pp. 200 n. 30). There were at least three translations in the 1790s, including *The Devil in Love* (1793).

20 Eliza Parsons's *The Castle of Wolfenbach, A German Story* (1793) was the earliest example. It seems, on the evidence of the spoof memoirs of a would-be female novelist in *The Ladies Monthly Magazine*, that by 1798 the attribution was *de rigueur*: 'Now for the title – let me consider – *The Apparition of the Castle* – No, that won't do – Flat, common, and insipid. – *Infernal Mysteries of the Bloody Banquet, a Tale from the German.* – Delightful to a degree'; 1 (Aug. 1798), p. 114.

21 These were: *Leonora. A Tale* by J. T. Stanley; *Lenora, a Tale* by Henry James Pye, the Poet Laureate; *Ellenore, a Ballad* by William Taylor of Norwich; *William and Helen* by Walter Scott; and *Leonora* by W. R. Spencer. See Stokoe, *German Influence*, pp. 65–7 and appendices II and v. Anna Letitia Barbauld (née Aikin) decisively re-enters the history at this point. William Taylor had apparently written his version of the poem some years before, around 1790, and it circulated privately in Norwich. Barbauld brought a copy when visiting friends in Scotland: 'At a party at Dugald Stewart's house, she produced a copy of Taylor's *Ellenore* ... and read it to the assembled company, who were "electrified"' (p. 66). Walter Scott was not present, but a friend's account of the tale and repetition from memory of the lines:

> Tramp! tramp! along the land they rode
> Splash! splash! along the sea!

inspired him to obtain the original. Although Scott knew very little German at the time he completed his own free rendering in a white heat of enthusiasm, working non-stop through the night.

22 Bürger was apparently inspired by 'Sweet William's Ghost' in the English collection, see S. M. Conger, *Matthew G. Lewis, Charles Robert Maturin and the Germans: An Interpretive Study of the Influence of German Literature on Two Gothic Novels* (Universität Salzburg, 1977), p. 136 n. 89.

23 See Conger, *The Germans*, pp. 2, 7 n. 10, who cites William Preston, 'Reflections on the Peculiarities of Style and Manner in the Later German Writers, whose Works have appeared in England; and on the Tendency of their Productions', *Edinburgh Magazine*, in four instalments, ns 20 (1802), pp. 353–61, 406–8; 21 (1803), pp. 9–18, 89–99. Cf. Hugh Murray, *The Morality of Fiction* (Edinburgh, 1805), pp. 120–1. See *British Critic*, 3 (1794), p. 207, judging the loose morals of *The Devil in Love* better 'left to its French readers'.

24 See *Critical Review*, 19 (1797), pp. 194–200 (attrib. Coleridge) and *European Magazine*, 31 (1797), pp. 111–15.

25 E.g. *Critical Review*, on *The Abbey of St. Asaph*, 2nd ser. 14 (1795), p. 349; *Monthly Review*, on *Santa Maria*, ns 23 (1797), p. 210; *Monthly Mirror*, on *Santa Maria*, 4 (Nov. 1797), p. 38.

26 A Persian tale entitled 'Santon Barsisa', a German folk legend for the story of the Bleeding Nun, and Spanish and Danish antiquarian material for two of the ballads. See M. Summers, 'Santon Barsisa', *Notes and Queries*, 175 (1938), pp. 174–5.

27 *Monthly Review*, 23 (1797), p. 451.

28 Definitions of intertextuality, a concept which forms part of the post-structuralist critique of the Romantic artwork, can read, symptomatically, like descriptions of the degenerate other, the formulaic pulp fiction of which Gothic is the archetype. See R. Barthes, *S/Z*, trans. R. Miller (New York, Hill and Wang, 1974), p. 20: 'The code is a perspective of quotations, a mirage of structures; we know only its departures and returns; the units which have resulted from it ... are themselves, always, ventures out of the text, the mark, the sign of a virtual digression toward the remainder of a catalogue (*The Kidnapping* refers to every kidnapping ever written); they are so many fragments of something that has always been *already* read, seen, done, experienced; the code is the wake of that *already*.'

29 Cf. Coleridge, *Collected Letters*, 1, p. 379: in a letter to Wordsworth (23 Jan. 1798) he remarks that Lewis's play *The Castle Spectre* is 'a mere patchwork of plagiarism' but 'admirably managed for stage effect'.

30 See Lewis's introduction to *Adelman, the Outlaw* (London, 1801). The hunt for sources of *The Monk* continues to the present day; Conger, *The Germans*, has the most exhaustive examination of the evidence, revealing both the breadth of Lewis's reading in German – he seems to have gained access to an unpublished manuscript of Goethe's *Faust* – and his complete lack of inhibition over word-for-word borrowing. In this light, the efforts of Lewis's modern biographer to defend the integrity of his subject can only appear misguided; L. F. Peck, '*The Monk* and Musäus' "Die Entführung"', *Philological Quarterly*, 32 (1953), pp. 346–8; '*The Monk* and *Le Diable Amoureux*', *Modern Language Notes* 68 (June 1953), pp. 406–8 – the latter article does however expose an ingenious plot spun by the 1810 translator of Cazotte's novel in order to discredit Lewis: *Biondetta, or the Enamoured Spirit*, was dedicated to Lewis 'without permission' and passages taken from *The Monk* were reproduced as if they were translations from the French novel, the 'original' (Cazotte) therefore being a copy of the 'copy' (Lewis). Cf. Tompkins, *Popular Novel*, p. 245 n. 1, for the claim, which Conger misses, that 'two-thirds of the book are taken, almost word for word, from a German romance' (*Die Blutende Gestalt mit Dolch und Lampe*); apparently demonstrated by Georg Herzfeld in *Herrigs Archive* 111. *The Monk* was plagiarised in turn in *Father Innocent, Abbot of the Capuchins, or The Crimes of the Cloister* (1803) and *The Demon of Sicily* (1807) by Edward Montague.

31 Foucault, 'What Is an Author?', p. 101.

32 In the preface to *The Victim of Magical Delusion* by Cajetan Tschink the translator Peter Will coolly attributes *The Ghost-Seer* to the same author

(the *Monthly Review* corrected him). The Minerva Press seems to have traded on the confusion of the novelist Mary Anne Radcliffe with her better-known namesake. The former was the editor of a Gothic chapbook compilation, *Radcliffe's New Novelist's Pocket Magazine* (1802) and author of *Manfrone, or the One-Handed Monk* (1809); two earlier novels have been attributed to her, *The Fate of Velina de Guidova* and *Radzivil*, both published 1790. See J. Todd (ed.), *A Dictionary of British and American Women Writers, 1660–1800* (London, Methuen, 1987), p. 265.

33 See Altick, *English Common Reader: A Social History of the Mass Reading Public, 1800–1900* (University of Chicago Press, 1957), pp. 52–4.

34 See R. D. Mayo, 'Gothic Romance in the Magazines', *PMLA* 65 (1950), pp. 762–89.

35 See William W. Watt, *Shilling Shockers of the Gothic School: A Study of the Chapbook Gothic Romances* (Cambridge, Mass., Harvard University Press, 1932). Montague Summers has evocatively described the bluebooks swarming 'from the parasitic presses of Houndsditch and the Borough and Finsbury Square, from Tegg, Dean and Munday, Roe, Harrild, J. Ker, and Anne Lemoine' and listed a number of chapbook titles from his own collection, the earliest dated 1797 but most of them post-1800: *Gothic Bibliography*, p. xiii.

36 See A. Parreaux, *The Publication of 'The Monk'. A Literary Event, 1796–1798* (Paris, Librairie Marcel Didier, 1960), p. 69, on other extracts from *The Monk* in chapbook form.

37 *Monthly Magazine*, 4 (July–Dec. 1798), p. 517; Parreaux, *Publication*, pp. 64–6: the second plot involving the Bleeding Nun was presented in the form of the ballet 'Raymond and Agnes' at Covent Garden from 16 March to 1 June 1797, and in the same year as a drama entitled 'Raymond and Agnes, The Traveller Benighted or the Bleeding Nun of Lindenberg', adapted by Henry William Green or, possibly, by Lewis.

38 See review in the *Monthly Mirror*, 4 (1797), where the critic is undecided between condemning the introduction of a ghost on Horatian grounds of dramatic impropriety, and applauding its success, 'the imagination is hurried away for a moment into the world of spirits, and all the fictions of the nursery, and the bugbears of romance become realized', p. 356. It may have been that critical disapproval was displaced by the anachronistic introduction of black guardsmen, one of whom launches into a condemnation of the slave trade. Lewis was himself the conscience-stricken owner of a West Indian plantation, and met the protests of the critics with the Wildean rejoinder, 'I thought it would give a pleasing variety to the characters and dresses, if I made my servants black; and could I have produced the same effect by making my heroine blue, blue I should have made her': M. G. Lewis, *The Castle Spectre*, pp. 102–3.

39 *Analytical Review*, 28 (1798), pp. 295–6. Cf. *British Critic*, 12 (1798), p. 73. 'To us, the originality [of the female spectre] appears not worth contending for. We would interdict the production of any *new* spectre

on the stage. This "reign of terror" is over: "incredulous odi". In a modern play, ghosts cannot be tolerated: they are generally mere substitutes for good sense and good writing.'

40 See Parreaux, *Publication*, for a detailed post-publication history of the poems.

41 See T. Castle, 'Phantasmagoria: Spectral Technology and the Meta-phorics of Modern Reverie', *Critical Inquiry*, 15, 1 (Autumn, 1988), *passim*.

42 F. Schiller, *The Ghost-Seer; or, Apparitionist*, trans. D. Boileau (London and Leeds, 1795), pp. 78–83.

43 Wollstonecraft, *Wrongs of Woman*, p. 75.

44 Castle, 'Phantasmagoria', p. 30.

45 Both Beckford's parodies doubled as protests against the British government's war policy and repressive measures at home. See A. Parreaux, 'The Caliph and the Swinish Multitude', in Mahmoud (ed.), *William Beckford*, pp. 1–15.

46 R. D. Mayo, 'How Long Was Gothic Fiction in Vogue?', *Modern Language Notes*, 58 (Jan. 1943), pp. 58–64; for a survey of parodies of Gothic, see A. B. Shepperson, *The Novel in Motley: A History of the Burlesque Novel in English* (Cambridge, Mass., Harvard University Press, 1936), pp. 154–81.

47 'Terrorist Novel Writing', *Spirit of the Public Journals for 1797*, 1 (London, 1798), pp. 223–5.

48 'Terrorist Novel Writing', pp. 223–5; 'On the Terrorist System of Novel Writing', *Monthly Magazine*, 4 (1797), p. 103.

49 For example, a reviewer of *The Italian* compares the ephemeral value of 'modern romance' with the lasting achievements of Fielding or Smollett, 'as its constitution ... was maintained only by the passion of terror, and that excited by a trick, and as it was not conversant in incidents and characters of a natural complexion, it would degenerate into repetition, and would disappoint curiosity'. *Critical Review*, 2nd ser. 23 (June 1798), pp. 166–9.

50 *Monthly Review*, ns 22 (1797), pp. 282–4 or *Critical Review*, 2nd ser. 23 (1798), p. 166; *Monthly Review*, ns 22 (1797), p. 93; *Monthly Magazine*, 4 (1797), p. 102; *Spirit of the Public Journals for 1797*, 1 (1798), p. 223; *Monthly Magazine*, 4 (1797), p. 348.

51 *Monthly Magazine*, 4 (1798), p. 348.

52 *Spirit of the Public Journals*, 1 (1798), p. 223.

53 From a review of *The Farmer's Boy* by Miss Gunning, *The Annual Review and History of Literature*, 1 (1802), pp. 722–3.

54 T. Gisborne, *An Enquiry into the Duties of the Female Sex* (London, 1796), pp. 216–17.

55 E.g. 'The Female Castle-Builder. A Picture from Real Life', *Flowers of Literature*, 2 (1802), pp. 215–17; cf. Drake, *Literary Hours*, preface.

56 W. Scott, *The Lives of the Novelists* (London, Dent, (1910)), p. 216.

57 See p. 101.

58 *Critical Review*, 2nd ser. 11 (Aug. 1794), p. 369.

59 Hugh Murray, *The Morality of Fiction* (Edinburgh, 1805), p. 40.

60 W. Benjamin, 'The Work of Art in the Age of Mechanical Reproduction', *Illuminations*, trans. H. Zohn (London, Fontana–Jonathan Cape, 1973), pp. 219–54, p. 241.

61 Murray, *Morality of Fiction*, p. 41.

62 *Critical Review*, 2nd ser. 14 (1795), pp. 113–14.

63 T. Medwin, *The Life of Percy Bysshe Shelley*, new edn (Oxford University Press, 1913), pp. 24–6.

64 T. De Quincey, *The Diary of Thomas De Quincey, 1803*, ed. Horace A. Eaton (London, Noel Douglas, nd), p. 156.

65 S. T. Coleridge, *Biographia Literaria*, vol. VII of *The Collected Works of Samuel Taylor Coleridge*, ed. J. Engell and W. Jackson Bate, 2 books (London, Routledge & Kegan Paul; Princeton University Press, 1983), bk 1, p. 48n.; cf. Wordsworth's analysis of the 'almost savage torpor' of the present-day mind, with 'frantic novels' among the contributing causes, 'Wordsworth's Prefaces of 1800 and 1802', *Lyrical Ballads*, eds. R. L. Brett and A. R. Jones (London, Methuen, 1986), pp. 241–72, p. 249.

66 See Murray, *Morality of Fiction*, p. 40.

67 C. F. A. Grosse, *Horrid Mysteries*, trans. P. Will, introd. M. Summers, 2 vols. in 1 (London, Robert Holden, 1927), pp. 140–1.

68 See Rosemary Jackson, *Fantasy: The Literature of Subversion* (London, Routledge, 1981).

10 CONSPIRACY, SUBVERSION, SUPERNATURALISM

1 De Sade, 'Reflections on the Novel', cit. and trans. M. Praz, Introductory Essay, *Three Gothic Novels*, ed. P. Fairclough (Harmondsworth, Penguin, 1968), pp. 7–34, p. 14.

2 J. C. F. Schiller, *Ghost-Seer*, p. 242. It seems that this conclusion, which the translator states is repeated from memory, was another instance of the British inclination to censor and moralise. The original story ends inconclusively, with the Prince morally and financially ruined by the plotters and about to seek asylum in the Catholic Church, and with the supernatural still not entirely explained away.

3 Schiller, *Ghost-Seer*, pp. 230–1.

4 *Monthly Review* ns 18 (Nov. 1795), pp. 346–7; see vols. 16 (p. 466) and 17 (p. 462) of the same journal for similar hints included in review of *The Necromancer* and *The Victim of Magical Delusion*.

5 J. Robison, *Proofs of a Conspiracy Against All the Religions and Governments of Europe . . .*, 3rd edn (Philadelphia, 1798), p. 14. Robison was Professor of Natural Philosophy and secretary to the Royal Society in Edinburgh. His book was first published in London in 1797, and its success is shown by further editions in Edinburgh (1797), Dublin

(1798), London and New York (1798); see J. M. Roberts, *The Mythology of Secret Societies* (London, Secker & Warburg, 1972), p. 208 n. 8.

6 But see below, for a discussion of the alarmism beginning as early as 1793 with the arrest and trial for treason of British radicals.

7 Schiller, *Ghost-Seer*, pp. 117–18, 119–20.

8 Roberts, *Mythology*, pp. 174–7.

9 Grosse, *Horrid Mysteries*, I, p. 80.

10 Grosse, *Horrid Mysteries*, I, pp. 82, 80.

11 The paintings of Jacques Louis David, notably the *Oath of the Horatii* (1785) and *Lictors Returning to Brutus the Bodies of His Sons* (1789), helped to form this cult.

12 Cf. the images of veiled (virtuous) heroines that initiate the narrative chain of events by provoking desire in *The Italian* and *The Monk*. For a formalist treatment of the trope, see Sedgwick, *Conventions*, pp. 140–75.

13 Grosse, *Horrid Mysteries*, I, p. 15.

14 M. Sadleir, *The Northanger Novels: A Footnote to Jane Austen*, The English Association, pamphlet no. 68 (1927), pp. 18–19.

15 Roberts, *Mythology*, p. 15.

16 R. Paulson, 'Gothic Fiction and the French Revolution', *English Literary History*, 48 (1981), pp. 532–54, p. 540; reprinted in a revised version in R. Paulson, *Representations of Revolution* (New Haven, Yale University Press, 1983), p. 223.

17 Grosse, *Horrid Mysteries*, I, p. 2.

18 Mathias, *Pursuits of Literature*, p. 162.

19 Mathias, *Pursuits of Literature*, pp. 248, 245n.(b).

20 Mathias, *Pursuits of Literature*, pp. 244, 248–9.

21 But compare Gillray's *London Corresponding Society, alarm'd,–Vide. Guilty Consciences* (1798), registering in a horror fiction mode the shift in membership from middle-class reformists to more radical elements – at last sufficiently paranoia-inducing.

22 William Godwin, *Enquiry Concerning Political Justice* (Harmondsworth, Penguin, 1985), p. 504.

23 Godwin, *Political Justice*, pp. 503–4.

24 W. Godwin, *Caleb Williams*, ed. D. McCracken, rev. edn (Oxford University Press, 1982), pp. 7, 113, 124 (cf. 296), 144, 159, 163, 202, 216, 319.

25 Carter, *Letters*, III, p. 341.

26 The writ of habeas corpus had emerged fortuitously as the chief legal safeguard of the liberty of the individual, out of the long-running battles over jurisdiction of the various courts of law from the fourteenth to the seventeenth centuries. Habeas corpus offered the means of challenging the validity of a committal. See W. F. Duker, *A Constitutional History of Habeas Corpus* (Westport, Conn., Greenwood Press, 1980), pp. 12–94; R. J. Sharpe, *The Law of Habeas Corpus* (Oxford, Clarendon Press, 1989), pp. 1–20.

27 See J. Barrell, 'Imaginary Treason and Imaginary Law. Treason Trials of 1794', *The Birth of Pandora and the Division of Knowledge* (London, Macmillan; Philadelphia, University of Pennsylvania, 1992), pp. 119–43.
28 E. P. Thompson, *The Making of the English Working Class* (Harmondsworth, Penguin, 1980), pp. 158–9.
29 Thompson, *English Working Class*, p. 161.

AFTERWORD

1 See Marie Roberts, *Gothic Immortals: The Fiction of the Brotherhood of the Rosy Cross* (London, Routledge, 1990), pp. 25–56.
2 Scott, *Lives*, pp. 234–5.
3 Coleridge, *Biographia Literaria*, II, pp. 6–7.
4 Works which investigate aspects of the historicity of Romantic Gothic fiction include David Punter, *The Literature of Terror* (London, Longman, 1980) and Victor Sage, *Horror Fiction in the Protestant Tradition* (New York, St Martin's Press, 1988). Especially interesting is Chris Baldick's *In Frankenstein's Shadow: Myth, Monstrosity, and Nineteenth-Century Writing* (Oxford, Clarendon Press, 1987), which shows the way Mary Shelley's monster exceeds the boundaries of the aesthetic in the form of myth, entering into the discursive field of nineteenth-century politics as a trope for diverse instances of creation run amok.
5 T. L. Peacock, *Nightmare Abbey* (Harmondsworth, Penguin, 1969), p. 68.

Bibliography

PRIMARY SOURCES

Periodicals

Analytical Review
The Annual Review and History of Literature
British Critic
Critical Review
Edinburgh Magazine
English Review
European Magazine
Flowers of Literature
Gentleman's Magazine
The Ladies Monthly Magazine
Monthly Magazine
Monthly Mirror
Monthly Review
New Monthly Magazine
Prompter
Quarterly Review
Spirit of the Public Journals for 1797

Books and articles

Addison, J., *The Drummer; or, The Haunted House, The Miscellaneous Works of Joseph Addison*, ed. A. C. Guthkelch, vol. 1 (London, Bell, 1914), pp. 423–90.
Aikin, J. and A. L., *Miscellaneous Pieces, in Prose* (London, 1773).
Anon., *An Essay on the Character of Hamlet As Performed by Mr. Henderson at the Theatre-Royal in the Hay-Market*, 2nd edn (London, 1777), n.p.
Anon., *The Spectre*, 2 vols. (London, 1789).
Aristotle, *Aristotle's Art of Poetry. Translated from the Original Greek, according to Mr. Theodore Galston's Edition. Together With Mr. D'Acier's Notes Translated from the French* (London, 1705).

Aristotle, Horace, Longinus, *Classical Literary Criticism*, trans. T. S. Dorsch (Harmondsworth, Penguin, 1965).

Ashton, J. (ed.), *Chap-Books of the Eighteenth Century*, 1882 (New York, Benjamin Blom, 1966).

Austen, J., *Love and Freindship* [*sic*], *The Works of Jane Austen*, ed. R. W. Chapman, vol. VI (Oxford University Press, 1963).

Northanger Abbey, Lady Susan, The Watsons, and Sandition, ed. J. Davie (Oxford University Press, 1971).

Barbauld, A., Preface to C. Reeve, *The Old English Baron, The British Novelists*, vol. XXII (London, 1810).

Barrett, E. Stannard, *The Heroine, or Adventures of Cherubina*, 2nd edn (London, 1814).

Baxter, R., *The Certainty of the World of Spirits* (London, 1691).

Beattie, J., 'On Fable and Romance', *Dissertations Moral and Political* (London and Edinburgh, 1783).

Beckford, W., *Modern Novel Writing and Azemia*, intro. H. M. Levy, Jr (Gainesville, Florida, Scholars' Facsimile & Reprints, 1970).

Vathek, ed. and introd. R. Lonsdale, revised edn (Oxford University Press, 1983).

Blackstone, W., *Commentaries on the Laws of England* (1765), 4 vols., 15th edn, with notes and additions by E. Christian (London, 1809).

Blair, H., 'A Critical Dissertation of the Poems of Ossian', [MacPherson], *Ossian*, vol. II, pp. 310–443.

[Blower, E.], *Maria: A Novel*, 2 vols. (London, 1785).

Bond, D. F. (ed.), *The Spectator*, 5 vols. (Oxford University Press, 1965).

(ed.) *The Tatler*, 3 vols. (Oxford University Press, 1987).

Boswell, J., *The Life of Samuel Johnson*, ed. G. Birkbeck Hill, rev. and enl. edn ed. L. F. Powell, 6 vols. (Oxford, Clarendon Press, 1934).

London Journal 1762–1763, ed. F. A. Pottle (London, Heinemann, 1950).

Burgh, J., *The Art of Speaking*, 2nd edn with additions (Dublin, 1763).

Burke, E., 'A Letter to a Noble Lord' (1796), *Burke, Paine, Godwin, and the Revolution Controversy*, ed. Marilyn Butler (Cambridge University Press, 1984), pp. 49–59.

A Philosophical Enquiry into the Origin of our Ideas of the Sublime and Beautiful (1757), ed. J. T. Boulton (Oxford, Basil Blackwell, 1987).

'Thoughts and Details on Scarcity', *The Works of the Right Honourable Edmund Burke*, introd. R. W. Rafferty, vol. VI (Oxford University Press, 1907), pp. 3–32.

Burton, John, *Lectures on Female Education and Manners*, 2 vols. (London, 1793).

Carter, E., *Letters from Mrs Elizabeth Carter to Mrs Montagu Between the Years 1755 and 1800*, 3 vols. (London, 1817).

Churchill, C., *The Ghost, The Poetical Works of Charles Churchill*, ed. D. Grant (Oxford University Press, 1956), pp. 63–191.

Coleridge, S. T., *Biographia Literaria*, vol. VII of *The Collected Works of Samuel Taylor Coleridge*, ed. J. Engell and W. Jackson Bate, 2 books (London, Routledge & Kegan Paul; Princeton University Press, 1983).
Collected Letters of Samuel Taylor Coleridge, ed. E. L. Griggs, 6 vols. (Oxford, Clarendon Press, 1956–1971).
Poetical Works, ed. E. H. Coleridge, 1912 (Oxford University Press, 1969).
Cowper, W., *The Poetical Works of William Cowper*, ed. H. S. L Milford, 4th edn (Oxford University Press, 1934).
Defoe, D., *et al.*, *Accounts of the Apparition of Mrs Veal*, intro. Manuel Schonhorn, Augustan Reprint Soc. no. 115 (Los Angeles, University of California Press, 1965).
Dennis, J. *The Critical Works of John Dennis*, ed. E. N. Hooker, 2 vols. (Baltimore, Johns Hopkins University Press, 1939).
De Quincey, T., *The Diary of Thomas De Quincey, 1803*, ed. Horace A. Eaton, (London, Noel Douglas, nd).
Diderot, D., *The Paradox of Acting*, trans. W. H. Pollack (New York, Hill & Wang, 1957).
Drake, N., *Literary Hours, Or Sketches Critical and Narrative*, 2 vols., facsimile of 2nd rev. edn, 1800 (New York, Garland Publishing, 1970).
Drelincourt, C., *The Christian's Defence Against the Fears of Death*, 5th edn (London, 1706).
Edgeworth, M., *Castle Rackrent*, ed. and introd. G. Watson (Oxford University Press, 1980).
Fenwick, Eliza, *Secresy, or, The Ruin on the Rock*, 1795 (London, Pandora Press–Unwin Hyman, 1989).
Fielding, H., *The History of Tom Jones*, ed. R. P. C. Mutter (Harmondsworth, Penguin, 1966).
Joseph Andrews and Shamela, ed. and introd. D. Brooks-Davies (Oxford University Press, 1970).
[Fuller, A.], *Alan Fitz-Osbourne, An Historical Tale*, 2 vols. (Dublin and London, 1787).
Garrick, D., *The Plays of David Garrick*, ed. H. W. Pericord and F. C. Bergmann, vol. 1 (Carbondale and Edwardsville, Southern Illinois University Press, 1980).
Gisborne, T., *An Enquiry into the Duties of the Female Sex* (London, 1796).
Glanvill, J., *Saducismus Triumphatus: Or, Full and Plain Evidence Concerning Witches and Apparitions*, 1681, intro. C. O. Parsons (Gainesville, Florida, Scholars' Facsimiles and Reprints, 1966).
Godwin, W., *Caleb Williams*, ed. D. McCracken, rev. edn (Oxford University Press, 1982).
Enquiry Concerning Political Justice (Harmondsworth, Penguin, 1985).
Goldsmith, O., *An Enquiry into the Present State of Polite Learning in Europe*, *Collected Works of Oliver Goldsmith*, vol. 1, ed. A. Friedman (Oxford, Clarendon Press, 1966), pp. 253–341.
Graves, Richard, *Plexippus* (London, 1790).

Grosse, C. F. A., *Horrid Mysteries*, trans. P. Will, introd. M. Summers, 2 vols. in 1 (London, Robert Holden, 1927).

Hazlitt, W., *Lectures on the English Comic Writers*, *The Complete Works of William Hazlitt*, ed. P. P. Howe, vol. VI (London, J. M. Dent, 1931), pp. 5–168.

Home, H., *Sketches of the History of Man*, 2 vols. (Edinburgh and London, 1774).

Hume, D., 'Of Miracles', *Essays Moral, Political, and Literary*, eds. T. H. Green and T. H. Grose, vol. II (London, 1875), pp. 88–108.

Hurd, R., *Letters on Chivalry and Romance* (1762), The Augustan Reprint Society, publication no. 101–2, 1st edn facsimile (Los Angeles, University of California Press, 1963).

[Hutchison, W.], *The Hermitage; A British Story* (York, 1772).

Johnson, S., *The History of Rasselas, Prince of Abissinia*, ed. and introd. J. P. Hardy (Oxford University Press, 1988).

 and Boswell, J., *Johnson's Journey to the Western Islands of Scotland and Boswell's Journal of a Tour to the Hebrides with Samuel Johnson, L.L.D.*, ed. R. W. Chapman (London, Oxford University Press, 1924).

Yale Edition of the Works of Samuel Johnson, eds. W. J. Bate and A. B. Strauss, 16 vols. (New Haven and London, Yale University Press, 1969).

Kant, I., *The Critique of Judgement*, trans. J. C. Meredith (Oxford, Clarendon Press, 1952).

Lackington, J., *Memoirs of the Forty-Five First Years of the Life of James Lackington* (London, Lackington, Allen & Co., 1803).

Lavater, L., *Of Ghostes and Spirites Walking by Nyght*, eds. J. Dover Wilson and M. Yardley (Oxford University Press, 1929).

Lee, S., *The Recess*, 3 vols. (London, 1785).

Lestrange, A. G., ed., *The Life of Mary Russell Mitford*, 3 vols. (London, 1870).

Lewis, M. G., *Adelman, the Outlaw* (London, 1801).

The Castle Spectre (London, 1798).

The Monk, ed. H. Anderson (Oxford University Press, 1973).

Lichtenberg, G. C., *Lichtenberg's Visits to England as Described in His Letters and Diaries*, trans. and notes M. L. Mare and W. H. Quarrell (Oxford, Clarendon Press, 1938).

Lonsdale, Roger, ed., *The Poems of Gray, Collins and Goldsmith* (London, Longmans, 1969).

Macdonald, A., *Vimonda. A Tragedy* (London, 1788).

[Macpherson, J.], *The Works of Ossian*, 2 vols., 3rd edn (London, Becket and Dehondt, 1815).

Mandeville, B., *The Fable of the Bees*, ed. and introd. P. Harth (Harmondsworth, Penguin, 1970).

[Mathias, T.], *The Pursuits of Literature. A Satirical Poem in Four Dialogues*, 12th edn (London, 1803).

Medwin, T., *The Life of Percy Bysshe Shelley*, new edn (Oxford University Press, 1913).

Melmouth, Courtney [S. J. Pratt], *Family Secrets*, 5 vols. (London, 1797).

Montagu, E., *An Essay on the Writings and Genius of Shakespear*, Eighteenth-Century Shakespeare Criticism 12, gen. ed. A. Freeman, facsimile of 1769 edn. (London, Frank Cass, 1970).

Montesquieu, C. S., *The Spirit of the Laws*, trans. T. Nugent, 2 vols. (New York, Hafner Press, 1949).

Murray, Hugh, *The Morality of Fiction* (Edinburgh, 1805).

Parsons, E., *The Castle of Wolfenbach, A German Story*, 1793 (London, 1835).

Peacock, T. L., *Nightmare Abbey* (Harmondsworth, Penguin, 1969).

[Polewhele, R.], *The Unsex'd Females* (np, 1798).

Pope, A, *The Poems of Alexander Pope*, ed. J. Butt (London, Methuen, 1963).

Radcliffe, A., *Gaston de Blondeville*, 4 vols. (London, 1826), with 'Memoir of the Author' by [T. Talfourd).

    The Italian, ed. and introd. F. Garber (Oxford University Press, 1970).

    The Mysteries of Udolpho, ed. and introd. B. Dobrée, explanatory notes by F. Garber, 1966 (Oxford University Press, 1970).

    A Sicilian Romance, ed. A. Milbank (Oxford University Press, 1993).

Ralph, J., *The Case of Authors by Profession or Trade* (London, 1758).

Reeve, C., *The Old English Baron. A Gothic Story*, ed. and introd. J. Trainer (Oxford University Press, 1967).

    The Progress of Romance, 2 vols. (Colchester, 1785).

Robertson, Joseph, *An Essay on the Education of Young Ladies* (London, 1798).

Robison, J., *Proofs of a Conspiracy Against All the Religions and Governments of Europe*, 3rd edn (Philadelphia, 1798).

Roche, R. M., *The Children of the Abbey*, 4 vols., 2nd edn (London, 1797).

Schiller, J. C. F., *The Ghost-Seer; or, Apparitionist*, trans. D. Boileau (London and Leeds, 1795).

Scott, W., *The Lives of the Novelists*, 1825 (London, Dent, [1910]).

Sheridan, R. B., *The School for Scandal and Other Plays*, ed. E. Rump (London, Penguin, 1988).

Smith, Adam, *An Inquiry into the Nature and Causes of the Wealth of Nations*, eds. R. H. Campbell, A. S. Skinner and W. B. Todd, 2 vols. (Oxford University Press, 1976).

    Lectures on Justice, Police, Revenue and Arms, ed. E. Cannon, 1896 (New York, A. M. Kelley, 1964).

    Theory of the Moral Sentiments, ed. D. D. Raphael and A. L. Macfie (Oxford University Press, 1976).

Smith, Charlotte, *Marchmont. A Novel*, 4 vols. (London, Sampson Low, 1796).

    The Old Manor House, ed. A. H. Ehrenpreis, introd. J. Phillips Stanton, rev. edn (Oxford University Press, 1989).

    The Romance of Real Life, 3 vols. (London, 1788).

Thomson, James, *The Seasons*, ed. J. Sambrook (Oxford, Clarendon Press, 1981).

Tucker, J., *The Elements of Commerce and Theory of Taxes* [Bristol?, 1755].

Walpole, H., 'An Account of the Giants Lately Discovered', *Works*, II, pp. 93–102.

'Account of My Conduct Relative to the Places I Hold under Government and Towards Ministers', *Works*, II, pp. 363–70.

The Castle of Otranto, 1964 (Oxford and New York, Oxford University Press, 1982).

The Castle of Otranto and The Mysterious Mother, introd. M. Summers (London, Constable & Co., 1924).

The Works of Horatio Walpole, 9 vols. (vols. I–V ed. R. Berry) (London, 1798–1825).

The Yale Edition of Horace Walpole's Correspondence, ed. W. S. Lewis, 48 vols. (New Haven, Yale University Press, 1937–1983).

[White, James], *Earl Strongbow: or, The History of Richard de Clare and the Beautiful Geralda* (London, 1789).

Wollstonecraft, M., *The Wrongs of Woman; or Maria*, ed. and introd. G. Kelly (Oxford University Press, 1976).

Vindication of the Rights of Woman, ed. and introd. M. Brody (Harmondsworth, Penguin, 1985).

The Works of Mary Wollstonecraft, vol. VII, eds. J. Todd and M. Butler (London, William Pickering, 1989).

Wordsworth, W., 'Wordsworth's Prefaces of 1800 and 1802', *Lyrical Ballads*, eds. R. L. Brett and A. R. Jones, 1963 (London, Methuen, 1986), pp. 241–72.

SECONDARY SOURCES

Adburgham, A., *Women in Print: Writing Women and Women's Magazines* (London, George Allen & Unwin, 1972).

Adorno, T., *In Search of Wagner*, trans. R. Livingstone (London, New Left Books, 1981).

Altick, R. D. *The English Common Reader: A Social History of the Mass Reading Public, 1800–1900* (University of Chicago Press, 1957).

Babcock, R. W., *The Genesis of Shakespeare Idolatry 1766–1799: A Study of English Criticism of the Late Eighteenth Century* (New York, Russell & Russell, 1964).

Baine, R. M., *Daniel Defoe and the Supernatural* (Athens, Georgia, University of Georgia Press, 1968).

Baker, E., *The Novel of Sentiment and the Gothic Romance, The History of the English Novel*, vol. V (London, Witherby, 1934).

Bakhtin, M., *Rabelais and His World*, trans. H. Iswolsky, 1968 (Bloomington, Ill., Indiana University Press, 1984).

Baldick, Chris, *In Frankenstein's Shadow: Myth, Monstrosity, and Nineteenth-Century Writing* (Oxford, Clarendon Press, 1987).

Barrell, J., *The Birth of Pandora and the Division of Knowledge* (London, Macmillan; Philadelphia, University of Pennsylvania, 1992).
Poetry, Language and Politics (Manchester University Press, 1988).
The Political Theory of Painting from Reynolds to Hazlitt (New Haven, Yale University Press, 1986).
Barthes, R., *S/Z*, trans. R. Miller (New York, Hill and Wang, 1974).
Benjamin, W., 'The Work of Art in the Age of Mechanical Reproduction', *Illuminations*, trans. H. Zohn, 1968 (London, Fontana–Jonathan Cape, 1973), pp. 219–54.
Bernstein, J. M., ed., *The Culture Industry: Selected Essays on Mass Culture* (London, Routledge, 1991).
Blakey, D., *The Minerva Press 1790–1820* (London, The Bibliographical Society at Oxford University Press, 1939).
Bogel, F., 'Johnson and the Role of Authority', *The New Eighteenth Century*, ed. F. Nussbaum and L. Brown (New York and London, Methuen, 1987), pp. 189–209.
Boorstin, D. J., *The Mysterious Science of the Law. An Essay on Blackstone's* COMMENTARIES (Boston, Beacon Press, 1958).
Briggs, K. M., *The Anatomy of Puck: An Examination of Fairy Beliefs among Shakespeare's Contemporaries and Successors* (London, Routledge & Kegan Paul, 1959).
Campbell, Colin, *The Romantic Ethic and the Spirit of Modern Consumerism*, 1987 (Oxford, Basil Blackwell, 1989).
Castle, T., 'Phantasmagoria: Spectral Technology and the Metaphorics of Modern Reverie', *Critical Inquiry*, 15, 1 (Autumn 1988), pp. 26–61.
'The Spectralization of the Other in *The Mysteries of Udolpho*', *The New Eighteenth Century*, ed. F. Nussbaum and L. Brown (New York and London, Methuen, 1987), pp. 231–53.
Conger, S. M., *Matthew G. Lewis, Charles Robert Maturin and the Germans: An Interpretive Study of the Influence of German Literature on Two Gothic Novels* (Salzburg, Universität Salzburg, 1977).
Cooter, R., 'The History of Mesmerism in England', *Mesmer und die Geschichte des Mesmerismus*, ed. H. Schott (Stuttgart, Franz Steiner, 1985), pp. 152–62.
Copley, S. (ed.), *Literature and the Social Order in Eighteenth-Century England* (London, Croom Helm, 1984).
Culler, J., *The Pursuit of Signs* (London and Henley, Routledge & Kegan Paul, 1981).
Dabydeen, D., *Hogarth, Walpole and Commercial Britain* (London, Hansib, 1987).
Darnton, R., *Mesmerism and the End of the Enlightenment in France* (Cambridge, Mass., Harvard University Press, 1968).
'Readers Respond to Rousseau: The Fabrication of Romantic Sensibility', *The Great Cat Massacre* (Harmondsworth, Penguin, 1984), pp. 209–81.

Davidoff, L., and Hall, C., *Family Fortunes: Men and Women of the English Middle Class, 1780–1850* (London, Hutchinson, 1987).

De Bolla, P., *The Discourse of the Sublime* (Oxford, Basil Blackwell, 1989).

Duker, W. F., *A Constitutional History of Habeas Corpus* (Westport, Conn., Greenwood Press, 1980).

Ellis, Kate F., *The Contested Castle: Gothic Novels and the Subversion of Domestic Ideology* (Urbana, University of Illinois Press, 1989).

Ferguson, Frances, 'The Sublime of Edmund Burke, or the Bathos of Experience', *Glyph*, Johns Hopkins Textual Studies, 8 (1981), pp. 62–78.

Ford, Edward, *Tewin-Water or The Story of Lady Cathcart* (Enfield, 1876).

Foucault, M., 'What Is an Author?', trans. J. V. Harari, *The Foucault Reader*, ed. P. Rabinow (Harmondsworth, Penguin, 1986), pp. 101–20.

Frankl, P., *The Gothic: Literary Sources and Interpretations through Eight Centuries* (Princeton University Press, 1960).

Furniss, T., 'Edmund Burke: Bourgeois Revolutionary in a Radical Crisis', *Socialism and the Limits of Liberalism*, ed. P. Osborne (London and New York, Verso, 1991).

Gadamer, H.-G., *Truth and Method*, rev. trans. J. Weinshamer and D. G. Marshall (New York, Seabury Press, 1989).

Garrett, C., 'Joseph Priestly, the Millenium, and the French Revolution', *Journal of the History of Ideas*, 24 (Jan.–Mar. 1973), pp. 51–66.

Grant, D., *The Cock Lane Ghost* (London, Macmillan, 1965).

Hartnoll, P. (ed.), *The Oxford Companion to the Theatre*, 3rd edn (Oxford University Press, 1967), pp. 428–9 for 'Harlequin' and 'Harlequinade'.

Hirschman, A. O., *The Passions and the Interests: Political Arguments for Capitalism Before Its Triumph* (Princeton University Press, 1977).

Hobsbawm, E. J., *Bandits* (Harmondsworth, Penguin, 1972).

Hopkins, J. K. *A Woman To Deliver Her People: Joanna Southcott and English Millenarianism in an Era of Revolution* (Austin, University of Texas, 1982).

Jackson, Rosemary, *Fantasy: The Literature of Subversion* (London, Routledge, 1981).

Jauss, H. R., 'Literary History as a Challenge of Literary Theory', *Toward an Aesthetic of Reception*, trans. T. Bahti (Minneapolis, University of Minnesota Press; Brighton, Harvester Press, 1982), pp. 3–45.

'Rousseau's Nouvelle Heloise and Goethe's Werther within the Shift of Horizons from the French Enlightenment to German Idealism', *Question and Answer*, trans. M. Hays (Minneapolis, University of Minnesota Press, 1982), pp. 148–96.

Jones, Vivien (ed.), *Women in the Eighteenth Century: Constructions of Femininity* (London, Routledge, 1990).

Kaufman, P., *Libraries and Their Users* (London, Library Association, 1969).

Kendrick, T. D., *The Lisbon Earthquake* (London, Methuen, 1956).

Ketton-Cremer, R. W., *Horace Walpole*, 3rd edn (London, Methuen, 1964).

Kirkham, M., *Jane Austen, Feminism and Fiction* (New York, Methuen, 1986).

Klancher, J. P., *The Making of English Reading Audiences 1790–1832* (Madison, University of Wisconsin Press, 1987).

Kliger, S., 'The "Goths" in England: An Introduction to the Gothic Vogue in Eighteenth-Century Aesthetic Discussion', *Modern Philology*, 43 (1945), pp. 107–17.

    The Goths in England: A Study in Seventeenth and Eighteenth Century Thought (Cambridge, Mass., Harvard University Press, 1952).

Knapp, S., *Personification and the Sublime* (Cambridge, Mass., Harvard University Press, 1985).

Linebaugh, P., 'The Tyburn Riot Against the Surgeons', in Douglas Hay *et al.*, *Albion's Fatal Tree: Crime and Society in Eighteenth-Century England* (Harmondsworth, Penguin, 1977), pp. 65–118.

Lowenthal, L., and Fiske, M., 'The Debate Over Art and Popular Culture in Eighteenth Century England', *Common Frontiers of the Social Sciences*, ed. M. Komorovsky (New York, The Free Press, 1957), pp. 33–112.

Lukács, G., *History and Class Consciousness: Studies in Marxist Dialectics*, trans. R. Livingstone (London, Merlin Press, 1971).

Luyendijk-Elshout, A., 'Of Masks and Mills: The Enlightened Doctor and His Frightened Patient', *The Languages of the Psyche*, ed. G. S. Rousseau (Los Angeles, University of California Press, 1990), pp. 186–230.

McIntyre, C.F., *Ann Radcliffe in Relation to Her Time*, Yale Studies in English vol. 62 (New Haven, Yale University Press, 1920).

McKendrick, N., et al., *The Birth of a Consumer Society: The Commercialization of Eighteenth-Century England*, 1982 (London, Hutchison, 1983).

McKeon, M., *The Origins of the English Novel 1600–1740* (London, Century Hutchison, 1988).

Mahmoud, F. M. (ed.), *William Beckford of Fonthill, 1760–1844* (Port Washington, New York, Kennikat, 1972).

Marx, K., *Capital*, trans. B. Fowkes, 3 vols. (Harmondsworth, Penguin, 1976).

    Early Writings, trans. R. Livingstone and G. Benton (Harmondsworth, Penguin, 1975).

    Grundrisse, trans. with foreword by M. Nicolaus (London, Allen Lane–Penguin, 1973).

Mayo, R. D., 'Gothic Romance in the Magazines', *PMLA* 65 (1950), pp. 762–89.

    'How Long Was Gothic Fiction in Vogue?', *Modern Language Notes*, 58 (Jan. 1943), pp. 58–64.

Mellor, A. K., *Romanticism and Gender* (London and New York, Routledge, 1993).

Miller, D. A., *The Novel and the Police* (Berkeley, University of California Press, 1988).

Moers, E., *Literary Women*, 1963 (London, Women's Press, 1978).

Moretti, F., 'Dialectic of Fear', *Signs Taken for Wonders: Essays in the Sociology of Literary Forms*, trans. S. Fischer *et al.* (London, Verso, 1983), pp. 83–108.

O'Faolain, J., and Martines, L., *Not in God's Image: Women in History* (London, Virago, 1979).

Parreaux, A., 'The Caliph and the Swinish Multitude', in Mahmoud (ed.), *William Beckford*, pp. 1–15.

The Publication of 'The Monk'. A Literary Event 1796–1798 (Paris, Librairie Marcel Didier, 1960).

Parsons, C. O., 'Ghost-Stories Before Defoe', *Notes and Queries*, 201 (1956).

'The Interest of Scott's Public in the Supernatural', *Notes and Queries*, 185 (1943).

Pateman, C., *The Sexual Contract* (Cambridge, Polity Press, 1988).

Patey, D. L., *Probability and Literary Form: Philosophic Theory and Literary Practice in the Augustan Age* (Cambridge University Press, 1984).

Paulson, R., 'Gothic Fiction and the French Revolution', *English Literary History*, 48 (1981), pp. 532–54.

Representations of Revolution (New Haven, Yale University Press, 1983).

Peck, L. F., '*The Monk* and *Le Diable Amoureux*,' *Modern Language Notes* 68 (June 1953), pp. 406–8.

'*The Monk* and Musäus' "Die Entführung"', *Philological Quarterly*, 32 (1953), pp. 346–8.

Pocock, J. G. A., *The Machiavellian Moment: Florentine Republican Thought and the Atlantic Tradition* (Princeton University Press, 1975).

Poovey, M., 'Ideology and *The Mysteries of Udolpho*', *Criticism*, 21 (Fall 1979), pp. 307–30.

The Proper Lady and the Woman Writer (University of Chicago Press, 1984).

Porter, Roy, 'Under the Influence: Mesmerism in England', *History Today*, 35 (Sept. 1985), pp. 22–9.

Praz, M., Introductory Essay, *Three Gothic Novels*, ed. P. Fairclough (Harmondsworth, Penguin, 1968), pp. 7–34.

Price, Cecil, *Theatre in the Age of Garrick* (Oxford, Basil Blackwell, 1973).

Prior, M. E., 'Joseph Glanvill, Witchcraft, and Seventeenth-Century Science', *Modern Philology* 30 (1932), pp. 167–93.

Punter, David, *The Literature of Terror* (London, Longman, 1980).

Reed, Amy L., *The Background of Gray's Elegy: A Study in the Taste for Melancholy Poetry 1700–1751* (New York, Russell and Russell, 1962).

Richardson, R., *Death, Dissection and the Destitute* (London, Routledge & Kegan Paul, 1987).

Roberts, J. M., *The Mythology of Secret Societies* (London, Secker & Warburg, 1972).

Roberts, Marie, *Gothic Immortals: The Fiction of the Brotherhood of the Rosy Cross* (London, Routledge, 1990).

Sabor, P. (ed.), *Horace Walpole: The Critical Heritage* (London, Routledge & Kegan Paul, 1987).

Sadleir, M., *The Northanger Novels: A Footnote to Jane Austen*, The English Association, pamphlet no. 68 (1927).

Sage, Victor, *Horror Fiction in the Protestant Tradition* (New York, St Martin's Press, 1988).

Schaffer, S., 'States of Mind: Enlightenment and Natural Philosophy', *The Languages of the Psyche*, ed. G. S. Rousseau (Los Angeles, University of California Press, 1990), pp. 233–90.

Sedgwick, E. K., *The Coherence of Gothic Conventions*, 1980 (New York, Methuen, 1986).

Sekora, J., *Luxury: The Concept in Western Thought, Eden to Smollett* (Baltimore and London, Johns Hopkins University Press, 1977).

Sharpe, R. J., *The Law of Habeas Corpus* (Oxford, Clarendon Press, 1989).

Shepperson, A. B., *The Novel in Motley: A History of the Burlesque Novel in English* (Cambridge, Mass., Harvard University Press, 1936).

Skinner, A. S., Analytical Introduction, *An Inquiry into the Principles of Political Oeconomy* by J. Steuart, ed. A. S. Skinner (Edinburgh, Scottish Economics Society, 1966).

Smith, Olivia, *The Politics of Language 1791–1819* (Oxford, Clarendon Press, 1984).

Spacks, P. M., *The Insistence of Horror: Aspects of the Supernatural in Eighteenth-Century Poetry* (Cambridge, Mass., Harvard University Press, 1962).

The Poetry of Vision: Five Eighteenth-Century Poets (Cambridge, Mass., Harvard University Press, 1967).

Spencer, Jane, *The Rise of the Woman Novelist* (Oxford, Basil Blackwell, 1986).

Stokoe, F. W., *German Influence on the English Romantic Period, 1788–1818* (Cambridge University Press, 1926).

Stoll, E. E., 'The Objectivity of Ghosts in Shakespeare', *PMLA*, 22, 2 (1907) (ns 15, 2), pp. 201–33.

Summers, M., *A Gothic Bibliography*, 1941 (New York, Russell & Russell, 1964).

The Gothic Quest, 1938 (London, Fortune Press, 1968).

The History of Witchcraft and Demonology, 1926 (London and Boston, Routledge & Kegan Paul, 1973).

'Santon Barsisa', *Notes and Queries*, 175 (1938).

Sutherland, J., 'The Relation of Defoe's Fiction to his Non-Fictional Writings', in *Imagined Worlds, Essays on Some English Novels and Novelists in Honour of John Butt*, ed. M. Mack and I. Gregor (London, Methuen, 1968).

Swedenberg, H. T., 'Fable, Action, Unity and Supernatural Machinery in English Epic Theory, 1650–1800', *Englische Studien*, 73 (1938), pp. 39–48.

Tanner, Tony, *Jane Austen* (London, Macmillan, 1986).

Taylor, G., '"The Just Delineation of the Passions": Theories of Acting in the Age of Garrick', *Essays on the Eighteenth-Century English Stage*, ed. K. Richards and P. Thomson (London, Methuen, 1972).

Taylor, John Tinnon, *Early Opposition to the English Novel* (New York, King's Crown Press, 1943).

Thomas, K., *Religion and the Decline of Magic* (Harmondsworth, Penguin, 1971).

Thompson, E. P., *The Making of the English Working Class* (Harmondsworth, Penguin, 1980).

Todd, J., *The Sign of Angellica: Women, Writing and Fiction, 1660–1800* (London, Virago, 1989).

   (ed.), *A Dictionary of British and American Women Writers, 1660–1800* (London, Methuen, 1987).

Todorov, R., *The Fantastic*, trans. R. Howard, 1973 (Ithaca, New York, Cornell University Press, 1975).

Tompkins, J. M. S., *The Popular Novel in England 1770–1800* (London, Constable & Co., 1932).

Tulloch, J., *Rational Theology and Christian Philosophy in the Seventeenth Century*, 2nd edn, 2 vols. (Edinburgh, 1874).

Vincent-Buffault, A., *The History of Tears* (London, Macmillan, 1991).

Wardle, R. M., 'Mary Wollstonecraft, Analytical Reviewer', *PMLA*, 62 (1947), pp. 1000–7.

Watt, I., *The Rise of the Novel* (London, Chatto & Windus, 1957).

Watt, W. W., *Shilling Shockers of the Gothic School: A Study of the Chapbook Gothic Romances* (Cambridge, Mass., Harvard University Press, 1932).

Weiskel, T., *The Romantic Sublime: Studies in the Structure and Psychology of Transcendence* (Baltimore and London, Johns Hopkins University Press, 1976).

Wellek, R., *The Rise of English Literary History*, 1941 (New York, McGraw-Hill, 1966).

West, R. H., *The Invisible World: A Study of Pneumatology in Elizabethan Drama* (Athens, Georgia, University of Georgia Press, 1939).

Westcott, I. M. (ed.), *Seventeenth-Century Tales of the Supernatural*, Augustan Reprint Soc. no. 74 (Los Angeles, University of California, 1958).

Whitney, L., *Primitivism and the Idea of Progress* (New York, Octagon Books, 1965).

Williams, E. N., '"Our Merchants are Princes", the English Middle Classes in the Eighteenth Century', *History Today*, 12 (1962), pp. 548–57.

Wilson, J. Dover, *What Happens in Hamlet*, 3rd edn (Oxford University Press, 1959).

Wright, T., *Caricature History of the Georges* (London, Chatto & Windus, (1867?)).

Zimbardo, R. A., *A Mirror to Nature: Transformations in Drama and Aesthetics, 1660–1732* (Lexington, University of Kentucky Press, 1986).

Index

CAMBRIDGE STUDIES IN ROMANTICISM

Titles published